OUTSIDE
OF EDEN

Helen Nathaniel-Fulton

To Donna
from
Helen
≈
x

**PUBLISHED IN
SILENCE PRESS**

Published by Published in Silence Press.
Flat 9, 32 Greenlaw Drive, Paisley. PA1 3RU.
www.grahamfulton-poetry.com

Helen's website address is
www.helennathaniel-fulton.co.uk

Typesetting and layout by Graham Fulton.
Front cover photograph by Helen.
Printed by Merchant City Print,
261 High Street, Glasgow. G4 0QR.

A catalogue record for this book is available
from the British Library.

ISBN 978-1-7399434-2-4

To my husband Graham
who made me believe in Eden again

Acknowledgements

Thanks are due to the editors of
the following publications where some
of these stories first appeared

'Two Fat Ladies' was first published in *Laldy!*

'Purification' was first published in *Southlight*

A version of 'Warrior' entitled 'Bridge
Over the River Neckar' was published in
the anthology *Bridges or Walls?* (Dove Tales, 2019)

Versions of 'Ghost Workers' 'Slavery'
and 'Memory Chip' were first published under
the single title of 'Memory Chip' in the anthology
Of Myths and Mothers (Fly on the Wall Press, 2022)

'Warrior' and parts of 'Nestbreaking' were
first published in the pamphlet *Da Vinci's Cuckoos*
(Something Like Chalk Press, 2017)

CONTENTS

Prologue

Living in Eden

Some years ago, as I barely clung on to sanity in a brain-busting, stressful job, I felt a compulsion to try something different and write short stories. Fairly soon into this therapeutic 'hobby', I found a good number of them coalescing into the start of an autobiographical novel. It felt I was being pushed, not jumping, and even as more chapters started to jostle against each other to get out, three questions dogged me: why attempt this at all (when it was bound to tie my brain and emotions in knots); where to begin; where to end.

As for the first, it felt as if some of the funny, achingly sad, often lonely, adventurous, scary and extraordinary experiences from teens to mid-thirties were clamouring to be heard, and, truth be told, I couldn't silence them. In these years (late 1970's to 1990) I fled Swansea, first to Aberystwyth, then West Germany, and from there to Kenya. In 1990, I chose to return to the UK.

I knew I didn't just want to write a travelogue though: it would be more interesting, as we are so rarely able to get under someone else's skin or into their minds, to share feelings and the impact of experience as I studied, travelled, loved and worked in these different places. We always feel we are the only ones, say, to have a particular thought, experience, defect, problem or grief, and it can be cathartic in itself to find you're not. No-one knows better than I, too, how we can sleepwalk through aeons of our lives – maybe if more of us describe their gradual awakening to this sad fact, it may help other somnambulists.

As for questions two and three, I thought the place to begin had to be at a point I started more consciously to observe, live, learn and be challenged, and, on reflection, the place to end (for now) was my mid-thirties. By then I was almost grown up at last, and on the cusp of waking, of being able to admit there was something I had hidden – even from myself – for a long, long time. A process of discovery and recovery followed. If anyone should have an interest in that though, the harrowing but hopeful tale is for another day.

1

Though it may have appeared I was charmed and indeed spoilt (the only child, grandchild and niece four times over in mum's close family) it was only true up to a point: It would be a lie to say my childhood was perfect, as the first years were full of nebulous anxiety and nightmares and I spent as much time as possible alone. Alone, I felt safe. Dreaming and reading were safe. This was not the fault of my parents or my mother's close family: they nurtured and supported me to the absolute limits of ability: there was a limit, however, as admitting to having emotions or physically showing affection was hard for them. They had been brought up in such frightening, macho times and in a stoic, narrow working-class South Welsh society. As a result, love had to happen by osmosis and was usually 'shown' only through deeds. Telling someone you loved them, along with any other kind of emotional expression, was namby-pamby: *English. Middle class.* Such things were shown on TV but didn't happen in the everyday world – well, not to *real* (i.e. working class Welsh) people.

Because their language was emotion, things like poetry and classical music were actively embarrassing. *Real* people just worked hard and got on with things. Despite this, with their osmotic love, irrepressible sense of fun and encouragement to work hard at school, I developed as a seemingly well functioning person with a love for history, poetry/literature/art and all kinds of music, and when I left home at 18 to live and take a degree at Aberystwyth University, this was a BIG DEAL: not only as I so longed to be independent and to continue my studies, but because in our branch of the family, I was the first to achieve this. Mum and my lovely uncle Fred had been grammar school and university 'material', but like so many of those born in the twenties, they had to leave school aged 14 to help support their families in a time of deprivation and then war and an even deeper deprivation. My family was proudly working class, displaying all the best aspects of that culture, being hardworking, respectable, respectful and respected. When I passed the 11 plus and got a place at a girls' grammar school from which almost everyone did move on to university, it was as if all their hard work and sacrifices had been rendered worthwhile. Though they had accepted their own fates, I would escape their early poverty and lifelong drudgery, would have choices. I know they both loved and, despite best efforts, envied and almost resented me for that.

Before leaving home, however, the grammar school I attended was my Garden of Eden: A Field and then TB hospital from the Great War on, it was a wooden building around a huge quadrangle and all the classrooms (wards) had one side made of folding doors that opened onto verandahs and gardens. I thought often of the patients who must have lain in bed or sat on the verandahs, drinking in fresh, sea air AND the fragrances of soil, grass, buds, leaves, flowers, feeling the gentle or harsh touches of seasons, circles of sun, rain, frost. Watching snow or leaves drift and disappear into earth while they recovered – or died. Waking if they survived the night to blue hazes of dew on summer mornings and settling into sleep soothed by the powerful but quick-fading perfume of flowers.

Oh, those gardens were beautiful, and always more than just a fragrant, humming summer backdrop to our lessons. In winter, of course, we suffered for our pleasures: the classrooms were freezing despite radiators, the open verandahs were our only corridors and (very poor) shelter. Not many pupils learn in a garden, but also there are few who have to dress in full woolly winter garb to move between classes, often starting a new lesson damp or shivering. But we didn't care: the sunshine days made it worthwhile. We were young, strong and would survive. Even now I annoy people by wanting windows open, summer and winter, and only noticing cold when the North wind blows.

These years were purely happy, like something in the *Bunty* comic I loved to read. I made friends and spent less time alone. I enjoyed the lessons (well, except sciences, in which I was however not the only puzzled and bored-to-coma pupil), and spent the rest of the time laughing fit to bust at not very much with my all-female class-mates, singing ridiculous songs, playing practical jokes and sneaking off at lunchtimes to the local bookshop to spend hard-earned wages (more of this later) and pocket money. It was a blessing to be encouraged to immerse in the world of history, literature, languages – a *blissing* in fact. I very happily did at least 2 hours homework a night: with no boys in classes and no boyfriends, there were no distractions, no troubles. I was always top of the class, indeed of all the classes, at the end of the year. Not a hopeless speccy swot though, by any means, as I indulged in the nonsense described above with gusto and in summer I would also run, almost tumble, down the hills after lessons to lie under the biggest tree in Singleton Park watching sunlight dapple and listening to soughing leaves until the cool sea-breeze made me shiver, or with a few good friends watch the last hours of a county cricket match with time tocking away hypnotically on long, late afternoons. This paradise of friendship, learning, laughter, pleasures and dreaming was of course punctured sharply by rounds of exams, but even that didn't torture me as it seemed to do my classmates. If there were some malady that had caused those early childhood anxieties, Eden soothed or even seemed to cure it.

As certain as Death, however, is that an Eden simply cannot last. We don't deserve it. Years after I left, the school was finally demolished and smart detached houses built on the site. They left the outer stone wall and some of the great trees, but otherwise there is no trace. Do people in those houses at least smell ghostly flowers, the sticky dark creosote used on the wood in summer, hear bells and laughter, running feet, slamming of desks? Gradually from the age of 16, the warmth and security it afforded leached from my psyche – even after I then found a second Eden. This too would be ripped away when Adam gave the Apple to Eve. Still, that's a few years away yet, and it's always best to begin at some kind of beginning.

Daily Bread

In my people's house there are still many sins. The Bible decrees seven, but I can think of at least a dozen things Good People don't do in working-class ramrod-straight-back respectable South Wales. If you're *decent*, you don't have sex (or, of course, children) outside marriage or get divorced. You certainly don't enjoy sex. You don't drink or swear to excess or, even better, don't drink and swear at all. You never take part in any criminal or violent activity. You keep yourselves, your children, your house and your garden fearsomely clean and neat. You don't bet or get into debt. and above all you never fail to work for your daily bread. Small wonder, you might say, that work is important when all other kinds of human activity appear to have been forbidden. But being out of or unwilling to work is without any doubt the Greatest Sin, and this is programmed into children of respectable families from birth. Not surprising, then, that I got my first job before I was ten years old. No: you don't need to go back and read that again: I was coming up to ten, and, to be honest, it seemed quite natural at the time.

Let me begin by saying it wasn't down a mine or in a factory – I'm not that old. It *was* over fifty years ago, however, and fifteen shillings (75 of those pees they have these days) was a FORTUNE. Quite a number of kids on our estate did the same kind of work, and, given it was illegal to employ us, we were paid in cash and had to pretend to be helping a parent or relative out. Doing it for a lark. Unlike some of the kids whose families were a lot poorer than mine, and definitely not doing it for a lark, I got to keep my wages. The work was also much sought after because it involved delivering bread and cakes, and we – the bread-boys – and girls – got to eat a fair bit of what remained on the shelves.

At that age, you're hungry all the time, and vigorous exercise sharpens the edge of hunger to a glinting and murderous stiletto point. We knew how the products we sold were made back at the factory, but we effortlessly blanked it out. Up at six, running up and down hundreds of steps and steep driveways (Swansea is built like Rome on many hills) with baskets of goodies for shops (heavy as coffins) and private customers (lighter, but you had to deal with mad dogs) and usually fighting cold and rain, you had to refuel regularly. At ten I was still quite child-plump, but, despite our gluttony, we all burned off what we ate by the afternoon and still had room for more. At eleven, I was suddenly stick-thin, with my St Trinian's type school tunic draped over coat hanger shoulder blades.

That's by way of an introduction. Now I am seventeen. I'm still doing it, you see: in school holidays, I find a full time job, but in term time I'm happy to help out delivering bread on Saturdays. I'm in the sixth form now, and the money is still good and it pays for a surprising number of books. For me, they have replaced food as a pleasure and an aching necessity. My daily read had become a thousand times more important than my daily bread. I can't expect my hardworking parents to buy them as well as supporting me in so many other ways, and, frankly, I would kill for access to books. I need to own them, jealously hoard them, have books of my own that I don't have to give back . . . six hours hard work on a Saturday seems a small price to pay.

Anyway, this particular day is the mid-winter kind when the light barely changes and bleary headlamps squint through veils of misting rain until the greyness melts into black again. Nothing has an edge except the wind. Exposed to the relentless fall of rainwater and blow of gritty salt gusts, you're soaked in a way people seldom are any more. Your hair is slicked to scalp and face despite pulling your hood tight. Your underclothes are icy and hard and scrape your skin. Your shoes squelch embarrassingly. There are, you learn, ways of withstanding it. Mind over matter. If you can make yourself not mind, it won't matter: in just a few hours, you'll be home and into a hot bath. Wrapped in a fluffy dressing gown, eating a hot meal and feeling a kind of glowing animal bliss some people never enjoy. All is contrast. Make it your mantra. Indeed, I feel generous, so have two mantras: this will soon be over, and all *is* contrast.

. . . And if you believe that sixties shite you'll believe anything. I'm so miserable and cold now, I'm weeping, but, fortunately, the rain acts as camouflage and no-one will know. I've torn a nail badly too, and one hand is throbbing hot. We have nearly finished the round, however, and I must admit there is a strange kind of satisfaction – even a twisted pleasure – in endurance. We've delivered tons of bread, performed prodigious feats of mental

6

arithmetic, dodged the few vicious mutts insane enough to venture outdoors, and I'm climbing the steps to a smart, middle class house in a smart, middle class area of town. My school is in this area, by the way, and a lot of my friends live here. This lady and her children know some of them. She has a large family: I've never counted, but there seem to be at least half-a-dozen children of Junior and Secondary school age. They never look at me when I stand at the door. If one of them answers, he or she calls for mum in a slightly panicked way and scuttles off. For some reason I embarrass them. Normally, that doesn't bother me and I don't try to analyse. Our encounters are too short and unimportant.

Today when the door opens, they all seem to be in the smart, middle class kitchen, and there's a kind of mass panic. Before they can bolt, the mother stops them. I'm literally standing here with water running off my nose and chin as if I'm a gargoyle. I probably look as attractive as one. Now what's going on? Why doesn't she just take what she wants, give me the money, and I can run away as her kids so clearly want to do? The eyes of her brood are pointing in unlikely directions at objects of no interest. They shuffle their feet. The mother looks very tight-jawed and determined, and I get the feeling they were having some kind of argument before I knocked. She calls me in. Now this *is* embarrassing: it isn't done! I'm a tradesperson. The rules are simple: I stand on the step, they pick and pay, I go. Out there, I am almost part of the elements and uncomfortable though it may be physically, I am still more at ease than I am in here where I'm making a pool on the tiles. The more they try not to look at me, the worse it gets. I can imagine too clearly now what I look like. I can see me for the first time as people see me when they open their doors. It's gone very, very quiet. The mother gears up for action. Her bosom rises like bread dough. What in the name of God is she going to do?

"I want you all to look at this girl. Go on! Look!"

I'm speechless now, trying discreetly to rest the heavy basket on a knee, warming up as the heat of the kitchen and the sheer awfulness of it all have an effect and my skin burns, my clothes start to steam a little. In here, I know I'll smell of sugar, damp clothes, petrol, sweat. If I'd been allowed to keep going, I wouldn't have noticed, but now I become conscious of how much I'd like to take a pee. Nothing matters, however, except what she's going to say next. It all bursts out like jam from a threepenny doughnut.

"For all we do for you, not one of you does a stroke of work. None of you gets decent marks. None of you ever lifts a finger. You're take, take, *take* and treat me and your father like dirt! *This* girl got eight O-levels and she's got a scholarship to university! And she's not too proud to work! You ought to be more like her. I wish you were more like her. You should be *ashamed* of yourselves when people have to work to live!"

This is possibly the worst moment of my life so far. There've been one or two bad ones, but I wish now I could drop dead. Some teenagers do: there's a mysterious heart condition and they go with no warning after exercise. I've run around until my heart thuds this morning: it might, if I'm very lucky, happen to me now. My one consolation is her kids look more upset than I am. They are shrinking like my clothing, imploding with absolute shame. I don't mind them hating their mother, the silly cow, but I do feel bad to think how they must hate me. The mother is also upset, and though she looks about to weep, I hate her too. I don't see how this can get worse. I don't see how it can end. This madwoman has missed the point: she and the father they treat like dirt have programmed them as my family has programmed me. If I lived in a house like this, with wealthy parents and bookshelves that no doubt bend under the weight of their load, I would be lying on a chaise longue sucking a slab of chocolate and reading poetry – and maybe one of them would be standing here. Dear God: does she really think using me as a model is going to make them miraculously become industrious and motivated? After this, they'll all probably become vagrants or junkie whores just to spite her.

Silence and Time are stretching out and I wonder when one or both will snap and how long I can stand here dumb. One of the older boys clears his throat and swallows convulsively. I notice his Adam's apple is huge. It's like a ping-pong ball. He's a bony individual altogether, and looks ugly and desperate. The mother closes her eyes and then re-opens them. She blinks, makes a visible effort, and smiles. It's a ghastly smile because the corners of her mouth still droop miserably and her eyes are glassy and red -rimmed. But I can tell she's back in her right mind, and that has to be good news.

"A large tin, two large brown sliced, a small batch and two Battenburgs please."

We always guess right what to put in the basket, as most people don't vary much from habit. I have all she needs, hand the items over, take the money and go. This is *better*, though even now I think of how I'll have to come here again next week. Sufficient unto the day, however . . . as the door closes, I turn my flaming face up to the rain, steadier now, needling hard, and looking set for days. Of course the only plan is to pretend that never happened and forget it as quickly as I can. In there, they'll do the same. Somehow Isis' veil twitched a little, and we all saw things that should remain hidden. Mad, mad . . . I run down the steps, and I'm comforted to see Pete the Deliveryman is in the van, tapping on the wheel and humming the number one song. I like Pete: a salt of the earth type, genuinely kind and funny. Not subtle – his favourite comedian is Benny Hill – but a Good Bloke. There aren't many.

"What took you so long? She's not normally the type to chat and you're the fastest bread-girl in the west."

I shrug my shoulders.

"No idea, Pete. She just wouldn't let me go."

"Selfish cow in this rain. They're all the bloody same round here, the women: strings of pearls and no knickers. I bet she never did a day's work in her life. Husband's a bigwig at Morriston Hospital, they say. Rolling in it. You should see his car now."

I nod.

"We're still a bit early, mind. Tell you what, we'll finish and have a cuppa from the flask and two of those cream cakes you likes. If we goes back now, the buggers'll only think they can add to the round."

Though I nod more eagerly, my appetite is gone. I know I won't forget today's humiliation however hard I try. I'm trembling with anger that I was exposed to it, but I don't know who is to blame so it has nowhere to go. As usual, I'll have to work it off. But one day I can expend my energies in a proper job. I might even become a bigwig and rolling in it. Someone has to. Pearls will definitely be out of fashion by then, but a man like Pete is bound to look at me and say: "They're all the same round here, the women. Look at her: all lah-di-dah and long words and probably never done a hard day's work in her bloody life."

Two Fat Ladies

Work all week. Take your leisure at the weekend. Whoop it up on your Saturday night out – now that makes SENSE. But in this bomb-wreck of a Welsh town decaying quietly by the sea, all the laws of logic are denied. Work is supposed to be the boring bit, and leisure the thing you look forward to. What you long for as you eye the clock. The pleasure you're torn from to go back to work. Simple! So where *are* the drunken winking lights, the pneumatic seventies drill music, the delirious clink of glasses and nerve-end screech of urban relief? In this tense, sweating silence, I wonder if other people feel the same when they're this bored. With me, tedium teased to an extreme makes my head feel it's about to explode. God – it would be such a relief if it did! I want to open my mouth and let the thick swell of dark frustration OUT. It would be like someone in a midget submarine smashing a porthole when the pressure gets to be too much. The whole thing would implode and, when the chaos subsided, only a silent-space of waters would remain. Either that or I suppose stuff would have to squeeze out of every orifice like vomit through an optimist's fingers.

Ah, no . . . let's stop it there. I don't like that image: I have a thing about vomit, which was the theme of a whole other story. Let's just say for now my skull really does feel like a sphere under unbearable pressure. If it won't blow apart from the external weights, something really will have to force itself out. I suppose that explains having to fight this elemental urge to yawn, to crack my jaw in a cavernous ROAR, to scream and swear. I almost wish I had Tourette's at times like this. I could spill it all out then and the people around me would have to accept. But this being Wales, even as they did, they would shake their heads in that maddening kindly but cruel way they have. They would say something like 'Aw, love 'er! She can't 'elp it!' The tone would sink to a whisper. 'She's simple, see. They're all a bit funny, you know, in that family.' Though you wouldn't think it possible, the voice would drop lower for the final soft stab. 'It shouldn't be ALLOWED. People like that should be PUT AWAY.'

As a veteran now of summer factory work, I thought I'd learnt to control this feeling quite well. But of course I've been kidding myself that I've developed a high tedium threshold. I feel embarrassed to recall playing the expert with my friends. Boasting that the trick is to switch your mind off, to sleep while standing or sitting amidst the machines and belts, or focus on ways to spend the money you're earning. The trouble is I can't do either of those things here, tonight. There's no guarantee of money at the end of *this* late shift, and, despite what non-aficionados might think, you really do have to concentrate at this game. If you don't, you lose the thread as the numbers patter out like bullets from a gun. The caller's voice might be all Blackpool-Pier-jaunty, but this is serious stuff. Groups share if they win, and people in those groups eye each other covertly. Ergo, if I drift, my co-players will know! Not only will that put a win in jeopardy, but also worse – much worse – they'll guess I don't want to be here. The other women around us would form their conclusions too, and – believe me – they wouldn't be kind.

Suddenly, I can hear a ghostly whispering in my head like echoes in a cold cave. 'She's a *snob*, she is. A fucking SNOB . . . thinks she's too cowin' good for us. Thinks she's got better things to do . . . do . . . do . . . would rather 'ave 'er 'ead in a book with words a foot long or watching some fancy bloody film, all talk and no trousers or even one of those Frenchy subtitles things. Never been like us. . . ss . . .ss! Hoity-toity piece – keeps herself to herself. Does no good spendin' all that time on your own! It's not NATURAL. It shouldn't be ALLOWED. People like that . . .'

There'd be all of that, and more.

And so I sit here doldrummed in a fog that stinks of cheap cigarettes, dark bitter-beer shandy and stale sweat. Of the knock-'em-dead perfumes purchased by husbands and fiancés for Christmas ('Ruinous bloody price – you wouldn't believe it – and the woman serving 'ad 'er nose right up her own arse. But that's what She told me to get, see, or else!'). And my bum sweats on a plastic bench. My hands rest on a formica table-top with cigarette burns melting into the once-shiny surface. Stinging eyes peer at the numbers dancing on the pink sheet of paper. Fingers fiddle with the felt-tip pen. Jesus wept it's not even eight o'clock! There's hours to go yet, plus making it through the break with a face made of glass that might shatter at any time because I have to keep smiling and trying to say the right things. Pretend I'm enjoying myself . . . that I want another shandy . . . that I would love a warm pie even though I deliver them to shops and people's homes on Saturday mornings to make a bit extra and I KNOW WHAT'S IN THEM. Have to avert my eyes from all the fat ladies cramming chips and pies and pasties and crisps and chocolate into their mouths, puffing like chimney-stacks, gulping down shandy or rum and black or bacardi and coke, leaving greasy pink and red and orange kisses on plastic glasses.

Have to pretend I can't hear that real whisper behind me: "I only wanted one last week! Ten numbers I waited. I never 'ad such a sweat! We would 'ave 'ad the 'undred pound. We would 'ave 'ad the fuckin' 'UNDRED. And that greedy old cow only comes once in a blue moon and she scooped the lot – she never goes shares. Shouldn't be ALLOWED."

Someone more powerful shushes the woman quiet, and the game rolls on.

All that and more.

At long last, the fun is drawing to an end. My aunt whom I love as fiercely as I am able to love touches my hand with rough fingers that always have bitten nails. She smiles but there's a little worried line between dark brows. She loves this game, this evening out, more than anything else in her hard-working week: she it was who asked me to come - or I would have found an excuse.

"Alright my love? You're not bored are you? Is the smoke too much for you?'

I smile and shake my head. Semi-lie with ease. I'm very good at it by now.

"Tired, Sylv, that's all!"

The last game is about to start. My mother finishes talking to a friend from work, who always sits beside her and is part of our group. My mother winks across the plastic divide at me. I smile. The microphone screeches a little. Then the only man in the hall, the high priest of the tombola, beams down on his devotees:

"Eyes down, ladies! This is the big one, now. The Saturday Night Golden Jackpot! Five 'undred notes for the lucky winner, fifty for a line! Think how many lacy knickers you could buy with that."

A few obedient titters stir the hot sea-soup around us, but we all cast our eyes down. The atmosphere changes a little as if the temperature has climbed several degrees. I feel I'm suffocating. That's an ENORMOUS amount of money to people who slog their guts out in shifts to pay the rent, clothe the kids, put food on the table. There's never anything left over at the end of a week: Not much, anyway. If you have a good 'win', you can afford something really nice for the house or even a holiday. Maybe in Spain! My palms are wet and I start to feel nauseous. I have to find a way to control, to concentrate, to care, because there is no greater crime than to miss a call and maybe lose that fortune, scupper those dreams of ruby Dralon sofas and matching curtains and golden beaches striped with regiments of umbrellas. I have to concentrate while I'm here. I have to forget how I yearn to be sitting in clean, cool air and perfect silence, opening a book, plunging into infinite otherworlds of my own choice.

The falsely-cheerful voice is still calling out the numbers. What's happening now is hard to believe, but I have to believe it. My heartbeats have speeded up, far exceeding the rapid tick-tick-tick of the balls popping out of the machine. I'm going hot and then cold. Pricked by sweat, needled by ice.

"Two fat ladies . . ."

My aunt, who can mark eight tickets and make sure she keeps an eye on all of ours, shouts with me before the caller can finish: "House! HO-O-OUSE!"

I see my mother and her friend look up, stunned, and then start jumping up and down and waving their cards. My mother runs to me, gives me an enormous hug. She never does that, and I'm as startled as if she's shouted a four-letter word. I can still feel her breasts pressing into my shoulder as she dances back to the other side of the table, singing a little tune she always sings at times like this.

"We're in the money, we're in the money . . ."

Everyone is laughing, and I'm pushed towards the front of the hall where I have to show my (temporary) members' card and pick up the brown envelope. It's a lot of money, this. So much more than people earn in a month. One or two of the women are muttering, sending little lapping waves of malice towards me, but

13

I hear someone hiss that it's *OK*: it's OK. It's Chris' daughter, and Chris never misses a session. I sit down, and my mother and her friend and my aunt beam at me. That was the last house, of course, the BIG ONE, and everyone else is putting on coats in the too-sudden dislocation after the climax, making for the doors.

"Legs shakin', love?"

My mother's friend who usually seems shy of talking to me – she may be Chris' daughter but she's not like us she's goin' to be a STUDENT! – comes up close. I nod.

"It's always like that the first big one. Mind – you never gets used to it! I'm always the same when I calls, even if it's a couple of quid on a line. Oh, bloody well done, love!" She's so happy her eyes are glowing like lighthouse lamps through the murk. "I can 'ave that new piece of carpet now. My old one's got 'oles in it you could drive a soddin' number twenty-six bus through."

But I know it's the euphoria and that she'll be too shy to talk to me when I see her again. I still don't belong. I never will: funny how I really know it now. I have to get up and go, and, as I slip on my coat, I know I can't make the pretence much longer. I know the headache I have won't shift entirely until I'm on a bus heading north to university and – no matter what – I'll have to find a non-hurtful excuse for next week. As my tired mind bobs about, I almost jump out of my own skin when an octopus arm slips around my waist. It's the caller. He pulls me so tightly to him I can smell salty perspiration mingling with the chemical reek of *Hai Karate* (bought by mothers and daughters and girlfriends for Christmas – it's on the telly, see, yet it's lovely and cheap!). I shudder. This man's a joker: the ladies love him. He thinks he's a sex god: I think he's as attractive as a long-dead fish. The few women left around us shoot more envious glances in my direction, but – caught on the hop – I pull away for once without caring about giving offence. I'm not quite sure why, but panic is my only imperative. The man's mask slips too and his expression darkens. I know this beast has seven other arms, and will not give up easily. He talks to my breasts.

"Shy, eh? Ah, well – soon 'ave you out of that, won't we? You got a lucky look about you. Clean me out, you will. Oh, don't worry: I'll find out your name, love, and I'll be looking out for you next week."

I smile, but it's only a small crack appearing in the glass. I steady myself by remembering that I am indeed supremely lucky, because I can make bloody sure I'm not here next week. Two very real fat ladies block my path for a few painful skips of the heart, and then I move fast. The night air cleans my lungs like sweet soap, and I can't wait to get rid of the money crackling in my pocket and to run.

Tourist in Hell

God, how I hate vomit! You'd be entitled to roll your eyes and snort, mutter under your breath: 'Well, who *doesn't*, and what's that got to do with anything?' – but if you are to understand the story, I need to explain why. I had a *phobia* about it you see when I was young. I don't think it's too strong a word: I'm still disgusted by vomit now, but back then it was a waking and sleeping nightmare. Just the thought of seeing someone do it, of hearing the strangled noises, would leave me choking – panicky as an asthmatic – on the imagined greasy acid smell. I would try to block out all images of it. If I thought someone was going to be sick in life or even on a screen I'd run for the hills. At night, however, in the dark, when conscious will is suspended, I'd sweat hailstones as I woke panting if it even lapped up warm to the unravelling edges of my dreams. Last but not least, however unwell I felt, by a superhuman effort of will I would always manage to hold back my own vomit.

So it's not quite as daft a statement as it first seemed, and may explain why I feel uneasy even as I write this down. Phobias are supposed to be illogical, not based on actual experience, but, in a way, my response was actually quite reasonable as it obviously stemmed from my poor dad getting so ill when I was young. His sickness made him fall over, vomit till he was empty and then convulse until the grey little Scottish doctor known almost admiringly by his patients as Andersen the Butcher came tutting his way into the house, tapping a syringe even as he ran from the car. Afterwards the house was utterly silent as my father slept for days. Mercifully, he would wake, and appetite would return . . . but then the cycle would begin again. My mother had to follow him up the stairs with a bucket when he was brought home from work on the worst days, but, as a young child, *I* had a choice. So I chose to shut my eyes tight, put my hands over mouth and nose and pray for it to stop. It didn't of course, and was too all pervading for me to succeed in screening it out. As I grew, I ached to help him, them, but had become hopelessly trapped in my own paralysis.

I didn't realise this would be important the day I came to work here at the crisp factory. It sounds so innocuous, doesn't it? I'm seventeen, young and fit. Starting another summer job in a factory to save up for a holiday and university, another job that will be hot, numbingly tiring and tedious – but soon over, and, ultimately, someone else's daily reality. And few of us can resist the reconstituted, deliciously flavoured 'potato snacks' there's an infinite variety of and market for – so they create well paid jobs galore. I used to love them myself, chomping my favourites – beef and onion - until the telltale lick of fat and salt-trail like gunpowder appeared around my mouth. We all seem – whatever our age, culture or class, wherever we are, whatever we should be doing, to be crunching the things between gums or teeth. I suspect baby food will soon come in Smoky Bacon Crisp flavour. Who knows how many packets are sold? When did *you* last eat a 'potato snack'? Are you eating one now? Knowing what *I* do now, I'd advise you to stop and read this first.

On the first morning at 6.00 a.m., you get issued with overalls and a snood. You get a demo on clocking on and off followed by a long lecture on safety and hygiene. Then you are hustled around like tourists in hell. The first thing you notice – even before the usual deafening industrial cacophony – is the smell. Vats of cheap, stale fat are bubbling somewhere, and the stink is made manifest as the invisible steam settles as a slick, fast-congealing film. Gradually, dust, dirt and insects are drawn to it, and high or otherwise unreachable surfaces are so dirty you would stick to them if you touched. By the end of the day, even the floors are so tacky you can't lift your feet if you stand still too long. And there's a hit-you-in-the-face-and-knock-you-flat aroma coming from vats of thick sauces. Mm-mm! Orange cheese that never knew a cow; pig-free scarlet bacon; pale, plastic chicken flavour; Barbara-Cartland-pink prawn that never bathed in the sea and pure black chemical beef. You can judge the additive content by how much the smell makes you cough, but the supervisor says we'll soon get used to it. We can wear masks if we like, of course, but it does get hot! And in a place powered by vast engines, intelligently constructed of metal and glass beneath a flaring sun, surely it would be easier to learn to breathe through your mouth?

We're all dazed by the sensual assault on that walkabout. It's probably less stressful being inducted into the SAS. None of us looks at each other, but suddenly I catch a glimpse of one of the other students. She is very pale, clammy, and her hand is clapped to her mouth. Jesus! Sweet Jesus! She's going to be sick! My own gorge rises with the wall of panic, and my mind races away. If she's sick, so will I be. If I'm sick here or if I run away, *I'll* be the laughing stock. I'm young but have worked in factories before, and it's a macho culture where you are advised *never* to show weakness. If you do, you may as well take off your overall and go home. You work hard – not too fast, not too slow – and you don't complain. Don't be too friendly; avoid the gossips; trust no-one. Now I feel the awful paralysis creeping, the tug of war – hold it in, stay, run, just let it go – but the tension snaps as the girl runs awkwardly but very fast for the toilets, and when she's through the door we can all breathe again: through the mouth, of course. I thank God for – apart from my phobia! – a strong constitution and nerve. Surreptitiously I wipe the sweat off my face, make myself relax my shoulders and look unconcerned as we move on.

Next we're in the deserted canteen, where the aromas of real food cooking are a temporary relief and blessing – bacon from a real pig smells so good we even revert to using our noses again – and then the locker rooms. They're very grubby, grey and bare. Because our guard has slipped, we note they smell of sweat, old urine from the toilets adjoining, dirt, cheese sauce and stale smoke. The supervisor has broken his own rule too and as his nose twitches, he frowns. He tells us to remember smoking is strictly forbidden and those caught will be sacked. No-one looks at him. We know and he knows if they even try to stop the smokers, the crisps will pile up on the belts until they cascade onto the dirty floor and form great brittle mountains that'll take over the world: the next unnatural disaster. Meanwhile, back on the factory floor, several bored-looking women wait to take us to our work places and get us to start earning our wages. The money is far better here than elsewhere, you see, and it's the fatal lure: every extra pound earned means a better 'lifestyle' for the workers' families, a debt-free existence and perhaps even a holiday on a Costa!

So here I am, at what will be my second home for the summer. A belt in the shape of an angular roller coaster winds around the high-ceilinged space. At the moment, it's moving but empty. Despite that, it's covered with the slime and the smell of cheese sauce and stale, dirty fat is very strong. The cheese smell wins every time . . . and of course it's just like that of vomit. I open my mouth wide and suck in the thick, hot, tainted air. Despite everything, it helps. Averting my eyes from the giant violet flytraps buzzing and sparking as Kamikaze insects roast and cling or sometimes drop, I am taken to a rather lonely station where I will stand on a wooden dais. *Why*? I don't like to ask. I am handed a pair of elbow-length rubber gloves and a mask. My sour-faced mentor clicks her tongue as I stare at them. Her industrial South-Wales accent is as broad as it gets.

"For fuck's sake, pur 'em on, will you? I 'aven gor all day. Fuckin' stewdents! Look, the things comes down yere, see? There's been a problem down the line and the fitters is fixin' it so they won't come again for a bit. When they gets to yere, you picks out the bad ones. You gorra keep up or they ends up in the bags, Moaning Minnie on quality control goes mad and we're all in the shit. OK?"

I swallow and pull down the mask to squeak: "*Bad* ones?"

"Thass wor I said, din I! I dunno – big ones, black ones, ones with fucking flies on . . . mutant ones Mair calls 'em. She's a reel wag, Mair is. Found a big one in the shape of a cock the other day and chased Iris with it. Iris never got married an' she's old-fashioned-like. She nearly *fainted*."

I smile for the first time today, and her round, worn face creases up: it softens her a little. Everyone warned me women here are the coarsest on the estate – 'common as muck' was the phrase used – and can be the nastiest. Some nice ones, of course, but some real bullies too. I suspect now it's one of the few pleasures they get. I'd go on a serial killing spree for fun if I worked here permanently.

"Yeah . . . first one she's ever seen probably! Well . . . you'll be orlright, lover. Just chuck 'em in the bin. Breakfast is at 'alf nine. They does a good breakfast yere, 'cos we're all bloody starvin' by then. Wait 'til Mair comes to take over, mind. She can do all the jobs. She's been yere longest."

She's gone, and I don't know her name. I wait. I reflect Mair must be a very tough cookie as well as having a Carry-On sense of humour. I don't think I ought to move, as the other women stationed at various points about the huge space are just standing and staring at the belt. We wait. The smell gets suddenly stronger, painful as the huge swell of an orchestra. An uneasy moment of anticipation, and then the orange snacks covered in molten vomit tumble joyfully down a rubber slope to begin their switchback journey around the room, blindly heading for the bright hygienically sealed bags and their intestinal nemesis. I'm first to see them and touch them, and I'm so glad I'm wearing the gloves and mask, even though I've never sweat as much as this before.

I glance quickly around and my fear is confirmed. There are only two of us wearing gloves, thus only two to pick out the mutants, and I can't believe how many there are! Too big. Too small. Hideously misshapen. Burnt black. Broken. Fly-and beetle-spotted. My arms are windmilling and the other woman's arms are a blur too. After a short time, it feels as if someone with a crowbar has broken my spine as I have to bend down and arch over to cull them all. She'll feel the same – or do you get used to it? This then is the reason for the dais: without that extra height, we wouldn't be able to reach across the belt, and it saves having to have two other people on the other side . . . the belt seems to be speeding up. The things keep tumbling. My gloves are soon covered in thick filthy gloop like a poison-yellow oil slick. The smell makes its way through the mask – of course it does! It impregnates everything, clothes, hair and skin – until at last it dawns on me that trying to avoid it is pointless.

Time slows down while I force myself not to sense or think or feel, but suddenly I'm being washed by waves of heat and cold, my legs grow hollow and saliva is running in my mouth as if a tap's been turned on. Oh God – I *know* it's coming. My legs are weakening and I'm going to fall. I know now my father feels like this most of the time, and the knowledge is like a stab in the heart. A strong hand pulls me down off the dais and shoves me towards the locker room doors. It's Mair: the Queen of the Conveyor Belt, the Veteran, the Joker. She has tight curls moulded to her narrow head like a brassy helmet, and lines deep enough to mislay things in scored into her skin.

"Run you silly cow! You'll be orlright when you've chucked. We all does it in yere. I'll fill in 'til you gets back."

I have no idea how I make it, but I do, and soon I'm splashing my face with water, trying to get my breath and stop the trembling of my knees. I'm in shock, I think. My meagre early

20

breakfast of toast and coffee and anything else that lingered in my stomach is on its way to the already polluted sea, and I'm shivering a little as it's much cooler in here and my underwear and overall are soaking with sweat, starting to cling. The woman who showed me the ropes comes in. I make myself stand upright and dry my face.

"Mair said you was going to chuck. Drink some water and have a fry up later and you'll be *fine*. We all does it sometimes, 'specially if we 'as 'angovers or mornin' sickness, like. My daughter used to keep a plastic bag in 'er pocket when she was carryin' as she used to get taken so sudden. Then she'd go on 'til break. 'Ave tea and dry biscuits for breakfast – that always 'elps 'an all."

This somehow is the last blow, and I can't force even a single word out. I've already made my mind up to look for another job. I'll find one – anything would be better! – and I'll be out of here in a couple of weeks. It doesn't feel like cowardice, just plain common sense. And I'm so lucky to have a real choice, the possibility of escape. This makes me more determined than ever to make use of it. Her face creases again.

"Yere."

She gives me a polo mint and I accept and smile my thanks. It'll take the taste away and make my breath smell less like potato snacks. Suddenly, however, I wonder where and how these little sweets are made and can't wait to spit it out.

"Go on, then! Get back to the belt! Mair's coverin' but ole Wanky Williams will notice if you're gone too long. Watch 'im an all – he'll put 'is 'ands where the sun don't shine. He's the randiest bugger yere, an' ugly as sin. Nobody'd touch him with a pole. You'll be orlright now, tho'."

And the strange thing is I am! It's happened, the thing I feared most, but I survived. This bizarre place has opened a cell door in a way, and I know I'm getting – for better than free, because someone's paying *me*! – a successful course of aversion therapy. It feels oddly good now to put the mask in my pocket, pull on the dripping gloves and march out, set on doing the best I can 'til I can make a relatively dignified exit. It will feel strange too after so many years not to dread going home at the end of the day. My father, who between his attacks loves chips and potato snacks, will be sorry when I can no longer take freebies home. I suspect the stink of this place will cling for weeks even after I leave, and I'll be paranoid others will be able to smell it. I'll throw away the old clothes I've worn here, and shower 'til I squeak. I'll feel a lot better, but I will wonder if some ghost of a taint ever quite disappears even if you scrub yourself raw.

Table Dancing

I love waitressing. I hate waitressing; both these statements are true. But even at the bad times, it's an improvement on working in the crisp factory . . . still, clearing up slime after a snail orgy would be better than that. The job I'm doing now is the best of the rest at this stage of the summer. Though it pays peanuts, I'm already finding I can enjoy it immensely if I can get it all right. Another plus point is that punters that go away cheerful and satisfied often leave substantial tips, which can add up surprisingly quickly: some days they outstrip your actual wage. When I hate it are the moments we're so rushed we're not touching the ground, when we fly about like demented grease-fairies. When orders all merge into one overwhelming jumble and tempers fray and spark like a fuse wire. When you can't please anyone and the tips left under saucers wouldn't buy a tin of beans.

Amidst the dizzy whirl, I have time to feel surprised by three phenomena: the first is that you're surrounded by food – some of it very appealing, as this is a decent quality Italian-owned restaurant – but you have no appetite. The kitchens here are better than most, I suppose, but it's still hard to cram down even free lunches and dinners when you've seen and smelt the cook and experienced the train crash that is the food preparation and storage area. Something else I didn't expect is quite how much your feet hurt. At the end of a shift, I'm in real pain, and when I get home and plunge them into cool water, it almost steams and hisses as in a cartoon. I must admit I'm also a little taken aback by how we waitresses are such a ragbag of all ages and classes and types, each with their own story of how they've ended up accepting this exhausting work for 30p an hour.

The most popular amongst us is called Evie. She's a salt-of-the-Earth woman with enormous heart, a great sense of humour and make-up as thick as greasepaint. She's in her thirties, a loud, peroxide blonde, rather sparrow-like, worn down thin under the brassy hair and slap, seeming too small to contain the big personality. She has four children and no perceivable husband. She's never been qualified for or done anything but waitressing.

By now, she's bloody good at it, but she's generous enough to help us newcomers learn the skills quickly. I keep wondering how she can possibly make the meagre wages and the unpredictable tips we earn stretch to housing, feeding and clothing herself and four others. I also wonder how she can have so much humour, energy and endurance: her feet must be like blocks of wood covered with old leather.

In a lull before the business picks up one Friday evening, we're all rather jaded and fed up. Evie puts her hands on her hips. "Cowin 'ell, you miserable lot! Cheer up, for Christ's sake. You'd think some poor old sod had died and been put in the bolognaise."

Her chivvying doesn't have much effect. It's been a busy week, but however hard we've all pushed ourselves, returns have been very poor. Suddenly she has a strangely fixed and determined look on her face. She glances around the dimly lit space, and, finding no sign of the owner or his manager (both profit-driven martinets), she startles us all by leaping from floor to chair to table like a mountain goat. We are paralysed, gazing up like devotees at a shrine when the Virgin's statue starts to weep. But Evie doesn't cry: she dances. It's a neat, fantastically adept little caper, and suddenly we're on the set of an old Hollywood musical. She's good – really good – and I imagine that a big band will strike up, and soon everyone will be on the tables, dancing like Fred or Ginger, belting out ridiculous but irresistible catchy songs in perfect harmony. Instead, only Evie and the cutlery on her table dance amidst the warm silence, her light and oddly graceful movements culminating in a baroque flourish before she jumps back to earth.

After a stunned moment or two, pulling our jaws back up, we all laugh and cheer. Evie curtseys, and her red lips part to make a wide gash. Her eyes shine. Suddenly it's hard to tell if she's grinning like a maniac or about to weep. There's no time for anything but straightening the table quickly, however, and we all get through a long evening so much more easily for our spirits being uplifted.

It's two weeks later and I'm getting quite professional at this job already. I'm learning to manage the rush, the heat, the demands, the changes of order, the complaints, the kitchen jostle, the flash tempers, three steaming plates up each arm, the occasional soup-in-the-customer's-lap disaster. But one thing I have learnt above all others is that we're here to serve no matter what the response or provocation. I've learned you have to work hard and *smile* to get tips. You smile and smile, even if the people you're serving are greedy, arrogant and obnoxious bastards that you'd personally like to force feed with a huge rubber tube. You bare the pearlies even if they make unjustified complaints, rude or suggestive remarks or pinch your arse blue. You serve and smile. Smile and serve. Like so many other things, I have Evie to thank for learning this very fast indeed. And this particular lesson stuck with me more than any other, because Evie doesn't work here anymore.

A few days after her spontaneous dance, a middle class nuclear family sat at one of her tables. From the first moment, they ran her completely ragged. They enjoyed doing it just because they could. They knew about the unwritten serve and smile rule, and they exploited it to the full. When they had stuffed themselves with four delicious courses, after they had swilled wine and coffee and liqueurs like the porkers they were, they all – including the two precocious children – went smirking towards the exit. While Daddy paid at the cash desk, Evie moved to clear up the indescribable mess, garnet-cheeked and sweating. As she lifted a saucer, she found her tip: a penny.

Maybe all the years of serving and smiling finally got to her. Something certainly did: I saw her eyes. In seconds, she had reached the man, roughened fingers yanking at his sleeve. In her very loud and common Swansea accent in front of all the customers and the martinets, she sneered: "'Scuse me, I think you dropped this, and I wouldn't like you to be short now! It's a lot of money, see: you looks like you couldn't afford to lose it."

Then it was like High Noon without guns as she stared the man, his hideous steel-tipped wife and bloated progeny down 'til their cheeks bled red as hers. Finally, when they lowered their eyes, satisfied in a different way to our well-fed customers, Evie stalked away to finish her shift, very tight-lipped and with a look in her eyes that made even the martinets avoid her. We never saw her again. I often wonder if she walked or was pushed. I hope she walked, but I do worry where she is now, a waitress without a reference in a surprisingly small city. I wonder if she's smiling

25

and what she's serving to put enough in her purse to house, feed and clothe herself and those four kids. Meanwhile, those of us who remain have learned another lesson: to keep quiet, keep frantically serving, keep our jobs. As we smile and serve, we hear the jingle and plan what to do with the growing weight of coins in our pockets. No-one will dance on a table again, and we keep our thoughts to ourselves.

Interlude

Eden to Eden

There is a very queasy mix of fear and excitement churning away inside me now. I've won a History scholarship to Aberystwyth, and I am going there! For at least three years! On my own! I hug myself. I will make it work, I will. I have known for over a year that I want to go to this odd, remote Welsh town on the West Coast. I couldn't truly tell you why, but I do. Family and friends say they are glad for me and are stiff upper lipped. They are all helping me as I try to keep any of my doubts at bay by being undemonstrative, accepting this as the natural turn of events. Except David.

David is a lad I met at cricket matches when 15 years old. Our relationship grew in a very gentle way, but was and is platonic. We have played at going on some 'dates', ending in chaste kisses, and I believed we both knew something more substantial was unlikely to develop, especially if we go separate ways. He has decided to study medicine at Cardiff but I have my secret yearning for Aberystwyth, to absorb history along with ozone air. I am of course, not for the first or last time, utterly wrong – and clearly not very good at this relationship malarkey.

I can't fail to notice how genuinely shocked he is when I burst the bubble and admit I have put Aber as first choice, but he rallies to say it won't matter too much: Perhaps it *is* a good idea. We can both study hard, meet as often as possible, get engaged when it seems right, marry when we finish. I am mentally open-mouthed and screaming, but somehow manage to look calm. I quake inside. This is *insane*. I don't know what love is: I feel it for my family and some friends, but even then it is if I am honest a halting, often semi-strangled thing. I certainly feel nothing like that for David. I didn't realise how much, if unwittingly, I've been using him to experiment with what it is like to have a 'boyfriend'. Getting engaged even is a horrifying thought, marriage worse: something for a far distant future with someone else, maybe not at all. But I can't say anything. I am a complete coward. I despise myself, but my strategy, if it deserves the name, is to cut, run and stay out of contact. He will get the message, be hurt, and hate me. He will call me names, but that is better than being brutally honest. Why do I think this? I don't know. I don't know. For now, only the panic counts. I will disappear, throw myself into a new life, a new place. It's all ahead, all in the future, and a clean break from any mess (my creation or not) is needed. I know that even if he writes, I will steel myself not to answer. Something tells me he will not.

I forget feelings of guilt in the excitement of packing my huge trunk and relishing the thought of my own room in an anonymous hall and truly leading a life of my own. I feel guilty again however when I realise how much my family is struggling to keep those upper lips stiff despite a lifetime of practice, but all I feel is mounting joy. Free!

Paradise Regained and Lost

I know the kind of happiness I'm feeling now is very rare, and words can barely do it justice. It may not sound like much to you, but it's all because I've made it to university, to Aberystwyth, and despite the happy years at grammar school, on an emotional plane it's as if I've come home to fresh air and green fields after eighteen years on a barren, alien world. The opposing forces of belonging and yet total release are making me dizzy. I can't really fathom why, but my body seems lighter, my blood is frothing in the vein, and I want to keep on hugging myself. Not only have I landed where I want to be, but I've also managed to win a scholarship to top-up my grant. If I'm careful with budgeting – and I always am – I'll be free to study and enjoy life unless I need to pay for some travel abroad. Right now, however, all I want to do is savour the moments as I walk down the long, steep hill towards the little market town that sleeps out of season and opens like a brightly coloured fly-trap to catch tourists in the summer. Someone told me recently that with a population of about 10,000, it has fifty-four chapels and fifty-five pubs: for some reason this pleases me inordinately, and I smile as I think of it now.

Distracted I may be, but I am speeding towards my goal, which is the decaying Victorian sea front and the old college building that looks like every child's fantasy of a mediaeval castle. There should be knights tilting in the courtyards, and ladies in very pointy hats trapped sighing in round gothic turrets. But around me now, in this time, in this polished bronze September, the sky is blue, the breeze light but fresh, the sun still has real power. This weather cocktail turns the sea into a blinding metallic sheet reaching all the way to Ireland and beyond, into infinity.

You'll probably scoff, but, living here, it's easy to believe that behind the dark veils that so often obscure the horizon lies Tir na Nog, home of the Happy Dead, paradise of the Ever-Young. Strange how here I feel so much more Welsh, more Celtic despite my blemish of English blood. My mother's ancestors were Gloucestershire farming folk, who could see the Severn and mountain beacons of Wales from the village where they lived. Soon they were drawn across the river to live there. Truth to tell, it wasn't the landscape or close-harmony singing that seduced them, but the lures of industry: it must have seemed worth it to them to go from backbreaking graft for little reward to lung-rotting graft for a solid packet of money in the hand.

Strange that some spell cast by this magical place has performed the reverse operation on me, drawing me away from the urban spreads, making my bones sing and my (predominant) genes perk up and dance. I spend a lot of time listening in a dazed and happy dream to traditional harp and folk music these days – when I'm not busy with all there is to do here. I suppose if I must narrow it down, identify the chief enchanter, it's the air. It's so startlingly *clean*, and it smells and tastes of ozone and salt. This makes it more intoxicating than champagne or any drug, so that breathing in is like sucking down pure oxygen. It's a kind of tonic, and everyone coming here feels young and healthy, almost light-headed. You can see the magic working immediately as people step off the buses and trains.

I find I'm almost running now as my energy level rises, and I have to resist the urge to skip and sing. It's hard to hide that I have *become* Joy, but there are limits to how much eccentricity the sometimes dour townsfolk will take from students – and that would definitely be going too far. Good enough that I know I'm living in this lovely place, so remote from anywhere else, circled by sea and green hills, sky arcing above it all. Good enough that I'm here, freed to be myself, comfortable in my skin at last. Actually maybe I shouldn't try to separate off any one element: I love it *all* equally, water and rock and land, the town itself that seems – despite the influx of students and tourists – to be a time-locked, off-kilter kind of place. It's a little shabby, it's true, but that's part of its charm and makes it as lived in as a worn and comfortable slipper. I don't stop to analyse why I never felt this delight in my home town. But why dwell on it? Why dwell on anything? When you're blissfully happy, the immediate present is all that matters.

I speed up even more as I approach the inviting spread of the college along the shore, the ridiculous ramble of building with its huge cathedral-like library, its winding stairs and dusty lancet-windowed tutorial rooms. Having the chance to lose myself in there in historical periods that fascinate me is another kind of ecstasy. Sometimes I think I'll implode with it, especially when I look up from a page, catch sight of the sea creaming on black rocks below and actually shiver with pleasure. Don't get the wrong idea, however: I've never had trouble making friends, and I'm not leading a melancholic hermit's existence – far from it. I knew one or two people coming here, and am forging friendships, grabbing every social opportunity. I have a strong feeling that the only bad thing about my choice to come here will be that I'm going to find it next to impossible to leave at the appointed time.

This rapture doesn't wear off, and my love affair with my studies and the town only waxes stronger. Even when the last tourist has been blown away on strengthening autumn winds, even when vicious winter storms crash in from the Irish Sea, the attachment keeps on growing and I'm undaunted. After all, true love doesn't alter where it alteration finds! But something happens to bring on a change, something I don't expect at all: you'll think me incredibly naïve, but that something is *sex*. Ah yes: the old serpent in Eden stuff. It may sound mad, but I never particularly thought about it up to now. I attended an all-girl school where you worked and played hard and enjoyed a lot of intense but (in my circle at least) genuinely innocent friendships . . . And I'm a little embarrassed to admit that I only ever had one boyfriend. This was from the age of fifteen, and he really was never anything more than a companion.

Looking back, I can see this was – considering the rest of the world has undergone a sexual revolution and 'anything goes' – a remarkably chaste interlude. Cricket matches; the pictures; holding hands; kisses on the cheek or tentative pecks on the lips; enjoying the grown-up feel of going on 'dates' without any real commitment or having to face scary experiences and choices. Well, that's what *I* thought: he as I have already confessed was expecting an engagement. Best now to draw a thick cloth over his reaction to my declaring I am going to Aberystwyth and, well, that's that. After what is probably our longest and deepest conversation to date, we part. On his side, the silence of bamboozled anger and bitter disappointment: on mine, a kind of annoyance at his presumption, but most of all, shame at my own idiocy and guilt that I've hurt him and seen things only from my point of view. A part of me wants to write, stay in touch, remain friends: the other part wants to cut and run. I run.

So here I am then: a virgin in mind and body, a blank sexual page, almost unheard of amongst my peers. If people were pure when they arrived here, a state of innocence didn't last very long. I suppose there may be others like me, strangers from a near-distant past, but I don't seem to meet any of them. Perhaps I should choose to go on as I am, a happy, studious but surprisingly sociable Heloise. But once the serpent has pricked you with his fangs . . . my mind is constantly ticking: *ought* I to pursue an Abelard? It seems to be the Next Logical Step. I'm becoming a young adult, living independently, responsible for myself. A lot of people meet partners at university! A lot of people are married and starting families in their early twenties! With a jolt of recognition, I realise what an absolute child I am. Perhaps it's time to join the real world. The excitement of my thoughts catches at my throat, and, if I'm honest, my hormones have been sizzling for some time. A lot has been stirring in the dark, and I'm beginning to be tormented by painful black aches and desires, a physical compulsion that started before my mind started to catch up. My body and mind are clearly out of sync, struggling to fall into step alongside each other. It's an odd feeling until they do – like constantly catching sight of two selves in a double-glazed window.

Small wonder then that when a very attractive man called Lawrence in his final year starts paying me attention, I respond. I'm flattered. He's twenty-one, tall, dark-haired, intelligent. He's a little quiet and shy, definitely not a slime-ball. His friends think it's amazing he's so smitten, as he's led a quieter life than they do and his only aim is to teach. My friends think it's amazing I'm responding, as everyone knows me as the life and soul who doesn't take anyone home after the parties, the discos, the visits to bars. At this time, I'm slim and have very long blonde hair and men seem to find me attractive. I must say I'm not entirely convinced and usually wear long, hippy-type skirts and voluminous blouses, letting my hair fall forward to hide my face. But we are drawn to each other, and our friends push us closer. Double dates are arranged. Then walks together. Dinners. The pictures. Concerts. The theatre. Sitting. Talking. Getting closer. A small insistent voice whispering, urging me on: '. . . *it has to be sometime. Everyone has to do this at some time'*.

I no longer know what to feel or think, and there doesn't seem to be a book about this on the shelves in the cathedral-like library.

I don't want to front up about my pathetic doubts and fears to my seemingly sophisticated friends. I assume the attraction, the liking, the fact he seems so keen on me, the enjoyment of each other's company – all these things will make it work. They seem to be enough for other people to enter into sexual relationships: indeed, a lot of my fellows don't even seem to demand that – there are myriad drunken and stoned couplings every night all over the campus and town, people who don't know each other's names and want to forget them if they do: amnesiac sex, I call it. All my careful upbringing and instincts prevent me from indulging in that, but neither is – quite maddeningly – guiding me to any certainty about what I *do* want.

Because I drift in a fog of indecision, it all seems in the end to happen to someone else. I don't quite remember how or when the decision is reached, but I'm in a doctor's surgery and being prescribed the Pill. No-one seems to care about any rumoured side-effects and neither do I: it's just a modern miracle that means you can have sex without consequences whenever you like with whomever you like. Then at the appointed time, we plan a romantic evening. We want to do it right. So, like children painting by numbers, we have dinner by candlelight. We walk by the glittering sea. We drink a mediocre German wine. Then unlike children, we light more candles, go to bed, have sex. He enjoys himself enormously: I like the warmth, the stroking part, the intimacy – but in sexual terms feel nothing at all. I thought I might find it painful, might hate it, might love it, might just have the firework-exploding Hollywood experience or faint away with poetic raptures. It's true to say, however, that I would be hard pressed to describe any sensations at all, and realise I have had more pleasure out of a good meal, reading a book or walking along the cliffs.

Against instinct, I'm impelled to pretend. If I'm honest, you see, I'll have to face what's just happened. Admit I don't have a clue what I'm doing, that there seems to be something wrong with me, that I've made a huge mistake. I'll have to hurt Lawrence, burst his bubble. It will be messy and I want things simple and clean: indeed, I wish I'd never taken even a tiny step outside the gates of Eden. So I lie. And lie again. With my lips, my body, my behaviour. I find some positives in being part of a couple, doing all the other things we can both enjoy. There's pleasure too in

33

being seen by my peers as an adult, as normal, even as lucky. But there's a disgusting worm in the fruit, a spitting cobra hidden in dew-dropped grass. And all my pure happiness is receding with the spring tide.

I worry away at what is an already fragmented and dry bone. Would it be like this then with *any* man? Am I what people (men) call 'frigid'? How on earth do you talk to someone, anyone, let alone the person concerned, about this? Maybe this is the way it really is, and it's books and poems and films that are the liars! I remember my mother's mutterings about no-one in their right mind wanting to give birth and throwing out dark hints that sex is an experience only indecent women would seek out or enjoy. Snatches of other conversations overheard through the years make sense now, the whispers about lying back and thinking of England. Or rather Wales. Yet . . . yet I have read and read voraciously about so many people's positive experiences and look at other young women around me, at my friends: have they all been and are they still lying and pretending? Ridiculous! *He's* fine too, apparently, and has noticed nothing wrong. Ergo I am the abnormal one, the one outside the circle.

All the time the pretence and worry is diminishing me, I do know the only way to get my innocence back, to be happy again, is to tell the truth and do what I know is right for me and for him. But of course I can't, and instead I agree to spend the whole summer with Lawrence touring Dorset. I even agree at the end of the holiday to visit Kent, where he comes from, and to meet his parents and his brother. Sweat pricks out hot all over my body as I think of his excitement about this, and I loathe myself for my weakness. Still my mind tries to reason, to persuade me it may help the relationship work, this long summer together in the sun. I know it won't, but I go all the same, with the knowledge that if it doesn't improve, if I can't find the key that will help me enjoy all the things we do or rather that he does to me, then I will have to tell him.

Summer Term is over, and I've managed 'A's' in the all-important first year tests. My pleasure and relief is tempered, however, by the fact we have to drive off along winding roads taking us south. I am envied now by some, but they don't know that I'd far rather be working through the heat, would prefer to be safe amidst the sweat and chemical racket of a factory or wearing the skin of my feet raw on restaurant floors. As we hit a straighter stretch of the coast road than usual, I glance back, desperate to catch a glimpse of the old white town sprawling between sea and hills, but the morning mists are too thick. A huge lump swells in my throat so that I have to force back tears and pretend to be looking at something fascinating out of the window. It's raining lightly but persistently now, the windows are closed tight and it's too stuffy in here. There's no sound except that of the car engine and folk music tinkling softly, but I swear I can hear gates clanging shut behind me, and a wistful little plopping sound as a different kind of key drops into the waves. I jump as he speaks suddenly, and my head turns. Then I'm learning again to paint by numbers, furiously but neatly filling all the gaps to make something tawdry and not worth the doing.

What Lies Beneath?

I am now with my second 'serious' partner, a German exchange student two years older than I called Michael, pronounced Mee-ch -ay-el. Everyone calls him Mick but I like the German contraction of Micha. Though the seventies are ending, he is a man spiritually trapped in the '60s: he believes he's a sort of Teutonic Bob Dylan – except he can't write songs, sing even vaguely in tune or play the guitar well. He also isn't rich and famous, and, instead of a few stray hairs wandering in a stoned kind of way over his chin, he has a full and shapely on-the-verges-of-a-Desperate-Dan beard. I don't know how other people feel about them, but I just don't like beards: they irritate me aesthetically as well as physically. I just don't see the point: we've come a long way since we dwelt in caves. Razors are cheap and no longer cut throats. You can even get electrical ones which don't cut your skin at all.

At first, it seems of very minor importance as, when he begins courting me, I am completely indifferent to him and all his body hair. After the upsetting split from my first partner Lawrence, I do not want to have a man in my life AT ALL. At the end of a summer holiday, when talk turned to an engagement once again, my own feelings being so eerily disengaged, I panicked and ran. So I use that word 'court' very deliberately, Victorian as it is. I never imagined a man could be this persistent: it appears even German hippies are relentlessly efficient. To my growing embarrassment, he brings flowers, wine, chocolates, gifts. He reads poems to me, serenades me with music, takes me to dinner, writes notes, sends letters (though he lives about 200 yards away), makes date after date (as a rule fruitlessly). Eventually I am reduced to avoiding him as much as I can, and am even resorting to diving into doorways or sitting in my room with the light off holding my breath when he calls.

After what seems like years but is a matter of weeks, one afternoon, despite being busy working (with enormous but unlikely pleasure) on an essay about Mediaeval Welsh farming patterns, in a fit of daft compassion I let him in. And there he is, specially dressed for courting in black polished boots and trousers, a yellow jumper and a cravat (?), sitting in the single chair. He is very comfortable, droning away in his oddly Dietrich-y accent about music, sipping the cold wine he's brought me, and something clicks inside, like an engine catching. There's no rational explanation: some intangible force mutually connects, and falls into a rhythm. To my own surprise, we become quickly inseparable: people are calling us MickandHelen. He is joyful. I am swept up. Naturally the beard recedes ever further into the background as the bond between us grows and we see each other through a rosy mist.

. . . But time ticks and though still appearing inseparable, the mist burns off. Now I'm at a point where I'm eyeing that chin fur and mentally drumming my fingers. Yes: the time is come. I've put up with the thing long enough. I know it could be worse – it could be a ZZ Top beard, a Quaker beard, a John Knox or Gandalf or Mephistopheles beard or one of those appalling little triangles of hair on the chin. I know it is at least a beard with some shape and self-respect, but it's still a beard. I decide the campaign will begin today. For years I watched a mistress of manipulation, my mother, who could have nagged and confused my father into eating his own feet if she'd wanted to. So it's war. I will choose and use weapons carefully. I'll nag, wheedle, plead, erode, haggle, threaten, annoy, niggle, flatter, reason . . . I'll pop sugarplums into his mouth to take away any bitter taste . . . you have such a distinctive face, Micha, I'll say: it's a pity to hide it . . . losing the fuzz will make you look *younger*. You'll be so much cooler and happier without it!

At last, worn down and desperate, he's doing it. V for victory for me; V for vanquished for him. He's taken over the bathroom for what seems like hours. I imagine him in there being as efficient as ever, with the scissors, foam, shaving brush, razor, clippers, *Tabac* aftershave laid out neatly on a cloth as in an operating theatre. The strange thing is, I've begun to believe my own propaganda, and I'm excited, looking forward to the new clean-shaven Micha. He will look younger! He will be cooler! He'll like it. We both will. He'll wonder why he resisted for so long. I'll nobly resist saying I told you so.

But when the bathroom door slowly opens, and I catch sight of that perfectly naked chin, my own drops. When people write about jaws dropping, you know it's just a cliché, a lazy phrase. But this is shocking, and I truly have to make an effort to close my mouth again. He stares at me and I stare at him. I never knew and maybe after all these years he had forgotten: but his chin is exactly the same shape as the beard: it wasn't that his beard had been full and square, it was a layer of whiskers hiding a Hapsburg chin so authentic I wonder if he has a drop or two of real Imperial Blood. His reaction as I plead with him to grow it again is best not spoken of: it is very un-summer of love. For now we are shaken and silent: something oddly serious has happened and we both know it. Maybe our relationship will survive for some time despite this, and he can grow the fuzz again and welcome, but for now we both feel as cold and exposed as his white jowls at the slipping of a mask.

If this is a tragicomic test, however, then unknown to me the real killer exam is on its way. Our sexual life you could call active: I suspect radioactive would be more fitting. His friends all leg it like spooked sheep when I go into his room: they know what will happen when he grabs and kisses me in greeting. Honest revelations again, however: though I am relieved that he appears not to notice at all – my own invisible mask is so perfectly moulded to my skin by now – I still feel nothing except a kind of happiness at helping achieve such joy in him. It makes me feel a little more real, more normal. But all my caution in taking the Pill does not protect me from the consequences of these mismatch unions, and I start to suspect I am pregnant. I have heard this happens, but I can't believe it. Despite being such an adept at ignoring what is troubling, I have to acknowledge something is way off kilter, with my period weeks late and feelings of disconnection, nausea, fear and a kind of exhaustion taking me over. I feel sick all day till about 10 p.m., and it's super intense in the mornings. By midday, I have only bile left to ring up. I live on liquids. At 10 p.m., I yearn for something horrible like a hamburger and chips. In the end, even I can't pretend this isn't happening: I feel and look like an undead, and there's the myriad complexities and consequences to face and process.

38

I have heard people whispering about other students this has happened to and how they had to 'deal with' their unwanted 'difficulty'. Though the summer of love was a decade ago and this is the promiscuous seventies, it makes remarkably little difference in Chapel-going rural Wales. I swear they still keep their piano legs covered in some of the more remote areas. Such a situation is, simply, shocking. Implications are that such girls are not only loose but stupid. This feels suddenly ferociously unfair: I am neither! More than feeling the injustice, however, I am terrified. The end of my child-world looms, the facing of the ultimate responsibility! The ruin of studies, degrees, career plans! The shame of parents and family! Those whispers and assumptions! And, yet . . . a BABY: Imagine – A beautiful baby; warm, snuffling and heavy on your chest; looking up; so vulnerable, needing and loving you in equal measure. My heart contracts with the pain of intense, tangible, pure love.

With a kind of horror, I realise I have never felt this before: any resemblance to earlier 'love' even for parents and close family – let alone friends or partners – was pale compared.

To feel as confused as this . . . a baby . . . but dear God how will Micha react? He believes himself to be freewheelin' like Jack Kerouac and Neal Cassady, a fiery, wandering creative spirit like a beat poet or a spiritual quester like Castaneada. Babies are not – might never be? – on his road map. And when I find a way to tell him, he reacts oddly. He looks simultaneously puff-chested macho-proud, diminished, fearful, shifty, panicked. Though it is usually a cliché, his eyes really do shift from side to side. He certainly can't pretend to any happiness. The chest quickly deflates. He takes my hand, but not to express love and joy and optimism, not to reassure: it is to entreat me earnestly to get to a doctor and arrange a termination immediately. He rambles about how I am his 'lady' and his muse (as if he is a rock and roll star) and we – he – cannot lead the lives we need to and must with a baby in tow. He seems to think a termination is some sad yet romantic thing freewheelin' people have to do, and then of course, write and sing melancholy songs about. All is shock, confusion. An insistent voice deep inside me says he is advising wisely, even if for the wrong reasons but - but - but . . .

In a genuine daze, I make an appointment with a doctor. The test is positive. Her advice is mercifully without judgment and more even handed. She will be happy to go with my decision, and insists it has to be MY decision. She says I need to see another doctor and can think about it, talk more to him or her. There is time. More shock, more confusion. I can't think for the bloody nausea. I didn't know how weak you can feel, either, on a liquid diet. If this physical onslaught continues for longer than is usual, what will I do? A part of me knows too that if I feel I must go on, I will have to go home, to the village-y whispers, looks of disapproval, shaking heads. After the hard initial shock and disappointment, my family will accept and help, of course they will, but I will be back where I know I do not want to be. This will be cancelled out as I will have the golden, shining prize of a baby of course . . . but then I will have to leave him or her every day in any case to work in some dreary 9-5 job to support him or her. Him or Her. Already not an 'it'. The names in my head are – Heaven knows why – Gareth or Eirwen. Yes, I would be trapped loving and caring for little Gareth or Eiri. Trapped.

It really does feel as if I'm on a roller coaster that is speeding up and up. Up. Down. Round sickeningly sharp corners. Up and down again. Feeling mortally afraid, sick, sometimes exhilarated, but, in the end, weak, legs like water, just wanting it to stop.

In the end it does stop, and very suddenly. I wake the night before I'm due to see doctor number 2, sweating and in pain that makes my periods seem like amateurs. I am bleeding. I know immediately it's not my decision any more. I alternately weep, grit my teeth, moan. An ambulance takes me to the small hospital in this small town. Micha is somewhere nearby but I see only grey or neon blurs and hear disjointed sounds. When peace comes, I am empty and sore, but definitely alive. The oddest thing to think of at such a time, but God it is marvellous not to feel sick anymore and I am stupidly, ferociously hungry. Empty. There is a trail of a memory: someone nearby screaming. Was it real? Was someone giving birth in an adjoining area? Micha holds my hand. He has tears on his cheeks. For whom? I feel oddly displaced. The staff here is not as non-judgmental as my GP: indeed, they are hostile, as if I have personally offended them. One of the nurses tells me through thinned lips when Micha is shooed away that it was ME screaming. They were all spooked and clearly in the end deeply annoyed by this nuisance. No kindness to be hoped for here: I don't want it in any case and am as happy as they when I am patched up to be readied for home. Thin-lips at least brings me tea and toast, and nothing I have ever had ever tasted this good. For the next days, I eat and eat. I feel better.

They say I am young and healthy and will recover very fast. After the briefest examination, with no reason offered for what happened, there is only a clipped 'Often we don't know. No reason you shouldn't have other babies'. An unspoken: ' – at the right time and when you are married and secure'. They eye Micha with real distrust and the looks seem to say '. . . and not when you are with someone like THAT.'

Nestbreaking

There are lots of other relationships for me in Aber of course: it's so like a village, you get to know everyone quickly. Some people hate this and can't settle: I think it's because the flip side of that is there is little to no privacy and everyone knows your business in minutes. I have female and male friends in lectures, hall, the folk and cinema clubs, friends to go for a drink with or listen to music with or dance with, go on cliff walks, play darts, have lunch, coffee and so on and on. My closest friend is another Helen, of whom more below, but three who are important are what I can only call cuckoos, people who attach themselves to you with no invitation and seem to crash their way into your nest. I feel they are connected too by an odd thread: the first, Val, looks like a demented Mona Lisa, so I imagine the second looks like another portrait of a woman by Leonardo and the third is so thin he reminds me of anatomical drawings by the same artist. All cuckoos: all conjured by Leonardo. Here they are.

Not the Mona Lisa

Val is a history student like me and on registration day, when we are queuing on a grand, ever upward-winding staircase in the gothic Old Building, she attaches herself to my side and thereafter follows me everywhere. It makes me deeply uneasy, but we're all so new and nervous, any friendly overtures are hard to rebuff, so I smile and chat. Truth be told I'm puzzled and am never quite sure how I feel about it;

1   Why would anyone attach themselves to me? This in itself I find odd as I find it hard to believe in myself, let alone have what appears as a disciple. Though we are the same age, she must look like a dishevelled fluffy chick glued to the smoother feathers of mama duck.
2   She has such a wacky appearance and sense of humour. This makes me look very conventional and sane, of course, which are big plus points, but my self esteem is far shorter

42

than my skirts and I prefer to blend in just now. I've become very good at this, and I don't think I like the kind of eye-popping, jaw dropping attention she draws. If people stare at her, they will probably stare at me!

The trouble is it's impossible in *any context* not to notice her. Val has a shock of long, wild, mad hair fizzing around a pale, pointed face. Her hazel eyes are oddly narrowed and her eyebrows wonky strings. The eyes twinkle with humour and her long, taloned fingers are expressive, the nails a different striking colour each day, always creating blurred rainbow auras through the air. She is an odd shape, too, a rotund, stocky torso plonked on top of plump thighs with legs tapering sharply to super thin calves and ankles.

On those legs Val wears psychedelic leggings, and, over the leggings, knee high boots. Because I know what's under the leggings and boots I do have to smile. Though we hardly have enough money to eat well, Val buys expensive leg make up, the kind a svelte blonde model would wear to show off endless, perfectly shaped legs between a mini skirt and elegant strappy sandals. Val applies the make up with more care than Leonardo used to craft La Giaconda; it takes hours every morning for the three years I know her. Though she's up at dawn, it makes her late for breakfast, buses, lectures, her life.

When it's done and dried, she pulls on her leggings and boots, taking exaggerated care to smudge neither the leg make up nor her freshly stained hand-and toe-nails. Then she is ready, confident, striding out joyfully into what always seems in this small seaside town to be a golden ozone haze that could revive a corpse. Val does not need reviving: she is very much alive. She is always happy.

It's odd that familiarity doesn't help: indeed, the longer I know her, the less capable I feel of coping with Val's eager friendship. In our first year, she, I and another girl called Helen grow into a tight group. I'm tall, the other Helen short, so we are to everyone Big Helen and Little Helen. We three even go on amicably to share a flat for our second year. Halfway through the year though, Val, who can't cook and eats frozen – *really* frozen, popped straight from the freezer for a few minutes into burning fat! – pancakes every day and is scared of bills, loses courage. She prefers the easier and cheaper option of hall. Though she chooses to move out, we stay in good touch. We are friends, after all. It is after this that Little Helen and I become (mercifully) spectators rather than active participants as Val slides from wackiness into something that feels more sinister.

We go one day to take her birthday cards, presents and a little cake. There are a lot of cards on every available space. While Val makes us tea to go with the cake, I idly look through them. With a physical shock, I can see she has sent all but one or two to herself. Her handwriting is inimitable; it straggles in strange shapes like her string brows. There is no doubt. I say nothing. I tell Helen afterwards. We have no idea what to do so we do nothing. Val is just eccentric, isn't she? She is harming no-one.

On another visit – we've been too busy to see her for weeks – she tells us excitedly she has an American suitor. He visits only at night, driving his motorbike along the dark, winding and dangerous country roads to see her. With hearts sinking into our boots, we know of course he doesn't exist. We don't know what to say, so we say nothing. This story runs and runs until he dies tragically in an accident. After this we hear of how he wanted to leave her his fortune, his millions; his father contested this and won. Grudgingly, however, he is allowing her to keep a huge emerald pendant her suitor had left her. When we ask to see it, Val says it is secured in a bank vault in London.

I am at a loss what to do: I begin to worry at what point all this growing strangeness will be noted – who else has she told? – and could reflect badly on me. Val even looks wilder than ever. I start to cringe at the embarrassment of association. Still, though we have a circle of sane friends, Helen and I do stay loyal to Val, for whom we care too much to walk away.

Then, one day, with the face-slap shock of life's randomness, she meets and becomes deeply involved with someone my partner knows, another German exchange student called Wolf. His mad frizz of lighter brown hair frames a thin, pale, plain face. He is buck-toothed and big nosed, with one of those non-beards on his pointy chin, at best a *jolie laide,* but brimful of personality and painted with a streak of sun-bright madness the width of a German Autobahn.

Not long after we first meet, he slips a piece of paper with something drawn on it into my hand, whispering it's the Black Spot of Treasure Island. It is too. Glory be, he IS madder than Val! We all laugh, and I'm afraid it's at him not with him. The curse means nothing to me: indeed, I feel only the lightness of growing relief when he begins to take up all of Val's attention and time. Surely, if they are so happy, we can forget those cards to herself at birthdays and Christmases? Put out of our minds all the crazy lies about the American and the Emerald? And, best of all, though we do not say it aloud, bury our cowardice at not confronting the deceptions?

Even more so, we feel free of concern when they get engaged, he whisks her off to Duesseldorf and they get married there. Of course it's quite natural under those circumstances to lose touch. We're hellish busy with work and our own relationships and she is leading a brand new life. We truly hope she is happy.

Since this sudden dislocation, however, something of Val's sweet, generous and brave but weird spirit has haunted me just as Mona Lisa's smirk seems burned on the consciousness of the world. It's *always* there somewhere, eternal and mysterious, unsettling, as if she can still see me and straight through me. I understand Wolf's curse now: He immediately loved her and knew me for what I was, a fair-weather and cowardly friend. Somewhere I'm quite sure he's smiling into his bizarre non-beard because he knows that the Black Spot worked, and from the day he took Val away, there's been a psychedelic hole in my soul, and it will always let in water.

The Italian Girl: La Belle Ferroniere

She looks like that portrait supposed to be by Leonardo of La Belle Ferroniere – the ironmonger's beautiful wife. It's a very secular head, definitely not a Madonna, a lovely yet slightly imperfect face you would really see on the streets of 15th century Italy, or, indeed, of 20th century Wales.

As you look at the ideal and the real thing, you will be struck by how there is a dark, hard gloss on both young women, and something amiss with all the features too, something to make you uneasy, hinting at the character beneath. You understand why a painter would itch to paint that head. Why he would feel it worth the struggle to convey the sallowness of the skin, the enigma of the nose that is at the same time too narrow and yet too wide, stunted somehow, with no softness in it. Why he would sweat till twilight faded to capture in oils the sheen of the dark, straight hair matching exactly the glinting flat planes in her brown eyes. Why he would risk going mad to capture perfectly the unpleasantness of the mouth, a silent, pretty rosebud-bow with a sardonic twist.

And the real girl . . . None of us, her fellow students firmly anchored in 20th century Wales, likes her. None of us understands why she attaches herself particularly to us. We three are already firm friends of a year, petite pretty Helen who looks like a doll, mad Val who looks like a demented hippy and my ordinary self. Val attached herself to us at the start of the first year, but, though wary of some of her eccentricities, we love her. She is now one of us. At the end of this first year of university in Aberystwyth, we are already sniffing the delirious scent of freedom to come as we plan to move into our own rented flat.

It's no show-piece, but on the first floor of a tall Victorian house halfway up a very steep Victorian street. It's full of ancient but not venerable furniture. The carpets are threadbare and worn, the wallpaper tired unto death; Oscar Wilde would have rolled his eyes to Heaven and died on the spot. The landlord is called Percy. We call him Percy the Purse as he declares he doesn't care what we do if we cause no damage, keep the house reasonably clean and, above all, pay our rent.

Still, we love it. It's going to be *ours*. We will be free: free to cook and eat what we like, get up when we like. We will be free to have visitors of either sex at any time. There's space everywhere for us to stamp our personalities onto. Oh, the endless possibilities! We feel as excited as little kids and mightily grown up at the same time. Like the sea air outside the sash windows, the thought is purely intoxicating.

There is one issue troubling us but we aren't prepared to explore it yet; we will be paying rent and bills for the first time in our lives, and it is really a flat for four. There's no-one else we want to share with however, and we hope, with teenage vagueness and crossed fingers and toes, that three can manage with careful budgeting.

Around this time, the Italian girl begins to attach herself to us at lunchtimes in the student union. We know her by sight from lectures and seminars, but suddenly she is always close by. She chats about work, exams, music, the fact she is half Italian, that her father owns a cafe and she can cook real Italian food. One Sunday, the day we have to cook our own tea (usually beans on toast), she cooks us spaghetti the way she tells us the Italians do on a one-ring stove in hall. We are polite of course, but privately amazed that after 3 hours there isn't enough sauce and it doesn't excite us in the least. She mourns the fact she can't cook us other Italian dishes without a proper stove, without an oven; we could feast otherwise on homemade pizzas and lasagne!

Gradually we find our anxiety mounting as she talks constantly about all the reading and revision she's doing for the end of first year exams. In the first year, if you want to study a modern European language, one of the compulsory 3 subjects has to be a language new to you. If you don't then pass all three, you're out. Of course we are all nervous as cats – and now this. How does she find the time to do all the extra work on top of essays and presentations? However, we can't risk failing: if this is required, and if she can fit it all in, we can. We work harder and later to keep up. It's like an academic Keystone Cops. We read more books – faster, faster! We scribble notes. Learn by rote. Faster! Keep up! We've all chosen Italian as a new language, and she is of course helpful to us in this as we cram vocabulary and grammar like preppy schoolboys afraid of the swingeing cane. Stay awake!

Suddenly, though we don't know how and still feel uneasy in her company, she is part of the group. It's a bloodless coup. We are too busy and tired to fight it. The exams come and go. The floating-on-a-cloud relief to have them done is soon replaced by greasy nausea as we wait for the results. Then, as they always do, they appear, are posted, and we crowd round. We have passed, Helen, Val and I with 3 top grades. But the Italian girl has just scraped through. Just! We stare at each other. Suddenly, she is nowhere to be seen. So we hug, circling like three un-Graces in a dance of daft joy.

When we come to our senses, we reassure each other we are through. It is all real. In a few months we will be in our flat. Second years; proper students; independent adults. How will we get through the long, hot holidays until September comes again?

Well here we are, settled in, feeling as happy as anyone has the right to be. Val is eccentric and scatty, it's true, but she has a room of her own and we are used to opening windows to let out the smell of her Bird's Eye frozen pancakes that she fries so they are burnt on the outside and still frozen inside. She eats them every day, but lives. Helen and I are naturally neat and Val does her best. We are all easy-going too, so we have none of the usual spats of sharers. As we expected however, it isn't long before our student grants and money hard-earned in the holidays is being stretched to the limit. Glumly, we know we will have to find a fourth occupant. Percy will show no mercy to those who don't pay up.

Then there she is again, the Italian girl. Back at our sides like a shadow. Chatting. Amenable. Is she really so bad? Her empty boasting after all had spurred us on to great things. We will take her fibs with a big pinch of salt now. Val shrugs her shoulders at having to share a room; it's only for sleep after all, and better than losing our home. So she's in.

It comes quickly, the end of the honeymoon period. She is lazy and dirty. Not untidy or a bit slapdash, but a genuine slut. Cups and plates left in her room, growing penicillin. Dirty pots all over the kitchen too, so we have nothing to cook in or eat off or drink out of unless we do huge washing up sessions. She ignores our complaints and does that maddening thing of acting as if we are incredibly bourgeois and uncool to care. She comes and goes as she pleases. Val often can't get to bed at a time of her choosing or indeed at all if the Italian girl has a boyfriend in their room. At these times, Val sleeps miserably on the lumpy couch.

It's hard to explain how cowardly we are, and how we fail to get her to change or, if she won't, to tell her to go. Struggling financially would instead be a blessing. We could eat less and go cold in the winter. But this is irrelevant: we can't find the courage to tell her to leave.

By this time, whilst Helen and Val are going on dates and to discotheques looking for boyfriends, I am settling into a steady relationship with my boyfriend Micha. It feels serious, and, after a slow start as I hadn't been as keen as he, we are growing very close. Helen, Val and I notice with gritted teeth how the Italian girl changes dramatically if a male is anywhere near: the dark eyes light up as if from within, and she is like a car going into top gear. She could flirt for the Olympics and would undoubtedly win Gold.

On several occasions, I catch her flirting with Micha. He is like a hedgehog in headlamps, and she is very determined. I seethe. We are all seething most of the time as we are so sick of her. We are only happy if she is out. One day, I'm in the bathroom and Micha talking with Val and Helen in the living room. I hear the door of the flat slam, and the Italian girl's steps on the stairs. I finish what I am doing, and move to join the others.

As I enter the room, I see her perched on the arm of the old armchair my boyfriend is hammocked in, leaning over him, teasing, touching, flirting. I've heard people describe seeing a red mist when anger takes over your soul. I see a white light. I don't remember much after this, though the others tell me the ensuing scene was epic. I apparently give her a good slap, shout a lot, haul her out of the room physically and stand over her while she packs her bags. I tell her everything that we have kept in over several months. She leaves. She never darkens the door again. The flat is clean and peaceful. We can breathe.

I suppose I should be ashamed of my red jealousy, white anger and abuse of a fellow student, but I'm not. I am usually hopeless at expressing anger, pathetic and paralysed. I never did anything like this before and can't imagine doing anything like it again. I often wonder where she went. Is she is still much the same? She won't look very different, I suspect, though life will score some deeper lines into her skin. Whether they are laughter lines or scars of malice and bitterness will depend on her. Yes, the portrait will become crackled and a little faded with time, and to me it will always have no name.

Anatomical: Skinman

When I think of him I think of Leonardo's skeletal figure drawings, the limbs all taut-drawn skin, visible sinew, underlying bone. He looks like that. We call him Skinman.

He's a very tall young-old man, absurdly thin, gangling, beyond pale, blonde. He says little. He does share with us however that he makes and collects models of buses. Of that subject he has an encyclopaedic knowledge. As we are only interested in using buses to get from A to B, we only come into contact with him given he is loosely attached to a group of guys we get friendly with during our second year at Aberystwyth University. These friendships are genuinely platonic – and great fun.

The leader of the pack, Colin, looks like Woody Allen and can be just as funny. He is studying law: we all secretly mouth 'God help his future clients' when he is in full comic flow. He has arranged his room in hall like an office, the desk facing the door. Anyone not-in-the-know who knocks and enters sees a young man in a tweed suit and bow tie, glaring over his wire-rimmed glasses and barking 'Do you have an appointment?'

He might then – depending on who the visitor is and how much he wants to spook them – treat them to the sight of him shimmying up his curtains making monkey noises. Or he might blow his nose in his scarf. Or in the person's scarf. Or just look back down at what he is reading or writing and wave the poor person away peremptorily like a tycoon dismissing a minion.

I suspect Colin and his group have given Skinman a place to belong as he too is eccentric. A geek before there are geeks. A trainspotter by soul. A curio in a cabinet.

By this time Helen and I know our friend and flatmate Val is going to move into hall again for the third year, leaving us as two people in a four people flat. Scared we will lose our beloved freedom and independence, we have consulted with our landlord, the money-mad Percy the Purse, and he has been surprisingly helpful. He doesn't like the people in the top floor flat for two. He confesses he is in fact just about to throw them out. Of course we could have it! Clearly he likes us: we pay on time and we keep the flat orderly and clean. Bad luck for our neighbours (long-haired youths with spectacularly smelly feet who have never spoken to us), but good news for us.

We are both by now in steady relationships, but Micha has had to return to Germany at the end of his exchange period to try to extend his funding and we will only be able to meet up in the holidays. Helen is not very good at steady relationships: I who knew her well can already see a glint of panic behind her eyes. She might, I suspect, make a break for freedom quite soon. If we are both alone, I am uncomfortably conscious we might be seen as fair game for any Lotharios loose in the Welsh seaside town.

Helen and I begin to notice that suddenly Skinman always slides into Colin's room when we go to visit. He starts, as he never did before, to tag along when we go for a drink or a meal. Wherever we are, he sits silent and wan like a spectre at the feast. He doesn't bother us, but there is always an inexorable creeping movement towards us. By the time the evening has progressed to a certain point, there he is, sitting either next to me or to Helen. Often, as we are the only ones with our own place, the lads all come back to the flat for more drinks and music. Now Skinman comes too.

Suddenly he calls on his own, late-ish in the evening. We don't lead a riotous life and most evenings we stay in. We work, we read, we listen to music and chat. We are very happy with each other's company and tuned in to respect the other's privacy. When we finally hear the unexpected knocking at about 8 pm one windy evening, we squint out of our attic window and see his long shadow in the light from the porch. We look at each other with resignation and let him in. It feels awkward. He sits on the edge of an armchair, all limbs like a giant albino spider. We make him a coffee. We essay conversation. Helen and I make most of the going. We grow increasingly desperate for topics as he calls more often.

We speak of this to his so called friends and they snort with derision. What can they do? He is a mystery, a one-off; they have no control over his movements. So we begin, when he calls, to try hints. They are never subtle and soon grow desperate: running a bath; changing into our nighties; putting on the kettle and filling hot water bottles; yawning till our uvulae are visible and waggling. None of it works. He comes, he sits, he hunkers down.

Helen and I are at a loss. He does nothing wrong, is always polite, so can we in all conscience throw him out, hurting his feelings? We assume though he never shows any that he does have feelings. And how do you start an argument with a spectre? We are on our own. We are clueless. Stuck. We suffer the almost daily visits. We long for peace again.

One crystalline spring evening Helen walks to the window to look out for the first signs of sunset. She makes a clicking sound with her tongue. I look up and ask what's wrong. She calls me over. On the side of the Victorian street already moving into shadow, we can just make out Skinman standing very still, looking up at the house. We know he can't see us: our house is so tall, for us to be seen from the street, we have to lean out of the window. We feel deeply uneasy. Being watched by a still figure on a dark street only happens in movies. We can't even think of going to bed until we know he's gone. He is there again the next evening and the next. We agonise about going down, confronting him. We don't. Then we no longer see him in the street and he no longer calls.

Needing to find out what is happening, we call in to see Colin after a seminar, and find him in a reasonably sane frame of mind. He asks us outright:

"What the fuck did you do to Skinman?"

We stare at him. Tell him we haven't spoken to Skinman for some time, but confess to spotting him in the shadows a few nights running and how uneasy it made us. Colin looks serious for once.

"Well, he's gone. Just left. Said it was a mistake to come here and he was going home. His room is empty." He can see our shock was genuine. "Ah well. Nothing to do with you or us I suppose. None of us knew him really. All he ever wanted to talk about was buses."

Colin adopts his PG Wodehouse persona with no warning. He can do this in conversation to bewildering or hilarious effect. He pretends to screw in a monocle.

"Buses eh Cuthbert old bean? Something of a niche subject donchyer know. Like Finknottle's newts. Doesn't exactly get the old intellectual juices flowing or tickle the ribs. No talk for a man, what, what?"

Helen and I walk slowly home, feeling very deflated. As we turn into our street, Colin comes puffing up behind us, apologising profusely that he has forgotten to give me something. Something Skinman was insistent I be given as soon as possible. I look down at the package. It definitely has my name on it. Both look at me expectantly. I lead the charge up the steep hill and the 6 flights of stairs to our flat. Once safely inside, I open it.

It's a wooden model, quite perfect, of a red London bus. Every detail is crisp and clear. There are passengers inside. It's headed for Marble Arch. Tourist Central now, but once the site of Tyburn gallows, where so many people, innocent and guilty, died in agony, some of them expiring whilst looking at their own intestines burning in a bowl.

We all three gaze at the thing. I have a lump in my throat. Colin can surprise in many ways. Now he makes comforting noises, pulls a bottle of wine out of his capacious overcoat pocket so we can toast Skinman and wish him well. Later, I slip the model into a drawer. Looking at it makes me tearful. Looking at it makes me like myself even less. Like a skeleton in the closet it lives in various drawers and cupboards over the years, that perfect little red bus. Then I lose it in transit from one place to another and I am glad.

Solstice

Our mood is euphoric, comic. In the eerie not-dusk we're like a gaggle of old-style mummers dancing, or, rather, what Shakespeare would call mowing, in circles. Some would call us motley in every sense of the word, I suppose, a dozen or so students all with long, flowing hair draped in a jumble of equally long, flowing clothes. Finger-pricking embroidered silks, old velvets, worn satins and country cheesecloth are mixed with stained and patched denims. A smell like incense rises from warm bodies, and there's very little distinction in the blurring light between male and female. We've dumped on the sands the essentials for the ritual to come like guitars, wine, beer and tambourines, and we are unable to keep still, bubbling over with a common happiness and laughing fit to bust. It's not clear exactly why . . . perhaps it's because we're so *young*, and, at this moment, have no thoughts at all of work or study or futures. Maybe because it's June 21st, and we're on the soft west coast of Wales, having spilled out of cars onto this deserted beach as the sun starts to lose power and sink towards the silvering sea. There is a town submerged in this bay, people whisper behind drawn and stuffy curtains in the hard brass of firelight: a lost Welsh Atlantis – you can even hear bells tolling, they say, muffled by fathoms of water, at certain times of the tides and seasons. But we're not frightened by stories and sea ghosts: we're too young. We're happy and strong, and we're making enough noise to make the dead run.

Driven by some atavistic urge, we all know we must light a fire even though tonight it will never become completely dark. It's certainly not needed for heat on the longest, balmiest, most benign night of the Celtic year: tonight is true pure summer, the peak of warmth and light, life and hope, and winter is too distant to be real. But, for once, we're not thinking or analysing at all, and we just mill about in a kind of contented chaos until we slide naturally into roles. Some unpack supplies. Some look for wood. Some prepare a pit for the bonfire. Micha, my partner, strums his guitar to accompany our industry, with a peculiarly intent and faraway look. Suddenly, as we search for driftwood and sticks, I and a friend spot a sign in a dune saying: *Fires on the Beach Stricly (sic) Forbidden!* It's irresistible, of course, and to the lilt of a folk song about peace and love, we solemnly destroy the crumbling wood and set it alight. Slowly, the others return with a few branches and sticks, and we feed the St John's Fire until it blazes and we become devil-faced figures in the Inferno. In circles, we caper with glee, drinking, singing, laughing for joy. If this is Hell, then yippee! All the time, however, we are aware of the sky growing greyer but never black, and, beyond our noise, we can still hear the pounding bass of sea, the twang of dry wood and the background soar of flames.

Just as the fire and fun are at their fiercest, two of the group make our hearts leap as they emerge out of darkness after a long hunt. Absurdly pleased with themselves, they puff and strain under the weight of half a dead tree trunk. The fragile bubble bursts, and some of us are laughing so much that tears flow and we clutch at our stomachs. Some have to sit and gasp and hiccup on the sands. The two tired woodsmen are not amused by our reaction. They set down their semi-tree to walk with hurt dignity towards the stock of beer cooling and rolling in the froth of the Irish Sea. They turn their backs. We decide the trunk makes a wonderful bench for the musicians, however, and the offended ones relax, coaxed back in to the circle as their find is admired and put to a good use.

Later, when everything is quiet and drowsing, lulled by rhythms of waves and warm breezes rustling through shingle and coarse dune grass, we all lie or sit cross-legged to adore the moon. After a time, we can pick out with our gaze even the thin veils of stars and distant planets in a darkly luminous sky. We wait breathlessly for the change now, but it *is* imperceptible as we were told it would be: before we know it, the transformation is over and the sky is brightening again. My head is resting in Micha's lap, and he strokes my hair, leaning down to kiss the top of my head fervently. Fuzzed with wine, happiness and sleep, I try to fight the sudden heaviness like a child not wanting to miss out on sham Christmas magic. But nothing can stop my lids closing like blinds now, and I slip off the thin ledge between times and worlds, spinning out into cold spaces on a trail of smoke and sparks.

Passenger

I am the passenger, and I ride and I ride . . . Iggy Pop's hypnotic 20th century urban-waif anthem throbs out of the stereo system, and somewhere, at a distance, there's a person smiling at the irony. *I am the passenger!* A car is hurtling through the soft September dark like a tube train through a tunnel, making a claustrophobic shushing sound as it passes between an avenue of trees. They are a tall, grey blur. There and not there. I wish it would all stop, that there could be silence, but I'm leaden, dumb, helpless. I know there are three other people in the car, but each is in their own space, and we mustn't look at each other. We all have to be alone. The tunnel walls close in. The car seems to speed up even more. Micha always drives too fast. If I ask him to slow down, he calls me an old lady. My heart and mind race in minor panic like the engine, and I have to focus all my energies inwards, concentrate on staying calm. The faraway person smiles again and whispers encouragement: go on – just give yourself up to it! Isn't there something *wonderful* after all about the torpor, the way your body weighs you down, the sated mind wrapped in cotton wool? Just give in, don't fight it, let it all glide by!

Today, after each eating the 'magic' mushrooms that grow in the local fields, the four of us have been wandering in pale golden clearings and damp earth woods like grungy naiads, worshipping, wallowing, hugging trees and talking to animals, to plants. We've felt their pulses, sensed their feelings, recognised their personalities. It certainly felt real, real as my own blood feverishly pumping to keep me alive now. We loved them and they loved us back. It was an exquisite kind of happiness. Just for today, we four very ordinary beings seemed to creep closer to the divine than any fawning priest. For a few fleeting hours, we were the congregation of a church pillared with tall trunks and lit by beams passing through foliage transparent as glass. We drank pure rain drops from curving leaves and it tasted like honey. We stroked tree bark, rough and warm. We marvelled at how plants seemed to glow from the inside, green and orange neon with life. For one day, we were truly part of the natural world and not just seeing it through car windows and television screens.

But now it's dark. Now we're heading home, and the journey seems to be lasting forever. The panic peaks a little again as I wonder if it can ever end, or will each one sit here alone stunned by the speed and the song playing loudly over and over and the deadening white noise until . . . until what? *I am the passenger . . . and I ride and I ride . . .* I can't understand why the song is still playing. We've been travelling surely for hours. Perhaps we're simply on the wrong road. Perhaps we're heading north or east. I want to speak to Micha, but there's only a dark shape in front of me, and it's oddly unfamiliar. In any case, it's too much trouble. I can't speak. I can't move. My eyelids droop. A long day: on the inside and the outside, a very long day. And now, in here, away from the pure sea air and wind, it's far too warm. Fuggy. Airless. I may just sleep for a while. I may just close my eyes for a while.

The car has stopped, and so has the music. I have the silence I craved, and yet it's not a comfortable one. There is still, somewhere, a strong and irritating buzz. We trudge to someone's room – I only know it isn't mine – and we sit. We are all exhausted. Someone makes a cup of tea. It's hot, comforting. We stare ahead. Music plays again, but softly. It seems a long time, but someone speaks at last. It's Micha. He sounds strained, genuinely puzzled. I squint into the dim light. He's got a tiny frown between his eyes. It's unlike him: he's always very sure about everything.

"I have no idea how we got here."

Heads turn. There is a little thrill of interest, of fear. We all wake up a little. I force the words from my mouth. I can't remember the last time I spoke. I swear my lips creak. "Weren't you driving?"

"No."

I don't drive, you see. I passed the test and got the licence but I hate driving. It frightens me so much I feel sick. So I *am* a passenger, always, and our two friends are quite adamant neither of them drove us back. One says he was next to me, one says he was beside the driver he didn't see. We all swear in a solemn, almost holy way: they seem quite serious and truthful. We all know we came back in Micha's car, a rusty little beetle that is his pride and joy. Ergo we insist it must have been him who drove it. He is equally adamant he did not. I've never known him lie, and he doesn't play practical jokes. In the awkward moments that follow, we all try to rationalise. Cars don't drive themselves: someone has to be at the controls. Well, don't they? One of three drove the thing! But we can none of us cope with an argument, and we decide to go to our beds. As we are drifting off to sleep, I touch Micha's shoulder.

"Were you kidding them? You drove us there: it must have been you driving back."

He is uncharacteristically short with me, and I am left in no doubt he did not. It seems this journey will have to remain a mystery. We got back, didn't we? Safe and sound . . . it's enough. Micha can never sleep without music in the background, and once again Iggy Pop is singing, this time ghostly quiet, about the city's ripped backsides. My eyes are wide open now, and tears trickle hot down my cheeks. I have no idea why I am this upset. In many ways, it was a beautiful day. It was intoxicating – in more ways than one. Micha would rationalise it as coming down from a psilocybin high. But I have seldom felt as alone, and I know if I can just reach out a little further with my mind, just an inch or two more, there is a key I could grasp, turn . . . learn something very important . . . but it's not the time and sleep comes swiftly. In the warmth of the room, my tears dry. The passenger rides on and on.

Interlude

Aberystwyth to West Germany

For most of my last year at Aberystwyth, Micha is away as his scholarship has totally dried up and he has to resume studies at his own university or lose out on any funding at all. I do feel adrift without his presence, the way he can make me seem relatively real and solid. There is a part of me however that is glad to be alone again. I know he truly misses me dreadfully, and is, in his own way, suffering at the loss. I am undecided: Do I want to be with him in Germany or not? Should I settle into a decent job, build up a life of my own? First though, in this fifth and final year, after successfully getting an MA in History, I am encouraged by a favourite lecturer to join a class taught by his wife. It is in Palaeography and Archive Administration. There are only 5 of us (about 30 in the whole of the UK) and we will all, it is said, walk straight into senior archivist jobs. I like my fellows and the course keeps me busy. I enjoy in particular reading old scripts. At first, though written say in 16th century English, it looks like Chinese to me, to us all, but then we are taught to pick out words we can recognise, study the form of the individual letters, see it as a jigsaw puzzle. Eventually, you can put the whole picture together easily, even getting used to the phonetic and infinitely varied spelling.

It ends as everything does and I have agreed – without even telling Micha at this stage – to go for a job interview in Caernarvon. Basically, I would be in charge of the archives there. It's a good job, and my family would be delighted. With a lifelong and continuing obsession with History, it seems perfect. I could live in another slightly off-key sea-side town, too, absorbing the pure air and its history. I travel to this possible new home by bus and train, and am perplexed when a cheerful bus driver stops – in the middle of the countryside – and tells me this is where the bus for the last leg will pick me up. I have to believe him but feel very insecure standing in a shaft of rich afternoon sunlight at the side of an empty road without even a bus stop sign to give me faith. But here it comes, a green rattling beast empty but for me and the driver. He is even more cheerful that the last, and chats to me as we bounce along. "Ever been to Harlech, my love?" No, I tell him, but I love old castles and have always wanted to. He tells me we'll go there. I am stunned he can loop off in this ad hoc way from his route, but why object? So soon we are looking up against a pure sky at the most massive, most impressive and intact Mediaeval castle you can imagine. THIS is what a castle should be: it is like a huge, well muscled, handsome and shapely warrior. It would scare the shit out of any would-be attackers, make them shrug and give up, riding away cowed and whimpering if they had any sense.

The driver does take me to Caernarvon eventually, and, as it is too late to go out to Edward's elegant French-designed show-castle, I cosy down in my B and B, swotting a little for the interview next day. All too quickly I am in a book-lined room with my possible future employers, and I can tell they like my CV and seem inclined to like me. I look out the window and see the little town sheltering as it has done for hundreds of years in the lea of the castle. It is even sleepier than Aberystwyth, which is bustling and cosmopolitan compared. Getting here from any direction takes absolutely hours: I travelled from early morning till 5 p.m., and it is a distance of about 50 miles or less. The feeling of a trap closing is sudden but acute. Images flash of working in basements, shut off from life, from the sun. My breath is actually a little short. I know the answers to all their questions but begin deliberately to stumble on each one, trail off sentences, say of course I will learn Welsh but manage to look as if I'm fibbing. I won't get this job, that's for sure. Their eyes have glazed over. They have pressed a collective 'uh uh' button mentally.

Already I know I will do as Micha wants, and live with him in the beautiful old town of Tuebingen near the French and Swiss borders. There, when I visited, I was stunned that he lived in a hall of residence that was once a 15th century Abbey hospital. I have always dreamed of living somewhere as old as this. It is so organic, made from earth with veins of living wood, it seems more human than some humans. It overlooks twisted old cobbled streets and is within sound of the church bells, which chime every quarter. The town looks like a twin to Heidelberg, with rows of tall mediaeval houses and willow trees each side of a wide, glittering Neckar.

If I think much more about it at all, I hope it will be a new beginning in lots of ways, and perhaps our relationship will deepen, especially on my part. It will be exciting too, I must admit, as I will need to find work here in a different culture and become fluent in German. I only have an 'O'- level, so will have to work hard and fast on that. I suspect when we have any cash, we will travel more easily from there to different countries. To a divided Berlin. Pop across the border to France and Switzerland for wine or cake. Take a train through the Alps to Italy, fly to the glory that was Greece. But, despite the excitement that does build, this is, I know, in many ways the easier option: I know where I will live, who I am going to live with. I have met and liked Micha's German friends. I can get student status once fluent and work, they tell me, is plentiful. My family seems inured now, even if they will never understand it, to my need to live away from Swansea. They know I will keep in good touch and will visit several times a year. After 5 years in Aberystwyth, this is already the established pattern.

Thus a decision by default is taken, and Micha comes to meet me in London so we can travel to Tuebingen together. He is like the proverbial dog with two tails: he tells me nothing has been the same since we had to separate. It will all be better now.

Ghost Workers

We are like Olympic swimmers poised on the edge or racehorses in their stalls, and even the air around us seems to be vibrating. There is the same unbearable cut-the-air tension, the same controlled restlessness and the same panic-tick of anticipation as we control our breath, waiting for the shot. A pulse beats out that rhythm in my head, and I can *feel* my blood pressure rising. A tiny glimmer of humour – a shaft of light piercing a dark pool – makes me glad I'm not connected to one of the monitors: if I were, I imagine the needle would hit end point and the glass of the machine would shatter, making us all jump in our skins. But like the swimmers or blinkered horses, none of us looks at each other. Instead, we retreat into ourselves, eyes squinting against reflected light on a tiled floor. We're supposed to be working as a team, but each of us just wants to get it over now, do her part and get the hell out. Despite the lack of communication, however, our heads rise eerily as one when we sense the signal is about to be given. Yes: the last person has left the room, and we're off!

When you see scenes of surgery on TV or in film – the more realistic versions – you never get a sense of the level of speed or brutality involved. You certainly don't imagine the volume of blood, or the fact surgeons are like a gorged Henry VIII, carelessly tossing bits of bone and tissue to the floor as they whizz through another meaty banquet so fast it makes you wonder if they get paid per patient or by the hour. Those floors are no longer covered with herbs and straw, and if the person swabbing has been unable to keep up with the flow, the blood pools are surprisingly large and slick. Worse, if the operation has been a very long one, the stuff seems to get glued to the tiles and ever harder to shift.

But we are protected of course, or, rather, the room is protected from our contamination. Latex-gloved, booted and masked, each one of us thinks of nothing but hitting the deadline and how to ignore the irritation of sweat running in actual rivulets down our skin and into our eyes. I blink away its sting now, and note again that though muffled, the smell of blood is metallic, sharp and rotten at the same time as if it's already begun to turn a little under hot lights. Our conundrum: we are human, we think, we feel, I think we even have souls: but if we come trailing clouds of glory, we are also *meat*. In these secluded places, our inner secret is revealed. Our bodies are opened to vent their stinks. Here, meat is cut up and rots from the moment it gapes raw to the air.

The scene has become quite surreal now, as more than a dozen rubbery arms are flailing, wiping, scrubbing, spraying every surface in the greenish white light – we've become an oversized octopus, tentacles waving underwater. I refocus, follow what I've been told and finish at exactly the same moment as the others. We are a cleaning production line! Another signal, and we're out. There's an odd kind of satisfaction to it, as if synchronised swimmers have executed the most intricate routine in perfect formation, but my lungs labour, my muscles scream and though I could drink a river, there's only salt water drying on my lips. Then comes the familiar sound of the door swhooshing shut on the pristine silence, the crystalline clinical cleanliness. Ten minutes are allowed between operations, not a second more, and we go out as we came through a back door into the sordid disposal area. What is astonishing is no-one sees us, and no-one even imagines us. That makes us less than ghosts. Mad though it sounds, I think the staff here also thinks it's like the TV, like the films: they probably think these areas are magically self-cleaning. They're not. Nothing in the world of humans is.

We are allowed to rest, of course, if there is a lull. Allotted our own little room, bare and neon-lit, in which we wait. Naturally there are strict timetables, but sometimes several operations overrun, and we endure a stagnant period. You know, I think I'd rather it when the times are closer together. I think I'd rather work till I *drop*. We are all female, you see, and I'm the only one who isn't Turkish. My co-workers all look the same: not a lick of dark hair peeping from beneath their headscarves, olive skin, plump bodies wrapped in black drab, faces oddly middle-aged even if young, skin like apples left too long in a winter store. Almost all have bad teeth, and every one is haloed by a visible odour of salt-fresh perspiration mingling with choking-ripe old sweat. Am I?

There's no mirror in here, so we can't see what we look like. I can't look into the black mirrors of their eyes as they will not meet mine: the unfriendliness is in any case palpable. The women always speak their own tongue and pretend I'm not there.

Such an odd feeling: if no-one sees or imagines you, if you can't look at yourself and no-one speaks to or looks at you, how long before you don't just suspect but *believe* you're not there? Worse even than the alienation, however, is the knowledge they want me to fail. I know they want me gone because I make them even more uncomfortable than they're making me. I'm the foreign body. I'm the annoying spirit hovering between worlds.

The smartly dressed and coiffed German woman in personnel who hired me knew how it would be. She frowned fiercely. Heavens: was I sure? This just didn't seem right! Only the euphemistically named guest-workers, the *Gastarbeiter* could, would or should do this work. She confided that such work was given to Turkish women who had no education, spoke very little or no German, and were earning valuable *Deutschmarks* in the only way they could to send home. One had to admit they were *Eseln*, she whispered – real *donkeys*: they could carry any burden without buckling or complaining and plod on forever. She shook her head and her hair didn't move although the slick pink lips did. Words formed like dirty steam out of those lips. They are not like you, like me! They don't feel things as we do. Please believe me: I know them. I couldn't face challenging her, but explained patiently in my neat but still schoolgirl German that I'd arrived too late to get any of the better summer jobs, and I needed to earn. I told her I'd be very grateful to be taken on and wasn't at all afraid of hard work. She stared at me, and her expression said: 'My God, how naïve are you!' Of course, that made me more determined. I wanted to show her I could do it. Then of course I wanted to show *them*.

In this second, however, I don't know where that determination has gone, and I just feel like weeping. Nothing prepares you for being so tired, so overheated, so – dehumanised. I'm very good at hiding my feelings, however, and I sip at the water cooled by a hot, humming machine, pretend to read my book and try not to shift in the chair. If I do, they'll know I'm aching! Suddenly, there's a light, electrifying trill of a fingertip on my bare arm and it makes my heart skip. I look up, straight into eyes that aren't black at all, but a rich, moist-earth brown. With another shock, I see the woman is young – maybe even younger than me – but there are deep lines between her brows, and apart from the life in her eyes, the rest of her looks worn as a threadbare rug. The others are talking animatedly about something, and she rolls those dark eyes. When she speaks, her voice rustles and her German is execrable. We both know we mustn't look at each other and speak like ridiculous Hollywood gangsters out of the sides of our mouths.

"Was dein name? What you called?"

I blink, swallow and clear my throat quietly. After so many hours of silence, I've forgotten what my voice sounds like. I have to force it out to whisper back: "Helena."

"I Sofia."

We both glance nervously at the others, but their discussion is becoming heated, and they're taking no notice of us.

"Too hard, this work. You student? You German girl?"

"Student, yes, but British . . . English."

She looks at me now as if I've journeyed from Saturn's rainbow rings.

"But *why*? Why you work *here*? Ist nich gut."

"I must work. My boyfriend is a student too. We have no money."

She smiles and shakes her head slightly. I can see she doesn't believe me. Before I can think and stifle the stupid question, it comes. "Sofia, why do *you* work here? So far from home?"

The lovely eyes grow darker and the smile slides off pale lips like bright blood wiped up silently and swiftly from the floor.

"Same as you! Money. Father die, I have no brother. I old sister – only me to work. Big family. My mother say must come here." Her eyes stare at the table, but she inclines her head slightly towards my book. The words are beginning to flow. "I no read like you. No school."

A tear wobbles on dark lashes, threatens to spill but she expertly draws it back, glancing again at the women. One of them now looks fit to bust, and all are beginning to wave their arms as we do when we're cleaning. The Kraken wakes, and strangles itself with its own tentacles. Better than them extending out to me.

65

Towards *us*.

"They no like you."

"But *why*?"

"You take money of Turk woman. They think you – what is word? – not strong. You go soon. Not . . . not like us."

I can't help it: something combative stretches in me.

"I work as hard as all of you!"

She smiles, and it's a sad smile. We become aware the noise level has abated a little, and one of the women is staring in our direction. Actually only one of her eyes stares at us: the other points in a different direction. Does it mean she can watch the door and us? Sofia whispers almost inaudibly: "We talk later. I try speak English."

I look down intently at the page in front of me, but the German supervisor saves us by opening the door and spitting out: "Let's go – theatre five, then two. *Schnell*!" He looks at the women with breathtaking contempt, but ignores me. Of course he does – I'm not there. He signals with fingers. "*Understand*? F-I-V-E and T-W-O."

Two weeks later, and someone I know has found me a job replacing her as a cleaner in the Post Office. For some reason, they prefer to employ Germans – and I'm as close as makes no difference. As jobs go, she says it's hog heaven: the clerical staff has gone home, you do the offices, corridors and toilets in peace and at your own pace. An added perk is you get to eat practically for nothing in your break in the canteen. Best of all, if you work hard and fast, you can even sneak off to the toilets you have made super-clean to escape into a book. It's shorter shifts and slightly less pay than here, but that no longer matters a jot: once you've been in the dark, dirty and terrifying basement, the meanest room in the upper house looks palatial.

Of course I have to save face, and I tell Sofia and she in turn explains to the women who were starting to unbend a little that I enjoyed working with her and them, but I've found another job. It goes without saying it's a better job, so I don't say it. Even as I speak, I despise myself for lying. Truth is, if I had to go hungry I couldn't work here another hour. I know it. They all know it. They pretend to be supremely uninterested, though the least friendly one of all can't help smirking knowingly. Maddeningly. But I no longer care, and, tired as I am, I'm riding the waves. I avoid Sofia's eye as I head for the door: it's the kindest thing I can do.

I undress and shower in an echoing, empty locker room – the others as you've probably guessed have stayed to work another half-shift as it's more money – and the sense of relief is as delicious and cool as the water. When I'm finished, sparkling clean, solid and *free*, I pass the coats and jackets hanging in a row like bagging, shed skins. I know which one is Sofia's, and I place a hazelnut 'Milka' bar – a rare, favourite treat I've seen her slip secretly and greedily piece by piece into her mouth – in her pocket. Wrapped around it is a note telling her if she wants to learn to practice English or reading, I'd be happy to meet her whenever we have spare time. I know she'll guess immediately who's left it and will keep it hidden if she has to find a sympathetic friend to read it to her. I've written it in capitals in English and German, and made the address and telephone number very clear. But I've begun to suspect she lives with the evil-eye woman who turns out to be her aunt, and something tells me she won't get in touch as I know Sofia will never have any spare time. I realised some days ago that though I swear I felt her touch and warmth, Sofia is the ghost. She was never really there so of course we can never meet again.

Slavery

In this moment, I feel like an insect on a pin. Splayed and displayed. Transfixed, exposed, wings stretched paper-thin. I'm trying to imitate the discreet stillness of the recently dead, but all the observers know I'm very much alive, a splash of white and summer colour on a darker background. At least I *am* alive, I suppose, if in temporary stasis. And yet . . . yet perhaps I'm worse off than any captured butterfly, for I am *aware* of the gaze of dozens of eyes in a neon-lit surgically clean no-bloody-hiding-place restaurant that smells of Germany: potatoes, cabbage and vinegar, roast sausage and curry powder.

Here I sit, alone, body curving and trying to melt into the ergonomically shaped plastic chair. Even furniture is ruthlessly efficient here. Wood is unhygienic. Wasteful! This chair wastes nothing: it simply is and does its job to perfection. Meanwhile, I'm waiting with impatience for the strong coffee and steaming plate of sausages before me to cool a little. Yes – here I am in very post-war *Deutschland*: run like clockwork and awesomely affluent, finally *ueber alles* in economic if not the military terms she wanted! A country getting rich instead, in which there is money for nothing: money on tap . . . well, not quite! In fact, if you're at the bottom of the tall heap, you have to work 'til you want to sob with exhaustion just as you would anywhere on earth.

Still, due to a seemingly inexhaustible demand for gleaming Mercedes cars, there *is* at least money galore for manual labourers and students, for those desperate enough to do one of the jobs the robots find too unpredictable. Jackpot cash for humans prepared to perform the allotted tasks over and over on hundreds of dry metal skeletons until every brain cell and nerve begins to scream and beg silently for the end of an eight-hour shift. Tempting rewards for someone like me who won't eat unless she makes those little tweaks that need a human eye and judgement on a fast -moving production line . . . but no brain function: oh, definitely no brain activity required or desired. Here, your most vital human organ is deliberately starved of oxygen, and I feel the sluggishness of mine as it crashes into gear now and tries to size up the problem.

Male eyes: there's the rub, as Shakespeare would have said. Eyes black with red lust, the ones to fear most! Others treacle-brown, melting with a warmer, more sentimental desire: eyes to look into while real sugar burns and Gypsy violins play. The rest flash amber, inviting an answer-spark like plugs in an engine and then . . oh yes, I feel those unswerving stares of still young men from Eastern Europe and from Greece, Yugoslavia: men separated from wives and girlfriends, lonely and horny and hot as hell. Bored half unto death. Living (existing!) in hostels that make cheap motels look like the Dorchester. *Men.* Staring. Genuinely believing a young, liberated Western woman *must* be easy meat. Promiscuous. The only question is: which one of them will approach me first? It has to happen soon. The tension is terrible.

I know looking down at my food will not help. Pretending to read my book won't help. My skin is slightly tanned, but they will see the flush shining through as I've scraped long blonde hair back off damp neck into a bun. You can't cover up too much as it's fiercely hot, but I'm doing my best by wearing a baggy T-shirt and a mumsy cotton skirt with a hideous wallpaper flower pattern on it. But none of it will help. To believe anything else would be the illusion of Hope versus Experience. They can still see a bloom of youth on skin, those men, the poke of firm, nervous-tipped breasts when I have to breathe out. They can gauge the length and shape of a hidden leg. They've had a lot of practice. They may not have letters after their name, but that's their area of expertise.

The anger rises at last and my cheeks must be hot to the touch now. Fuck them all! I *have* to eat after seven hours up and six working and no appetite for breakfast. Until I get my pay cheque this is so cheap it's almost *free*, and I *have* to sit somewhere to eat it! Christ! To the hottest inner circles of hell with them! And yet . . and yet I'm bolting the food down now, swilling the coffee, annoyed by my cowardice, by the fact I'm giving in, but prepared even to spend the rest of my longed for break in the toilets. It's cool and quiet there, and I can read my book. As I'm about to push back the chair, eyes still demurely cast to the floor, a body plumps down opposite me and I have to look up.

The man sitting there searching my face with his eyes is in his mid-twenties, lanky, one of those so tall he'll always stoop a little. His hair is the colour of chocolate, his eyes hazel. The expression in those eyes is serious, but he has a very attractive smile that reveals the regulation bad teeth of the *Gastarbeiter*. The euphemistically named 'Guest worker': God, what a cruel joke! Unwanted but essential factory fodder fuelling an economic revolution, more like! A slave labour force sanitised by being well paid and legal, but still utterly despised by its superior, commanding hosts. Germans have made this very clear to me. They've told me *I'm* different, of course: they're glad to have me and are immensely impressed I speak German quite well. One day I could be like a German! They don't tell me how pleased they are that I'm as blonde, healthy and Aryan as they are. I know they think it.

"Boris. My name is Boris. You?"

His German is the usual pidgin type that people make such fun of and imitate. I try to clear my throat which is suddenly very dry. To walk off is impossible after a lifetime of being urged to be polite, always to remember one's *manners*.

"Helena."

"Pretty! You are pretty I think but too serious. You are English, I heard, and you are young. You shouldn't be here. Student?"

I can't help but stare. Though I quickly close my lips my eyes stay wide open.

"Yes. I'm a student. Well, sort of! It's easier that way. I really came here to be with my boyfriend."

He leans forward. The eyes seen close up have green flecks in them. They are lovely. Suddenly they darken a little. Will that reference to being involved with someone be enough to send him away? Will he think I'm just saying it? My stomach curls into a little knot and I wish I hadn't eaten after all. He looks angry.

"Your friend . . . he lets you work *here*?"

"Yes, of course!" I smile. I can't help it, but my face feels stiff. "He works here himself, but on the other site. We need the money."

"To live?"

I nod very firmly and look him direct in the eye.

"Yes. To live. To eat!"

In return, he nods slowly. This is not going at all the way I expected, and I feel more uncomfortable than ever. I know the other men are still staring. I can feel the beams very hot and searing into me. I'm amazed marks like cigarette burns aren't appearing on my bare skin. If anything, the level of tension has increased. Been tightened up like one of the wheel nuts on the assembly line. Everyone is waiting to see what happens next. *I'm* waiting to see what happens next. I can't explain it, but suddenly I don't want to run away any more, and I want to keep talking to the young man opposite me. I think he senses it, as he smiles very widely. This time it's a real smile, a one hundred percent grin, and his eyes light up with it.

"I work to send money for my wife Anja and my family to eat. If I work hard, we can get a better house. More land. Better land. Then I go *home*. My mother is widow and my youngest sister live with us too. I have two sons. *Beautiful* boys. I show you a photo later."

Now I don't know what to say.

"My sister – she wants to be a student. She is clever. Read all the time, like you."

There are no words. He leans forward and puts a large, roughened hand on top of mine. I'm paralysed. I couldn't stir now if someone tossed a grenade into my lap.

"You smoke. I saw you outside."

"Y-y-yes."

"You come out now. We sit on the steps. We smoke together. Those others - Boris glares at the men who are still openly or surreptitiously watching us – "*Turks!*"
He looks about to spit, but sees the look on my face and shrugs instead. "*Bastard* Turks . . . they treat women like cattle.

So you come out with me now. Then they think you are mine, you have been taken. They will leave you alone."

It takes me some time to reply. My voice sounds as if my vocal cords are being squeezed. "*Why?*"

He misunderstands, frowns. "I just tell you! They will think you are my girlfriend – *meine Frau* – they leave you alone. Men, they can go to a woman on her own – but not if she has a man. They can see then you have a man."

This time my smile is involuntary but still a little desperate. Such inescapable logic from an alien world! "I mean, why are you doing this . . . Boris? What . . . what benefit, what good can you get from it?"

As he beckons with an inclination of the dark head, I get up to follow him out into stifling smoke-tainted summer air and we both blink in the sunshine. Everything is metal, the colour and smell of fresh coin. It stinks of burning metal out here. The sun is brassy. We sit. The metal staircase burns through the cotton of my skirt. I wince and fidget, and I really am now gasping for a cigarette. Boris lights two companionably for both of us, and more eyes stare. But I can distinguish the heat of the stares from the metal branding my buttocks and legs and from the sun's rays at full power, and I swear it's cooling! Already, the thwarted eternal male sex-gaze is inexorably turning elsewhere.

"It's because of my sister. I think: what if my sister had to be somewhere like this?" He frowns again. "Or my Anja? Not that I would let them, dear God! But what if they had to be annoyed and insulted by *Turks*? *I* am a proper Christian man. Do you understand? While you are here, working here, I am your friend. You will be safe. My good friend here is Polish – Andrzej. He does the same. You will meet him. If I am not here, he will look after you."

I am mesmerised and I nod. I know he's telling the absolute truth and wants nothing from me. The staircase is as solid as anything on earth can be, and there isn't even a sigh of wind, but to me it feels as if it's swaying. I have never in my life felt as safe as this, and I marvel. To him – so natural and logical: to me, a revelation. What price freedom now? I feel embarrassed to admit that, obviously, but I must or be dishonest. It's also embarrassing that my eyes are filling up with liquid and my throat closing. I blink and I swallow hard, drawing deep on the cigarette. He returns the nod, and stretches his impossibly long limbs. His strong but very tired limbs. Now I'm so ashamed I can't even bear to look at him. In weeks I can count on my fingers, I'll be gone: how long will his sentence be? Will his beautiful boys know him again even if he can get away?

"Good! Now tell me about your home – do you miss it? – and I will tell you about mine and show you the photo . . . here . . ."

I stare at the slightly greasy, curling photo in my hand. The woman cradling two lumpy featureless infants is stocky and plain, face sketched roughly in tired lines though she must only be about twenty. The boys are gazing up at her like little idol-worshippers, however, and the dark eyes sending a message through the lens are dancing with love and mischief. I give up and let tears well, but of course the sun scorches my cheeks dry before they can drop. He frowns again, looks suddenly concerned.

"Careful . . . please! Is my best photo. My wife is beautiful, yes? And my boys – my boys! Anja says they look just like me . . ."

Do unto others . . . I hand the photo back carefully. For the rest of my time here, he will protect me, and I will do my best to encourage him not to stay here too long, living through a nightmare instead of waking up to his dreams.

Memory Chip

The sun today could melt the hair on your head, and it's exciting the other women in the house. Their voices rise in pitch as they talk of driving to a mountain lake at the weekend to bathe alternately in solid heat and ice-cooled waters. Then the sound of laughter recedes like an echo as they run upstairs to delve into cupboards. They'll find what they're looking for, and I smile to think of how the paint-blob-splash bikinis, the creased and slightly musty summer clothing, will whirl into the air and drop into heaps on the floor. To me, pearl-pallid, the heat signals months of discomfort. More importantly, however, it heralds the money making season has come again. When in the distance thunder rumbles, I imagine it's the Mercedes Benz conveyor belt calling me. Though I'm scanning the job columns in the newspaper for the area, I'm resigned to having to answer that call. Suddenly, my eyes widen and track back to an advertisement and my heartbeat – grown worryingly sluggish and blurred of late – quickens.

I don't exaggerate about the heat: in these landlocked foothills of the Swabian Alps, the summer months are so airless and oppressive that I visibly wilt. I'm drooping a little already, and assuming that's why my energy seems to be draining away as if a parched vampire is gulping his greedy fill. This good news that jobs are available at a local electronics factory literally perks me up. I even sit up straighter, as the key word resounds in my head like the sound of a nail tapping on fine crystal. Local. *Local!* This potential workplace, you see, clings to the skirt hems of the frumpy and utilitarian neighbouring town . . . but if I could get a job there, Reutlingen would look radiantly beautiful to me. It's only ten minutes away by bus, and, even better, the ad says that one can choose one's shifts!

I lick drying lips. As in all decisions, of course, there is hesitation and then the weighing up process begins. I would earn two thirds or even less of the wages paid by Mercedes Benz, granted, but would escape another endless summer spent as a Hell-factory android. To have a vivid imagination isn't always a blessing: I feel a greasy swell of nausea at the thought of getting up for the early shift at 4.30, and, suddenly, I'm back on the dawn bus again. I'm one of the many miserable, jaw-cracking drones, spending my own long, silent journey trying not to vomit up the cold milk that is the only breakfast I can tolerate at that hour. Staring down at the ad, I feel an actual swing of giddiness. Shit! As if it's not bad enough being drained by invisible vampires, the pull of that faraway conveyor belt seems to be sucking at my brain matter: it's like the moon-tug that wrenches bright metallic clots from the womb and lobotomises the weak minded.

As a rule, I'm an insanely cheerful person, especially in the mornings: I even tend to irritate my partner Micha, who's always grumpy until about eleven o'clock if he has to rise early. He wakes up as the day goes on, picking up a frenetic momentum as he vacuums up various substances we can't afford. Then he listens to music, plays guitar and/or parties like a Dervish until three or four a.m. This doesn't make for harmonious relations, as you can imagine, especially when one of you has to get up at 4.30. Oh, yes: helping Bosch keep the world's clothes whiter than white would definitely suit me better! I could still earn a perfectly decent sum without turning into a nagging, sleep-deprived, grease-monkey drudge, and it might well defuse the tension that always builds between Micha and myself when lifestyles and priorities meet head on to crash at high speed.

So, on the day and at the exact time stipulated, I enter the personnel department at Bosch Electronics Company. There's quite a crowd, but it's clean and quiet as a hospital. Serene. Odourless. No smell here of thick black machine-blood, of sun searing through glass into metal and hot rubber like a laser into flesh. No ceaseless daemonic din in vast, unholy Miltonian halls. In this intimate, hushed atmosphere, one feels the need to walk quietly and whisper. Employees glide about looking cool and unruffled. None of them has ever-expanding sweat patches on the backs and underarms of T-shirts! None of them is grimed with a slick of oil! I'm glad now I've worn some neat summer cottons, and that my German is pretty fluent. If I can get one of the jobs, it will make the summer less of an endurance test as well as easing our financial situation . . .

Good God, what sort of pathetic euphemism is that? We are as completely desperate for money as usual. Like everyone else in the so-called civilised world and in its star economy, we've become victims of our own material comfort. We're caught in a shower of rent slips and fluttering bills like white and brown confetti . . . and bills have to be paid. At least I believe so. I know opinions vary, but I'm terrified of owing money. Micha is happy to live on an overdraft the size of a developing country's debt. His bank thinks he's going to be a dentist, you see, and dentists here make unfeasible amounts of money. What he hasn't told them is he gave up the dentistry course after six months to study philosophy and the American Beat Generation. *I* know, however, and often wake sweating as I dream of what will happen when they find out. He's an extravagant and generous person with other people's money. It goes on booze, drugs, parties, his book and music collections . . . and gifts for me I usually neither want nor need. In many ways, he really is a boy: mundane things are worried about and paid for by grown-ups – such petty concerns have little or nothing to do with him. He thinks I'm hopelessly bourgeois to care, but the only way I can live with it is to make sure I earn enough for all my needs, and that we depend on that bank for nothing *vital*.

I blink in the bright light and smile grimly as I wait with everyone else to be called through, as I wait for something to *happen*. For years, though unsure of his worth, my family has expected me to marry Micha, but I've always held back instinctively. Now I know in my heart there'll definitely be no wedding, even if we could surmount the (already outdated) hippy principles of clinging to so -called freedom – a 'freedom' that can be as restricting as the bourgeois shackles he fears. I don't want to give these thoughts too solid a form, but I do know the compatibility I imagined existed between us is a lunar illusion. Like blue moonlight, it can be romantic but also unsettling. It's a thing of no real substance, after all: cold, second hand light powered by no life-giving core of earth and fire.

But if I'm an adept at anything, it's holding that dawning realisation at arm's length, and I push it away now. We've been through a great deal and we've been together quite a long time. He assumes we always will be, no matter what. I'm the more realistic, but, then again, I come from a long line of dedicated reality-evaders. I've been brainwashed in an old-fashioned South-Welsh upbringing to regard breaking a commitment as being a sign of weakness, even degeneracy. So I don't want to think about what I would do if I have to leave him and the life we've built together – however precarious it might be. There's so much *not* to think about, it takes at least 90% of my energy, and that normally boundless resource is shrinking fast. I'm so busy taking care of mundane things and pretending to be fine that I don't even stop to wonder why I'm so exhausted, or reduced to tears by things I would normally shrug off.

Mercifully, for the next hour, I can't think of anything at all, since, along with the other hundred or so applicants for about twenty jobs I have to go through a series of complex dexterity and memory tests. We're all a little bewildered, frankly: we've come to get factory work, not join MENSA. Part of me then starts to enjoy the challenge, relishing how my reactions gear up for it, while the rest of me feels anger at being treated like an unthinking lab rat. It rapidly becomes clear to all of us speech or language facility is of no importance in this silent place. What matters here, it seems, is response time, nimbleness of fingers and a near perfect visual memory. As we progress through the exercises, those who fail are escorted away around me but I'm mesmerised by the tasks, determined not to be beaten or get a low score. When I finally look up, I'm startled to find there are less than twenty of us left. A little dazed, we are issued on the spot with clean white coats to put in neat, clearly numbered lockers. We are shown silently around, and are duly impressed by the facilities. We're the chosen few, the winners. We're *in*.

Now I sit comfortably on a high chair at a sort of workbench cum desk, doing my job. The chair is at the exact right height and so carefully designed I feel no pain though I have to sit like this for eight hours with three short breaks a day. The desks are well spread out so no-one can talk, even should they be able or wish to communicate. Each desktop is individually lit, and when it's dark or the sun doesn't shine direct into the rooms, we sit in lonely, eerie haloes of light. In front of each of us is a circuit board with holes punched in it. Into each hole, a tiny component must fit and be connected to others. We have models to look at, but we no longer need to. We were chosen for our ability to memorise, after all, and we know each jigsaw pattern off by heart. We can fill one of the boards that are the brains, nerves, veins and tangled guts of a machine in seconds. It needs no conscious thought, and while we do it we become like the things we're helping to build.

I don't ask, naturally, so I don't know how the others feel, but I find it oddly comforting, and I rock gently and sing softly to myself as I create machine life. I croon a kind of lullaby to the rhythm of the soft mechanical clicks that are like hearts beating all around me. More and more it feels like being a priestess in a temple of futuristic worship, performing an intricate set of mysterious rituals. More and more I feel my own brain shutting down, however, as I make these circuits fit to fire up. More and more I find it hard to ignore the fact something is very wrong with me, but I'm sure if I can just focus totally on what I'm doing, it will act as a kind of anaesthesia and I can still pretend there isn't.

This afternoon, however, the bubble of pretence bursts. For days, I've been driven on only by a steely determination not to give in to the truth, to bodily weakness. But sounds and light are now behaving most oddly, rushing at me and then receding like rogue and skittish riptides. Though the beams spotlighting down from glass windows onto our islands are quite cool and silvery today, they're needling hot into my skull and pricking out sweat like acid rain on my skin. Gravity's pull seems to be dragging me down, down, and there's an odd buzzing sound as I fight to stay conscious, stay on the chair, ride the breakers of ferocious pain and nausea and panic. Jesus! My body *is* a machine after all, and it's going haywire, beyond my control. It's screaming for attention, breaking down . . . but we machines once stricken cannot help ourselves: humans give us life, after all, and only humans can maintain that gift or take it away.

More sunshine. My eyes smart as I come to. The fiery pain however has been doused and the all-pervasive dark nausea has gone. I didn't realise I was carrying a set of heavy weights, but I was, and my mind and limbs no longer feel leaden. There was a grey fog around me too, but I blink as the light hits my eyes and images are sharply focused again. A shadowy figure draws the curtains a little to shield my face, and the temperature instantly seems to drop. I sigh and sink back into pillows and into a mattress that moulds to my body even more efficiently than my chair at work. Work! My eyelids flicker in time to the runaway pulse of panic as I make a great effort to rise above some lingering wisps of fog like a plane lifts over ranges of cloud. I'm not at work, and I'm not at home! Someone has beaten me up, or so it feels, and yet I feel better than I have in many weeks. I'm even hungry again. In fact, I'm hollow as a barrel.

With increasing consciousness comes curiosity, and many questions to be asked and answered. I move a little gingerly, and find I really am sore. I'm oddly *bulky*, too, padded up in a sort of nappy as if I have a heavy period. Knowledge knocks a little louder on my skull to be let out not in, and then, just as dreamlike, the door to the room opens and closes quietly only to open and click closed again. A white-coated female takes a seat on the bed. But if I'm not at work . . . my brain moves at last into first gear. Ah: either I *am* dreaming, or I'm in hospital. Simple! And if in hospital, then this brisk little person is a *doctor*. No sooner do I have the thought, than she is indeed introducing herself in a gravelly voice as Frau Doktor Claudia Dickbertel-Bopp. What a totally ridiculous name! Laughter froths gaily in my throat and I smile. I *must* be dreaming after all: sometimes my dreams are startlingly real.

Yet, as she talks, her words solidify. They're very real. They rasp against the air and it feels as if they're sandpapering my nerves. I don't suppose she means to be accusing, but the tone is incredulous and hints strongly at blame as she informs and interrogates in equal measure. *Wie kann es sein . . .* how can it be that I, an intelligent person, didn't *realise* I was pregnant? The voice, long nails on a blackboard, scrapes on about something called Rhesus Incompatibility. Why did I not go to a doctor if I felt so ill? Hmm? Was I ever pregnant before? Why had there been no blood tests when I lost that first baby? It was the same father back then? Ah . . . then both babies inherited their blood group from their father (Yin) . . . not mine (Yang). Positive and negative are incompatible: the two eternal principles, contrary to myth, *do not fit*. My body it seems has been fighting my own child for survival.

Doktor Dickbertel-Bopp is getting more corporeal by the second. She is trying (and failing) to couch it all in acceptable terms. I don't have the energy to tell her I am an intelligent person after all and I've got the message: put simply, one of us had to go

– if I'm alive, my child is dead. I have to face it finally: another child is dead. She rattles on. An extreme case: not usually as bad as this. Despite my . . . er . . . lack of awareness (she means stupidity), nothing I did or didn't do caused it. She's very, very sorry. She sighs. What is very sad is there *could* have been a chance, if the doctors had been more alert and the right action had been taken when the first pregnancy ended. After that little twist of the scalpel, she finishes off like a kind but stern headmistress: there should be no more pregnancies – I must understand *that*. A third time could be fatal. That's another myth shattered, then: a third time, I might not be so *lucky*.

Hours later, I wake again and Micha is hunched miserably by the bed. He is haggard in the sick-white hospital light. I can see how blunted and ugly his bones and what he will look like as an old man. When he sees I'm awake, his features lighten, the blue eyes as lovely as a woman's sparkle and two lines etched deep between his brows disappear. I wince as he grabs my hand so hard it hurts, and struggle to understand as he babbles. It's so good to have me back again: God, he's been so *miserable*, so worried! It's all been like a bad dream. As if I wasn't there. As if I'd left him. He couldn't work out what was wrong – no-one could work out what was wrong. I wasn't myself, but everything will be just fine now. Everything will be exactly as it once was. We can go back to *normal*.

I feel absolutely nothing at all, but I nod and try to smile. I notice he's taken the trouble to pick and bring a great bunch of yellow wildflowers and grasses from the woods near where we live, the woods that I love so much. They're in water, but of course they're dead already: delicate and innocent victims of an impractically romantic gesture. But I'm well brought up, and I open my mouth to thank him. As I do, he startles me by leaning over and kissing me with some passion. There's no time to move away, and I go cold with distaste. How crass! How . . . disrespectful! I would like very much to hit him, but I can't. It feels as if we should both cry, but we don't. A part of my mind detaches from the scene, thinking of how it will help to dry those flowers and keep them in a box. Yes: that's what I'll do – then, wherever I go, just like Mad Queen Juana of Castile when she lost her weak but adored husband, I can keep them with me. She dragged her husband all over Europe in his coffin: my clinging

80

and mourning will be more discreet.

Because Micha seems happy to witter on, I nod and smile again so I can be alone with my thoughts. His lips move, but I hear no sound. He seems almost obscenely happy to me. Well, I know he never wanted children as I did. Though another observer might be touched by his devotion and think he's taking it rather well, a cynic might conclude he's a mightily relieved man, for more reasons than one. Someone who judges others harshly might go so far as to think him a little heartless. I know the truth, but I also know that within his limits he is at least genuinely loving and honest. From now on, however, I will sit in a cold lonely halo of light putting words, gestures and feelings into patterns I've learned by heart. If I concentrate and do it all just right, I can make the machine work, even though I have no real understanding of what I'm doing and why.

Have you noticed that now machines are so absolutely integral to our lives, we're just not conscious of them when they're getting on with their jobs? We only remember them and what they do when the noise stops, in that awful moment when a machine shudders and dies into a shocked stillness. Even then I suppose it can be a kind of relief: at least you know the worst, and can usually get on with repairing it or replacing it with new. If you can't do that, though, you'll try desperately to deceive yourself there's nothing wrong. You'll shut your mind and eyes and ears and pray to a god you don't believe in that it will keep going. Unwittingly, the machine can collude by teasing you and by going on relentlessly, even maddeningly – until, intelligent being or not, you're tantalised into believing your own idiotic untruth.

So who's *really* in control, do you think? I don't *know* the answer, by the way – I throw out the question in case anyone does. I do think machines have great advantages over us humans. I think it's most wonderful that despite its built-in memory chip, a machine actually lives in an empty perpetual present. It can't think or feel pain or remember and – most comfortingly of all! – it has no independence or ability to create and therefore no free will or decisions to make. A machine has no choices because it needs none. That's it. *So* simple: a machine just works or doesn't work, and it's up to its masters and slaves to take action either way while it just chugs along blankly, appearing to conform to whatever its creator dictates. That's what happens I guess when someone takes out their memory chip and throws it away.

The Sure Hope of Resurrection

I once heard someone say that after a major bereavement, it feels
as if your head is stuffed with cotton wool. Well, I have to say my
brain feels more as if some bastard sadist is surfing through it on
Brillo pads. Wiry and yet dense, greasy but gritty, their edges are
razor sharp. Because of the hurt and the chemical-pink fog, I can't
think, can't think. But why do I have to? Why am I trying to? My
brain is already under attack, haemorrhaging with the effort of
holding back a tide of grief, but there's something vital just out of
reach . . . ragged wisps of unwanted memories, receding echoes of
a bad dream? No . . . someone is urging me (again!) to take a
decision, to make a choice that isn't a choice . . . or am I just
endlessly circling in the dream-pool of what has happened to me?
Here in the white bright hospital room, I can no longer
distinguish between the buzz of heat, the hum of machines and
the echoes of faraway footsteps and voices: maybe time is
becoming blurred and unfocused too. I try to will myself into
sleep, forgetfulness, a state in which I can be here, but not here.

When at last I'm coasting nicely, a visitor comes. It's my friend
Susi. She has a wide mouth, tombstone teeth and a sparkling
smile that would melt the ice in a corpse's veins. When she kisses
me though, her lips are cold. She takes off her coat. I can smell the
winter air on her, on it. Patting her unruly hair into a bob, Susi sits
and nods at my hand. "Who's the letter from?"

I stare at her, and then down at my hand, at pink lobster pincer
holding the letter. Are they mine, the fingers? They're clenched so
rigidly, they won't obey my brain's signals and they remain tight
shut. My mouth, however, opens. An odd sound comes out as if
we're underwater.

"What's wrong?" Susi frowns fiercely. "D'you need a nurse?
Why on earth didn't you call one?"

She's kind but very practical. As she jumps up to reach for the
bell, my voice squeaks out some words: "No! Don't! It's . . . it's
about my uncle. I told you he was ill. He's dying now. This says
he's dying."

"I'm so sorry, Helene." The ugly-attractive face relaxes. Pale
eyes shine compassionately. She works the letter free from my

clutch. "I know you wanted to go before but it's not your fault you couldn't. They'll understand, surely?" She has an idea. "I could help you to the 'phone if you'd like to ring them, though. I've got plenty of change."

"I need to go home." Words are piling up now, spewing out. "They don't know about the baby. They're very . . . old-fashioned and they wouldn't understand. They've had all this worry with my uncle so I couldn't upset them anyway . . . I definitely can't now. And I have to see him before he dies! He's the most wonderful man, truly kind and loving." I struggle for words at last, my voice squeaking again. "*Er ist sauber und einfach.* A clean and straightforward man."

Susi stares at me. Then she smiles. It's a tight smile.

"Don't be so daft. You've been very ill and you've . . . lost a baby: you can't even *walk* properly yet. What would Micha say? You should tell your family why you can't come: it's crazy not to."

Well, Susi may be very stubborn, but I'm more so. Something muscular flexes in the void and my voice grows steadier. "Micha isn't here. He never is when I need him. I *have to* go."

I'm boarding a train now at Stuttgart Station. The Brillo pads have fluffed up into cotton wool after all, and I'm here, but not here. It's almost Easter. I'd forgotten. In Britain, the way we usually mark the miraculous resurrection of Christ the Saviour is by eating chocolate, watching football and bad films and shopping. I suppose some people still go to church in Britain, but probably not enough to fill Wembley Stadium. Here, Easter is on a par with Christmas, so everyone makes their way like lemmings to their 'loved ones'. That's why I couldn't book a seat when a reluctant Susi, at last accepting she couldn't stop me, took me to a travel agency. That's why all seats are filled, as are the corridors and every other space available. Most people are going to North Germany, so I might get a seat somewhere between Aachen and Ostend. That will take many hours, however. Around me there's a holiday atmosphere, and, ironically, a Blitz-type togetherness. Some fellow standees smile at me, and a young man in army uniform tries to talk. Wartime echoes are so strong I blink as if swatting the past away. He must think I'm a miserable cow I suppose or even a bit crazy. He's probably not far wrong. After a while, he gives up. Turns away.

In my mind, grainy pictures of my uncle run like an old film in the way you're supposed to watch your life just before you die. Light reflects in the bald pate I used to draw pictures on as a small child while he dozed. He wakes, looks up, and I see his rounded cheeks that always shine pink as a boy's, the slight facial twitch. I can faintly hear his stammer and the snort when he laughs: he's painfully shy in company, but totally at ease and humorous with close family, and especially with me. I see his earnest expression as he gives me books, knowing the right kind when no-one else would, then the head bent over a crossword puzzle while others watch telly, or over his favourite book, a doorstop called the Rise and Fall of the Third Reich. I remember his joking about me being a student (though he drove me miles to and from the university like a proud dad) and making fun of me going to live with THE HUN. I recall my gran looking sad then, and telling me later he went out with a German girl himself just after the war. She preferred someone else and he never asked another girl out, ever: that's why he lives with her still, this gentle, reliable, devoted son and brother, this kind and generous uncle. With him I always feel happy and *safe*. Safe.

With what strength I have over from trying to stay upright and awake, I try not to picture him now. I know he's unable to walk, talk, move. That he's incontinent, with all human dignity gone and only abstracts of Love and Death left. Pray just in case there's a god that he feels only the love rather than fear and humiliation. Pray he's not slipping away as fast as this train can slice through the cold of night, as fast as we're hurtling past city and station lights, then back out into empty, silent dark so that we're left staring at ourselves in black mirrors. I'm distracted from these thoughts by the horrible sensation of warm blood soaking out of me into the nappy-like pad I'm wearing. As I squeeze my thighs together, the oddest feeling creeps over me, the conviction I'm empty: a cool, empty shell. My skin, however, feels very hot. How can this be, when I'm so cold and my blood is leaching away? If I hadn't lost my child, perhaps I could have pushed out my belly and insisted on a seat. Eventually, leaning hard against a panel, unable even to sit on my bag as the space is too packed, I drift. Through my eyelids, lights and darkness alike are now arterial red. Showers of stars burst, float in my head. The rattle of wheels on iron soothes and drowns out all other noises. Their rhythm lulls: 'Endure, endure – endure, endure!' And, at last, I'm here, but not here. I've done this before! When? Why? I mustn't think. I return to my mantra.

Eons pass and then an altercation nearby is loud enough to rouse me. I start as a hand touches my arm. A middle-aged man with a sagging face but concerned and kindly look is motioning me to a pull-down seat. He seems to have shamed a scowling younger man into giving it up. I can only nod heartfelt thanks, and, as the need for exertion of Will is gone, my legs give way, my eyes close and I drop onto it. I'll worry about getting the ferry later, and then catching two more trains. For now, I can sleep. Awake, I'm dreaming: asleep, I find rest.

***

At a long journey's end, all I can think of is how cold it is in here, in this red-plush-lined fridge with a tiny stained glass window. I suppose they have to keep the bodies from going off. Surreal. Surreal. My uncle lies on a table in his best dark suit. His greatest friend, my uncle by marriage, told me he laid him out himself, as he couldn't bear the thought of a stranger doing it. I wish I could have done it, given some return of love and care before he started his journey. In the little Celtic village I come from, tradition dictates women can't go to the graveside at the funeral, so this is my chance to say goodbye. Why then am I wasting time fretting about the loud whispers I heard earlier that he wouldn't have known me anyway – recognised nothing and nobody in past weeks, not even his beloved mam? There are many kinds of chill, and the disapproval that I stayed away so long, didn't make it in time, is what's really freezing my blood and making me shiver. Everyone will *say* it's not my fault, but I know they think it is. I bend, talk into my uncle's ear like a Muslim murmuring the name of God, but he doesn't move and there's no hope of absolution. I kiss his forehead, smooth and colder than a marble slab. Strange that apart from the waxy complexion he doesn't look dead – he looks rather as if he's closed his eyes to work out some complex crossword clue. There's a rare photograph of him taken years ago when he was in the army, in which he smiles shyly, achingly young and handsome, envelope-cap at a rakish angle. I can see it more clearly now than the white cheek that no longer twitches, that shines only with my tears.

I expect depressed silence in my gran's house, but I walk into a war zone. I should explain one of my aunts converted to Catholicism recently. The whole shebang: bells, books, candles, incense and – to the equal disgust and amusement of my family – a phial of holy water in her pocket. In a pagan turned Protestant village, that's far more shocking than atheism or offering your soul to Satan at midnight. My family even goes to church reluctantly for hatches, matches and dispatches. It's very 'low' church too, as plain as chapel but more *respectable* somehow: all expressions of fervour – Fundamentalist Protestant or Catholic – are equally undesirable. Now my secret RC aunt – not the brightest pane in the stained glass – has let slip she's ordered a mass for my uncle's soul. I suppose it's to make sure it goes to the right place. Well, we all know if there is a heaven he's on his way or there already – so what's the *point*? I know he would have hated a mass beyond measure. He utterly despised God-botherers, as well as all fuss and hypocrisy – but if he knew some people want to chant Latin to make themselves feel better, he'd probably snort and then laugh. I feel like doing the same, and I'd certainly be prepared to let it go.

However, I don't voice this opinion as everyone bar my dad, my gran and my youngest aunt is in a state worse than any Pentecostal frenzy, and I'd never be heard. In any case, like my deaf father who sits locked in a room with perpetual silence, I'm here but not here. I move towards my gran and my youngest aunt, who are weeping hopelessly. My mother is made of tougher material, however, and her cheeks are as brilliantly red as her hair used to be. She's arguing fit to bust, and other relatives, encouraged by her fighting spirit, join with her so the voices swell to a crescendo. Finally, as my aunt stomps out into the night, the Catholic taint is exorcised and an uneasy silence falls after the shock of violent emotion spent. But it's not over yet. I've never seen my mother look grimmer, and am amazed that she has somehow gotten hold of the priest's telephone number. We watch fascinated as she picks up the 'phone.

After a tense pause, it's clear the Man of God is in. With next to no preamble, she tells him what to do with the Pope, his mass, his church, all its contents and congregation. Martin Luther would have bear-hugged her and signed her up on the spot as a Reformation Missionary. One assumes that at the other end of the line, the priest is trying to be reasonable, persuasive. He's probably used to the infatuations and worship of fawning middle-aged women who call him Father, carry holy water in their pockets and holiday in Lourdes or Rome. I could guarantee he's never come across a tirade like the one he's being subjected to now. When the 'phone is clapped smartly down again, my mother informs us that there will be no mass. She says my uncle would spin in his grave. There's a longer silence as we all remember he's not in his grave yet, but lying alone in a pretend-chapel under a piece of pretend-velvet that's no protection against even the most delicate of ice-frills on the air.

***

Well, I'm back in Germany and back at work. I think I am alive. I must be, as everyone tells me in their different styles that life must go on. To underline this message of hope, fate has dealt me an ace: ironically, when I appreciate it least, I've managed to get A Proper Job. It was just there waiting for me, this position in a university library department. They want someone fluent in English and German to sort, manage and translate their catalogue system into both languages. It's brain-cell-killing-dull, but I'm used to that, and it's a plus point now that I don't have to think. It pays so well I can work part time, and, by giving private English tutorials, I can supplement the regular salary and we're far better off. And so I work on. And so we do all the other things couples seem to do. Except we don't talk about our dead babies or the fact we'll never have a child; we don't talk about the cracks opening up at our feet; we don't talk about my uncle; we don't talk about anything important. I'm here, but not here. I'm always sad even if I appear happy and I eat everything I can garner and hide to fill the terrifying and cold spaces inside. Friends look relieved, complimenting me on how well I'm bearing up and how strong I must be. My family is very far away. Micha, of course, is still not there when he's needed most. Food is.

Time passes. And passes. Doors close, doors open. There's a feeling of restlessness, but now the pattern of it is reversed: in the daytime, I'm anaesthetised, too dazed to think of change, working hard, always busy, a cheerful marionette, head and body stuffed so no-one will notice I'm still bleeding. At night, however, I toss and turn, moan and mutter, my legs scissoring as I dream about running for trains. Of journeys. Micha complains I kick him and keep him awake. In my dreams, I have to catch a particular train, even if I'm not sure why the need is so desperate. This time the trains are quite empty, and, after a series of trials and frustrations, I always manage to claw my way on and drop into a seat. Each time, I'm borne away triumphant but afraid as I swhoosh into an unknown dark. Each morning I'm disappointed to wake. For a few fleeting seconds, in the no-man's land between night and day, I'm undefended against the stab of loss and the bewilderment to be breathing when no longer alive. Then I get busy, of course, and forget for another year the Easter story of a benign hand rolling back the stone and a corpse walking out into a blinding dazzle of light.

Warrior

John is a soldier. A GI. We don't exactly remember why but, from a deep south hotter than chilli and livid with anger, via the US barracks in southern Germany, he found his way to us. It seems so unlikely.

Years ago I saw this amazing portrait of a warrior-knight in the 15th century in the British Museum. It's by Leonardo, and as you can imagine incredibly finely drawn and detailed. He has no name, but I see his face has brutality, a brooding focus, but it is not ignoble or ugly. He is proud, and he wears armour that is like a work of art: is a work of art. Some of his underclothing is even tied off with jaunty, flying ribbons. Though he killed so he would not be killed, Battle and Death were an Art form then, and tactics a scientific game. But I remember also soldiers raped women until they bled to death and impaled babies on stakes.

Though it makes me think of him, John is nothing like this ideal portrait. He is graceless, stocky, his scalp shaven, face coarse, jowls slack, body broad and lumpy. His neck really is red. He has small eyes set deep and way too close together. He walks like a sure-of-himself-get-out-of-my-way gorilla even on sharp urban streets. Why is he so drawn to us? We are a group of typical hippy -ish students with lots of long hair and flowing garments. We study things like American Literature, Art, Philosophy, Mediaeval History, Music. We worship culture in all its forms. We are fey. Some of us do Yoga, others meditation. We read The White Goddess, Carlos Castaneda and the Egyptian Book of the Dead. We walk along Ley-lines on serious, pseudo-spiritual holidays. We worship the mind and life in all its forms. Most of us are vegetarians.

John in contrast doesn't read. We suspect he thinks only gay faggots do that. John doesn't look at pictures, except those in Hustler. John thinks women are for fucking and cooking biscuits and corn bread and grits, maybe having brats to keep the race going. He drinks only beer and whisky. He eats hamburgers or sausages. His idea of a holiday is a bar brawl or going into the woods to kill things.

There were one or two fringe members of our group who must have met him in a bar and decided to use him for the things he could get for practically nothing from the barracks' store. Like women using GI's for stockings and chocolate in the war John Wayne helped us win against the Hun: it's a nice irony. I suspect this strongly as he comes to visit with the myriad pockets of his shapeless khaki jacket bulging. Do they usually hold guns and grenades?

Whatever the reason, he found us, looked, and something in him stirred and keeps bringing him back. What *does* he get from this off-kilter relationship? I would have thought he wouldn't piss on us if we were on fire. If we are using him, what does he hope for in return? I think I'm the only one now who feels truly uncomfortable around him. Everyone else has grown used to him hanging about. The guys drink, smoke and laugh with him. They guzzle single malt whisky and suck deep on Marlboros. They also seem to enjoy his talk of training to become a killer, of the God Gun, and his ridiculous story of trying to smuggle his own pistol into Germany. The other women in our group seem to find it easy to ignore him. I wish I could too.

Though he knows I am with Micha long-term, and Micha drinks, laughs and smokes with him, I notice that he is too often near me. Whenever this happens, he chats awkwardly like dusty white trash thrown into conversation with a frilly and fragrant southern belle. Eventually he plucks up courage to ask me about myself. I would as a matter of course be polite, interested even, and would ask him the same questions in return. But the only imperative when he engineers these encounters is to get away. On one occasion he tells me I look like a blonde actress he saw in a thirties film. There is no answer to this.

One dark winter afternoon, he says we should all go along with him to Stuttgart. Taste a bit of reality. Get away from the quaint mediaeval university town where we live in a half timbered building, once a monks' hospital, romantically overlooking the river. Escape the rooms where we sleep safely in the shadow of the fairy tale castle lulled by the holy sound of the church clock chiming the quarter hours.

Where he takes us, this real place, is called The Strip. It's formed of two parallel lines of cheap thrown-up shanties flanking a dirt track. It's like a frontier town in the West just starting to be born, but there's no freshness or hope for something better in the future here. Inside, the shanties are very dimly lit bars where porn films show in a loop to a clashing juke box accompaniment. Thus Elvis is mourning the death of a child in a ghetto while prostitutes solicit the customers and penises on screens endlessly do what they do.

When I try to escape for a few minutes and go to the loo, whips and bras hang behind the door. I can still hear the groans of simulated pleasure. In these little hells on earth, you pay a high price for the drinks and the sad, faceless whores, but – hey! - the porn is free.

I go back and whisper to Micha that if we don't leave right now, I will walk off alone and he'll be personally responsible if I end up on a slab. He knows I mean it. We leave, though I know he's secretly loving this *nostalgie de la boue*. He'll probably write a song about it, feel a pleasant frisson of lowlife daring amidst the sheltered confines of his life.

However when we get back to the half timbered mediaeval building and our cosy room, he apologises for my distress and anger, hugging me until I relax. We have a glass of good red wine. Listen to some pseudo-spiritual music. We lie on the bed. We start to make love. It's very late now. We haven't locked the door, but no-one would call in the early hours. Suddenly, over Micha's shoulder, like a flash from a nightmare, I see John's stocky frame in the black doorway, silhouetted by the night lamps in the corridor. I can't see his face. He can see mine. Before I can even react, the door closes silently. I leap out of bed, lock the door, explain. God, I am mortified, and have even more reason now to feel uncomfortable with this outsider. I dread our next meeting. However, we don't see John the next day, though, or the next. It gradually dawns as a sense of relief we will never see him again.

I am glad yet also very sorry, even though I can't be sure what for. I think some miss his booty but no one can contact him. We don't even know his last name. He invaded our space. Now he's gone. He wasn't noble or special, not a knight-warrior: he was just John Doe, a sad and lonely soldier, fitting nowhere. Born to drift and die.

An Alligator's Eye

Florida. Now, what do you think of? Oranges; sunshine; beaches; Mickey Mouse; obese retirees called Abner and Dolores, dressed in 'lee-zure-wear' and sporting Chevrolet-type 1950's shades. Oh – and sharks and hurricanes. But we're not here as straight tourists, and proud of it.

We're definitely not here to visit the plastic horror of Disneyland, though the place we're staying at for six weeks is just as surreal in my view. Near the village of Waldo (I'd never heard of it either) on the moss-draped edges of shrill, shimmering swamps, there is a farm. And on that farm lives a community of American Marxists. Pete, the guy who owned it before he gave it over to the World Revolution, became a friend when he was studying in Germany. On this farm, people come and people go, but a core of believers stays and even those passing through must live by strict Marxist principles, holding everything in common and working the land. We soon realise 'everything' includes sexual partners and caring for the children born of stoned and sweaty couplings in the deepest, hottest dark I've ever known. Mind you, I rather think that quaint custom owes more to 1960's California than Moscow.

You soon learn all aspects of life in an ideal state have to be explored in tedious committee meetings: instead of TV, the modern opiate, there's a mind-paralysing meeting every night. In a weirdly mediaeval fashion, all behaviour and decisions are solemnly analysed and passed piece by tiny piece through the crystal Truth of the Teachings. To make it worse, these natural sleeping potions are brewed in shower room heat to a backing track of insects sawing wood and night birds screeching insanely. When they're over, millions of brain cells have died and there's no impetus to do anything very much except go to bed and make desultory Marxist love. I do wonder if there are accepted positions – the Lenin Lunge, the '1917', the Trotsky Thrust (ouch) – and if they're allowed to call on God or Jesus when it all gets too much. I'm curious, but not enough to want to find out . . .

As we arrive, the evening meeting's just breaking up, and all we can do is fall into an innocent if not very clean bed where in the heavy dark I dream uneasily of alligators circling the farm in silence, only their eyes showing green in milky moonlight. They glide through steaming waters and I can't tell if they're guards or predators.

So here we are at our first actual meeting, new arrivals, fresh off the bus. Pleasingly exotic – even Marxists just *lo-o-ove* my English accent – and providing unusual entertainment after the drudgery of the agricultural day. We or rather I manage to create two sensations . . . firstly I make it clear neither of us will be sexually available to commune members. Micha my partner tries not to look disappointed, as do one or two assorted Comrades. Well, they can like it or leave it: if that's unacceptable, I'll be gone. Communists seem thrown by this forceful approach – they oughtn't to be, of course, after Stalin – and before they can recover I create a *second* sensation by refusing to do any work on the farm. Before anyone can suggest I repack my rucksack, I use the sugarplum method to cover the bitter taste, volunteering to care for the children as needed, clean the place until it shines and to *cook all meals*.

These are all things I enjoy, and, by good fortune, are the three duties the comrades least want to do, they all being so dedicated to tilling the soil. People who work the fields while it's light get very, very hungry. Hunger bends principles, and few people *like* living in chaos or having cockroaches as big as any in a William Burroughs' hallucination stalking the unwary at night. They look at each other, slowly nod assent. Naturally they're vegans, but there's enough fruit, veg, nuts, pulses, corn flour, spices and brown rice here to feed a small state, and when I promise to cook for the freezer too, they're fully converted. They almost shout 'Amen!' and wouldn't care at this moment if I were a Wall Street Wanker or a robed and chanting priest: we're in!

Of course, I soon find I have time on my hands. The children are happy to play, sleep and occasionally be fed food and stories, the roaches are tamed as they ever can be for now, the wooden floors scrubbed and crisper cotton curtains billowing prettily at the windows. The porch is swept, mattresses aired, sheets laundered, dust conquered, lentil stew and (vegan) nut dumplings bubbling in the pot. The capacious freezer is stocked. So there's time to sit with Pete's most regular 'partner' who has a sense of humour the others lack and seems almost like someone from my planet. She is pouring herself a cup of freshly brewed coffee. She looks pooped. She is pooped. She tells me the combination of the heat, hard work, an exquisitely painful period and the knowledge her 'relationship' with Pete is terminal is bringing her down. To cap it all, she's due to do a shift at the Waldo Cocktail Lounge tonight and will have to go – the hard cash comes in handy and she'll lose the job if she lets them down again. Pete doesn't like her working there, but, hey, fuck him! There are things a girl needs to buy, Marxist principles or not.

My mind ticks. We have very little money left, and will need some for the journey back to New York, diamond gateway to a deliciously decadent Europe. I hate hitching in this One Flew Over the Cuckoo's Nest country, and we'd maybe have enough for both of us to take a bus. I ask – despite the fact it's strictly illegal – if she thinks they'd accept me as a sub. Her tired eyes kindle. She loves the idea. Perfect for both of us – we could share the shifts 'til I leave! Waldo is way off any track, and the wages and tips are in used dollar bills. They're pretty cool at the Lounge, and the local police wouldn't notice if half the population massacred the other half if they did it quietly. And they'll just l-o-o-v-e my English accent. It might even be a crowd puller: not a lot happens in this Everglades suburb.

The Lounge looks like a couple of battered titanic trailers mating, but inside it's quite attractive. Muted country music plays from the jukebox, people sit at covered tables in the glow of golden haloes of lamplight. Well dressed and groomed, they sip their cocktails. I'm encouraged. They even talk quietly, so the atmosphere is soothing and surprisingly civilised. Not unlike a cosy library with alcohol on tap. Mind you, I can't say I'm enamoured of the uniform: it's an eye-popper, as the dresses are very short, and we all have to wear a French-maid type apron. My new friend made me borrow a pair of decent shoes to wear with it. No self-respecting hippie ever dressed like this, but when in Sodom . . . and though I hate revealing them, other people say my legs are fine, and, after all – it's easy money, cash in hand.

I have some trouble with the drinks list: there are *hundreds* of cocktails, most with bizarre names I've never heard before. I'm startled and not a little spooked to find 'Tonite's Special' is called an Alligator's Eye. *My* eyes function very badly in semi-darkness, and I can't read the list without putting my nose close to it. I also discover I have no hope of understanding the clientele, who drawl the names in broad rural accents. But the cocktail maker is a sharp guy, and he tells me just to repeat the sounds I hear phonetically, and he'll know what I mean. He does, too, and we've done fine so far. Jeez, they all can't *believe* I'm from Eng-er-land – just imagine that! – and they do l-o-o-v-e the accent! I already have a pocketful of tips, and they keep on coming. People seem to be downing the drinks in one just so I'll go back to serve them, talk to them again and they can give me more money. I could do this forever! I'm like a salaried parakeet!

Three hours later: a live band has been on. They played the stand-by-your-man type of stuff at first, followed by what they call here shit-kicking music and now slow, mournful numbers again. People have drunk, danced, whooped, spooned, staggered out to be copiously sick and then crawled back in to drink, dance and whoop some more. Some couples gamely prop each other up, exploring each other's bodies and throats with the subtlety of drunken surgeons. Without exception the punters have turned into sweaty semi-human creatures, the men with red necks, shining faces and dark armpits and the women with streaked make-up and self-destruct hair styles. I and the other waitresses whizz to and fro as if on skates, our own cheeks hot enough to fry eggs sunny side up and our aprons limp. My feet feel as if they're being cooked too, and I've earned so much I've had to stuff a wad of notes down my bra. They're getting wet: I'll have to iron them dry later. People don't share their tips here – you grin and grovel for it, you get to keep it. Fair's fair: I'm using my greatest asset in a money economy, and by God I'm *earning* it.

Suddenly, the noise level rises in the area nearest the stage. We can hear it above a man in a Stetson singing about how his baby left him, done ground him down with her high heels. He's droning it out, and I've wondered what she saw in the miserable bastard in the first place. I would have shot him: grinding with heels would take too long, and I have a suspicion he'd enjoy it too much. Anyway, I'm watching from a few yards away with my mouth open as – with so little warning! – chairs are cracked over people's heads, punches are aimed at fat cushion midriffs and two women tumble to the ground like famished lovers, tearing at each other's hair and clothes. Tables turn, drinks spill, glasses and bottles smash. One man whoops and dives on top of the women to pull them apart. Two men roar like goaded beasts and dive less gracefully on top of him to pull him off. Amazingly, I seem to be part of it as I'm lifted clear off the ground and flung to the floor. The cocktail maker hisses: "Stay there! Face down!"

I've seen a lot of movies, so I flatten myself, head to one side. Eyes shut, I wait. I don't know for what, but I don't expect it to be good. My knees are shaky and I'm so, so glad I snuck to the toilet five minutes ago: even in this mayhem, someone would notice if you peed yourself. There's an odd kind of silence around me now, and I open one eye, sliding it sideways like an Egyptian dancing girl painted on the wall of a tomb. All the workers, welded to the floor as I am, are doing the same, eyes flashing messages of comfort as we wait. For me, at last, the light bulb illuminates! We're less likely to get hurt here – playing dead, no-one will knock you down and better flying glass on your back or legs than on your face . . . people don't shoot into the ground either. Someone really could pull a gun out here – everyone here seems to have at least one.

Eventually, above the noise, comes the demented wail of sirens. Ah: the laid-back sheriff and his men. Annoyed to have their evening interrupted no doubt, but welcomed by the staff if not by me. My knees grow even wobblier: will they check ID's and social security numbers? I groan. What *do* they do to illegal workers here: if people are having saloon-type fights: are lynch mobs still in fashion?

Closing time. No lynch mob, everyone's worked wearily but happily together, and the place is as it was when I arrived. There's a pile of broken furniture in the yard at the back and the bins are overflowing, but spare tables and chairs have been brought in and carefully arranged, tablecloths laid. There was blood on the floor, and clumps of dyed hair. Even something that looked like a flap of skin. But the place is clean again and ready to make good capitalist cash tomorrow. Someone turns down the lights and the golden glow blurs edges, making everything look better. Someone else puts a seductive song on the jukebox, and the manager offers everyone a beer. We sip the icy liquid, kicking off shoes, groaning aloud in relief. The cocktail maker flumps down beside me. I thank him for his timely action, and he gives me a dazzling smile.

"No problem. I guess that never happened to you before. I bet you won't be coming back!"

"My friend said I should do Saturday for her."

"Oh, my!" He smiles again. It really is an enchanting smile. You could warm your hands in front of it. "Stiff upper lip, huh? Like in the movies. Saturday . . . good tips on Saturdays, but then it *really* kicks off. Weeknights now – weeknights like tonight is *quiet.*"

We both laugh. I'm bone weary, but I'm happy. I'm *alive.* Thrumming like an engine.

"Then I think I'll do Saturday."

We chink beer bottles, and he winks.

"You gotta try one of these cocktails you been serving all night." He sees the doubt in my eyes, and his own twinkle. "Completely without prejudice, ma'am, and I'll even give ya a lift home – it's on my way. I ain't a serial killer – ask anybody. "

That man is an artist in his way, and the special tasted wonderful, though strong as rocket fuel. I had two, and don't remember anything about getting home or cooking breakfast for the Comrades. I must have done both, as I found myself sitting in the kitchen in weak shafts of sunshine coming through windows on the east side of the house, and there were dishes in the sink when my eyes opened fully and uncrossed. I 'did' many other nights at the Lounge, starting with the following Saturday. On that evening, there was a fight. One man died of a heart attack. Two were driven to the county hospital and quite a number hauled off to the jail. One of the cops looked me up and down and winked at me as he snapped the cuffs shut on a dishevelled, cursing woman. I discouraged him with a fearsome frown. It would be dangerous for him to hear my English accent, even though he would of course have l-o-o-v-e-d it. By now, I knew no-one would snitch – already I *belonged.*

Soon we'll be heading home, and I'm enduring these last days until we catch the bus. I have to say I've enjoyed my job at the Lounge a thousand times more than being on this farm where people are pickled in principle, dead already as they organise their thoughts and lives in the same way they pack and label the produce in dusty boxes and sacks. I can hardly wait to get out of this damp, worthy non-Eden. I'd rather be poking an alligator in the eye. I'd rather be crawling around the Lounge floor dodging chair legs or bullets. I'd even prefer to be in Disneyland, where I'd have my picture taken, grinning as if my smile will meet at the back of my head and the top fall off. Yes, sir-ma'am: that's me high-fiving Mickey with juices from a triple-decker cow burger tracking down my chin: Yup, that's me having the time of my life.

Purification

When that last straw breaks, it's usually important but symbolic, inaudible. When mine breaks, it is a loud crack that – finally – wakes me up. Through all the months of Micha-misery, I sleepwalk, struggling to summon up strength to cut the ties. I can't. I travel in circles. Stay. Go. When? How? Go. Stay. One thing that both keeps me sane and tied to the house of sadness is my beautiful cat, Sapse. From nowhere, she offers herself to me when my spirit is very low – and becomes a lifeline. She is a kitten, a soft, furry scrap, with green eyes huge in her sweet face with its delicate bones. She seems to grow quickly, filling out in all directions but still slim and elegant in frame. Our neighbours Arthur and Ulli got her just before they found out Ulli was pregnant. They weren't sure if she should stay – cats and newborns don't always go well together – but she takes the decision out of their hands by spending all her time with me. She creeps through a window that was ajar . . . and stays.

The adoration is mutual, and she is truly mine. There is an unspoken sympathy and trust so strong, others see and feel it. My job is part time, and if I do 4 hours a day, I can do them any time the University Library is open between 8.00 am and 10.00 pm. This means I both leave for work and come home at almost a different time every day: even if I leave, say, at 10.00 am, I might not get back 'til 5.00 pm, as I might meet a friend, go for lunch, spend some time reading in the library or give an English lesson. Sapse sees me off like a faithful dog each time, and the ladies in the local shop tell me that exactly five minutes before I arrive, she appears at the stop, sits and waits on the wall, looks longingly at the horizon.

Whenever possible, we play together, or she sits while I read or follows me when I do tasks about the house or garden. Like a dog, she even follows me when I go shopping in the village. I feed her, love her, give her a safe and comfortable home. Increasingly, she sleeps with me when I am alone, tries to comfort and cheer me. One day, we are in an empty house and I am indulging in the luxury of a good weep while no-one will see. She begins to touch me with her paw, walk towards the door, come back. She does this until I cotton she wants me to follow her. Just like Lassie! We go to the hall, where there is a lovely old wooden staircase and banister leading to the first floor. She streaks to the top, watches till I am paying full attention, then slides down the banister, does an alley-oop backflip and lands neatly in front of me. I laugh fit to bust and she seems to smile. A few of my housemates come in at the moment. I tell them excitedly, I beg her to do it again. She won't. I wonder if they believe me – they probably don't. They are kind, however, and pretend they do, are glad something has made me happy again for a time.

One day I come home from work and two of my housemates are waiting, with tears unshed and how-the-hell-do-we-tell-her looks. My heart leaps then sinks to the floor. Oh God, Micha! What has he *done*? An overdose! An accident! But no, Susi and Michaela tell me Sapse is dead. Dead . . . Dead . . . Dead. It echoes. They make me sit. We live in a farming village. Our right side neighbour put poison in his barn to kill rats. Though I feed her only the best, she ate some. It would have been instantaneous he says. He is sorry, they say. Sorry . . . sorry . . . sorry. I have no idea where Micha is. When I have drunk gallons of tea and smoked several cigarettes, have accepted the truth, all we feel we can do is wrap her gently in a favourite scarf of mine. She is stiff as wood, and this is more horrible than anything. No flicker of life, of soul. Rules are very strict here and you are NOT allowed to bury pets in gardens and there is a vet's we have to take her to where she will be cremated. My friends drive us there. All that love, intelligence, innocence, grace, playfulness, her generous little soul – all to be burnt and then scattered in the woods I love.

Next day, Micha turns up late in the morning. He looks as if *he* died some time ago. We tell him and his only reaction is to complain bitterly that we did all we had to do for Sapse without *him* there. He loved her too! It was thoughtless of us, of me. I can see my two housemates – especially Michaela who has grown to loathe him – have real trouble in not hitting him. Something does seem to break inside, and there is a rushing in my ears. I tell him very calmly I have reached end point, am going; that the sight of him makes me want to vomit; that he is the most selfish, self-indulgent and hypocritical pig that walks this earth on two legs. Everything I have wanted to say for months is said. He looks as if he will faint. Suddenly, though, I think only of Sapse and cry lakes of tears. When I am calm, he is gone and my housemates help me pack. Micha they say is distraught. Well, fuck him: he has had his cake and gorged on it, now the cake, plate, fork and napkin are taken away.

There are practicalities. I make various arrangements with Susi and Michaela, Achim and Hannes. They tell me they want Micha to go, but he has refused. I explain it will be better in the end if I go, as I will be leaving Germany as soon as I can and they will have lost two housemates at once. Bills are reasonable, but only with 6 sharing. I realise the gift Sapse has given me: she has achieved what I could not. Leaving now seems easy and natural. I am awake, seeing straight, and will not be back.

Today I'm already somewhere else, a kind of waiting room, pretending the cube I am in is the inner sanctum of a temple to Isis set on an island, surrounded by still, reflecting waters. In a courtyard, fountains play. No-one but the goddess herself and her high priestesses can enter this cocooned cocoon at the epicentre of her power. But even in this sheltered place I hide behind a triple protecting veil of closed lids, the fringes of my hair and a white curtain. The opaque scant light is blood-pink. I've returned to the womb where the peace is deepened by a trinity of sounds, the sh-sh-sh of running water, the ticking of breath, and a soft heartbeat chant: 'I have left Micha, I have left Micha, I have left Micha'. Despite all my best efforts, thoughts intrude. It's so hard to believe I have left him I need to keep saying it. Everyone else says it's about bloody time, but when it happened, I was like a baby born prematurely, expelled shockingly into the cold, into dangerous air when I've been content to live in the dark on second-hand oxygen.

Despite all my efforts of imagination, the X-ray eye of truth would see me in the shower stall of an apartment in a half-timbered building, a house of high ceilinged rooms full of light from windows that gaze out over a crumbling mediaeval town. Like the Goddess in her temple, this is not my home, but it's a sanctuary where I am tended by women, my friend Luciana and her lesbian feminist flatmates. My crutch and my stick they comfort me. All men are rapists they say solemnly, glad of my conversion, and of their role as my rescuers, nurses, champions. He tried to call here yesterday: the Furies practically threw him headlong down the stairs. I laughed but then I cried: I wanted him dead, I wanted him back. They have a point of course: Micha may not have raped my body, but he did score deep into my spirit 'til it gaped open and oozed pain.

I can never forget the shock of first reading in history textbooks of how soldiers of all nations over the ages have violated women and children until they bled to death beneath them. They're still doing it now, this second, all over the world. I know they always will. When we find life on another planet, they'll rape the alien females and babies, grunting, plunging, whooping like wolves to an empty sky. *Why*? The ecstasy, I suppose, of that primal power surge: the power and the glory and god-joy: you can create life and as easily destroy it – just because you can.

I have to wonder where it started to go so wrong for us. Drugs tipped the balance I think. In the end, after years of flirting, Micha chose drugs and drink as his life-companions: cocktails of drugs, fathoms of drink. And he and the other members of the band became quickly addicted to other thrills, picking out teenage groupies like gluttons in a cake shop, stuffing their mouths with the creamiest eclairs on the shelf. Sometimes, out of his senses, he started to bring one particular girl back to our house – or more kindly I suppose she followed him – and I was forced to seek another kind of sanctuary with an outraged Michaela in my own home. I thought I was a strong, capable person, but overnight I became a poisoned and groggy fly glued into a dark web.

I find it odd that my mind keeps working as all else fails. The water runs, my body feels as if it's dissolving, melting, slipping away, but my mind purposefully plays an endless film loop of memories and, even worse, my own imaginings. I'm being made to look right now at mental pictures of ugly, mechanical couplings leading to the deadly creep of disease for him – though, thank the White Goddess! – not for me as we were leading almost separate lives in any case. Suddenly, with no warning, things worsen as a secret door slowly opens to a side room of my mind. I can hear insidious whisperings. A memory eludes me but I must seek it out. I recall now that as a small child, I heard the same whispers around me in the dark. Too scared to sleep in my bed, I used to crawl out to sleep under a table. My parents comforted me, of course, but they found this habit in turns irritating and amusing – and they never wondered why. Anyway, it stopped and I forgot, but now once again I can hear those ghosts gossiping.

Reason returns, but slowly, and I quieten them for a while. Think. Why in any case am I surprised at all at what's happened? It's the way it's always been and there's no reason at all any man or woman should be immune. Betrayal as I worked to pay the rent . . put food on the table . . . slept or lay awake alone. Such a strange and cold forgetfulness of everything we've been and done and felt and promised over years and years . . . a disrespect of how our not-fully-formed babies died and the parts of me that died with them. The loneliness as he gambles with death for fun, carelessly putting up my life too as a stake. The water is whirling about my feet now and I worry if I can't hold onto my mind it will start to slip down the plughole with the flow. *Concentrate!* Think! Somewhere in this mess I've lost something incredibly, ineffably important, but I don't even know what it is. I seem to be weeping silently for every human loss and hurt there's ever been or will be. I'm so empty my legs tremble and the water enters my veins.

I become aware it is happening again. My skin is being sluiced not only with soap and water, but with tears, urine, snot and a weirdly thin liquid from my bowels. It's all flooding away to the sea in a froth of filth. My eyes are wide open and I am watching myself disappear. This release of liquids only happens when I'm in the shower and my only comfort is that *no one knows*. No-one sees. The rest of the time, I manage. I move and speak and work and shop and cook and chat to friends and pay my bills. I try to grip onto normality. I know I should get out of this sanctuary now, as Luci and the Furies will surely be home soon. But, suddenly, although the water is still warm, it feels like ice. I can't move. I can't switch off the water. Everything is going from me. I'm stretching to end point. Not one teardrop of dignity or will left. Too much is lost. All is lost. Let it go.

I close my eyes. My lips begin to move. I'm having a conversation with myself. Urging. *Urging*. Fight this. Turn off the water now. Get out. Dry yourself, dress. You can appear fairly normal by the time the Furies get home. This is the strong voice. It fades. The other is softer, sly. But what's *wrong* in staying here? All you have to do is just stay here 'til you're clean. You're still not clean. You may never be clean. There is a short, tense silence then both voices seem to alternate and that's even more frightening.

You have to go back into reality. What else is there to do? No, don't do it: until you're clean it isn't safe to go back. People will know. They'll know you're dirty. But why should they know? You know they will, they'll see through the scrubbed pink skin into the stinking mass inside. They'll *smell* it. They'll be sick with disgust. They'll know you for a bell-ringing leper.

The sly voice is getting stronger and though it takes an eternity, with my teeth clenched I send a shaking hand creeping up towards the shower controls and turn the jet off. Both voices and all the liquid flows have stopped. My eyes are open, the tiles stare back, other teardrops drip. *I* just did that. I turned the voices off. I'm choosing to face the silence, the rush of colder air that makes me shiver. I have been reminded that I am more experienced in these matters than I knew and I can deploy weapons of a kind. What's left of me must and will survive. For now I'm s*afe* here, if not sound, and, for this moment, it's enough that when the others get back they'll find me calm, smelling of roses, sipping tea. They'll ask how I feel. I won't tell them the truth and they will smile, be happy for me, the world will turn.

Interlude

To Africa –The Legion

Some changes are so seismic you feel the tremors as they happen. I have to hold onto invisible ropes as this one shakes me. I still don't know how, as it took every atom of will I thought I no longer possessed, but I've broken out of my self-constructed West German prison. I revived enough to hand in and work out my notice, pay my bills, say goodbye and heartfelt thanks to kind friends, buy a ticket, pack the little I need . . . and leave Micha drowning in a dirty puddle of self-pity. He cannot accept I'm going: I cannot accept he is dense enough not to understand why I must. As I've said before. he wants his Scwarzwald Gateau and eat it: I would like to stuff his throat with it 'til his eyes pop, till he convulses and dies. My anger is cold, however, an icicle dripping dangerously inwards, and I have nothing left to say to him. I am focused instead on a decision to choose life by doing something truly worthwhile – preferably on a far continent – and I keep taking out the letter in my bag that confirms a posting as a volunteer overseas. Each time I do the trembling starts. I'm not sure if it's due to excitement or terror.

My family to whom I have briefly returned is, quite naturally, just as torn. They all know something is badly wrong, that this is more than the break-up of a relationship due to simple incompatibility and/or unfaithfulness. But they don't express let alone confront emotions, and, just in case anyone should break with tradition and try, I've Sylvia Plath-ed myself under the thick glass of a bell jar. Inside it, I'm too mistily seen and distant with pride for them to ask questions. I can see out, however, very clearly indeed, and know they are at the same time deeply impressed and worried sick. I tell them all with a cheerful, brittle smile that it actually appeals to me that you don't get a choice as to where you go or what you do: if you're accepted by VSO, you are sent to wherever your skills fit best. I don't tell them that in some ways, it's the emotional equivalent of joining the Foreign Legion. I *want* heat. I want discomfort. I want disease, danger, death lurking in every shady place. Things that make you focus on survival and the now, things that inexplicably heal the wounds of the mind.

Still, on the surface the wounds heal over surprisingly fast, and I'm recovered enough to be delighted when I hear I'm not being sent to some desert hell-hole but to *Kenya* as an English teacher and librarian. Kenya! Impossible even to convey now the romantic impressions in my mind as I sleepwalk through about half a dozen courses, prepare and pack and re-pack my bags – but anyone who watched *Daktari* as a child or has seen *Out of Africa* can probably imagine how I'm transported by visions of golden grasslands and teeming game, white-capped mountains and dun plains on which Maasai warriors herd cows and drink their steaming blood. Of course this is the twentieth century, and there's a very modern slant to *my* idyllic Kenya, where heroic westerners quietly try to atone for the twin colonial sins of arrogance and exploitation by working with the people for the people. Serving where once we had been served. It will be pretty rough in some ways, I'm told, but I'm looking forward to it. Escape and adventure. Choosing to live but risking illness and death; suffering to comfort oneself; atoning for being fool enough to be the victim of second-hand sin . . . yes – the Legion. Undoubtedly the most dramatic and yet quietly efficient way invented of forgetting yourself and being forgotten. You don't realise until you're in it that it can take so many different forms.

Arrival of the Queen of Sheba

So here I am at last at Nairobi Airport. Our straggle of volunteers sees little of it or the country we're to live in for two years as we are ushered through customs and driven to a quiet compound east of the city. With the pace of change registering at least 6.5 on the Richter scale, there's no time for much excitement or romance on the short, in-country induction course we are required to do before we are unleashed on the people of Kenya. We rise each day relentlessly at 5 a.m. to learn basic Swahili and advanced cultural awareness. After a few long days, conversant with Swahili and very, very culturally aware, six of us heading north-westwards are packed off to catch the train for Kisumu on Lake Victoria. At Nairobi station, we are each given a huge cardboard box by the field staff. The boxes have 'VSO – essential equipment' stamped on the side. They are very heavy and big enough to blot out the sun – and that's no mean feat, as here it often appears as the gigantic, flame-shooting gas ball it is. We don't know what's in the boxes, and there's no time to ask, but if it's *essential* . . .

When the train manager catches sight of our boxes and luggage, he goes stark raving bonkers. In no uncertain terms, he tells us there's no room on the train for the boxes: he doesn't care how essential they are! We're travelling second class, and we gaze yearningly at the third class carriages, where, it seems, people are allowed to take on board anything they like, including enormous wicker cages of chickens, horned goats, metal trunks like coffins and bedsteads. We point this out. He tells us as if we're two year olds that that's *different*: those people are *peasants*! A lot of them will do the overnight journey standing up as there's no room to sit down. In his part of the train, *Things Are Done Properly*.

At some point during our heated exchange, our vehement protests slide into piteous but fruitless begging. Eventually silence falls amidst the chaos as we stand confused and angry on the anthill platform. A man in the window of a first class carriage – an exquisitely tailored Kenyan who looks like a rich businessman or lawyer or maybe even a government minister – has been watching the scene gravely. He beckons one of our party over. She's someone I liked on sight and am fast developing a friendship with, an Anglo-Indian woman called Sandra. He clearly recognises we're not from round here, and that Sandra is the most assertive one among us, and, leaning out, he speaks low and earnestly to her. She nods, marches back, demands ten shillings from each of us. Puzzled but beyond caring, we give up our cash. She takes the train manager aside, a roll of notes changes hands, and he calls over porters to heave our boxes on. The other passengers complain loud and long about our luggage blocking the corridors and areas next to toilets (noisome holes in the floor, no water) and bathrooms (rusty taps, no water), but a mood of hilarity takes over. In one moment of Bunty-comic boarding-school type larks, Hazel – a rather drippy individual – sees her ticket slip down a gap between the window (stuck shut) and the little sink (no water) with a cover on it that acts as a table when not in use. Silence falls again.

We've been warned that if train managers are strict, ticket collectors are even more so. Thrice woe unto you unless you sit in the carriage with your names on the window – all mis-spelt, by the way, mine as 'Elena McTraniel' – and you have a valid ticket or you get off. We can try the same trick as at the station of course, but what if this train official is incorruptible? Panic breaks out, and we try every which way to reach into the gap, but, eventually, we accept the ticket is lost. We all look at Sandra. Can she do it again? With narrowed eyes she looks at Hazel and says matter-of-factly: "Hide".

Everyone stares, frozen in position like a waxwork tableau. Hazel breathes out as if she's been asked to eat a baby for breakfast: "*Hide*? Where?"

Sandra points at one of the top 'bunks'. We have already realised we won't be able to sleep one to a 'bed' as our luggage takes up racks, floor space *and* the top bunks. Hazel swallows. "It won't be comfortable."

Sandra's eyes roll. "It's better than getting off! We'll keep a look out, so you won't have to go up 'til he comes round. After that, we can bring you some food from the dining car and you'll be safe enough till morning. You can go back up if he comes around again." My new-made friend has a wicked sense of humour. She grins, showing tiny white teeth contrasting starkly with deep olive skin. "Even if he sees you, you honkies all look the same to them, I suspect. It'll work. Trust me."

Hazel is a very earnest person. She doesn't smile, but she nods reluctantly, and we share 'watches' after the long train pulls rather impressively out of the station. When he comes into sight, we heave her up and when he's gone, she clambers back down. We are all cheerful again as the train gathers speed and settles into its wonderful chockety-chock rhythm: this is going to work! We have (tarnished) silver-service dinner in a (down-at-heel) Orient Express type dining car to look forward to, and then a long, deliciously cold night toiling up into the Highlands through the Great Rift Valley. This is where Karen Blixen really did have her farm in Africa and her dashing Dennis! Though we can't see out, we are – at last – all caught up in the romance and excitement. Even propped up against each other like leaning skittles, we cocoon ourselves in the crisp linen sheets and fluffy woollen blankets available only to first and second-class passengers and fall into a dreamless, warm sleep.

Kisumu. It looks and feels like the seaside, though Lake Victoria is bluer than any sea, very still, brushed with silver. Again we are too bewildered to note any details as we are hustled by the local field officer and his staff to the bus park, where, horror of horrors, we are separated, each of us to go our own way. My stomach clenches. Suddenly, I'm on my own and going into the unknown. 'Up-country' city people call it. From the tone of people's voices, for 'upcountry' read 'dark side of the moon'. The field officer's secretary, a woman with the friendliest face I've ever seen, calls me 'honey', and tells me the deputy headmaster will meet me in Bungoma. She says it's a three hour journey, and, as I've done since I was a kid, I start to worry I'll want to go to the toilet. Oddly, however, I feel no warning stirrings in the nether areas, and allow myself to be thrust into the seat next to the driver. I see the friendly lady slip the driver a note. He winks. This time I understand why I'm clearly in the best seat while everyone else is crammed onto two wooden benches in the back of the van called a matatu. My luggage – including the huge box – is fitted onto the roof rack.

With startling suddenness, we're full and we're off at high speed. Then the brakes screech, and if I didn't have a bag jammed on my lap, I would break my head on the windscreen. My eyes bulge, the driver grins and winks again. The conductor opens the back door, brutally shoves a few more people in now everyone's been thrown forward, and we're off again. With time, this will be routine to me. Now, it makes everything feel even more surreal.

The misused and sweating passengers are still grumbling bitterly as we climb and we climb until we're on a high ridge and the whole of the town and the lake stretch out below us. Apparently migrating tribes stopped and praised the gods here in thanks for bringing them to the lush basin and infinity of water they saw below. They came from where I am going. Is this significant? And how much higher can we *go*? Before I have finished the question the road levels a little, and we are picking up speed. The rest of the journey goes by literally in a blur. People drive very fast here. There are no road markings, no road signs. Right of way is gained by intimidating other drivers. Heart-stopping risks are taken overtaking and we often lurch as if to tumble over into ditches or down slopes or into rivers. At times we veer off the tarmac onto dirt, and throw up clouds of choking dust. To my absolute horror, my box keeps falling off the rack. Whenever it does, however, someone yells, and we screech to a halt as the conductor good-temperedly jumps down to retrieve it.

By the time we approach Bungoma, I have a brain-tumour headache and feel sick. I'm now worrying that I don't want to go to the toilet. I haven't peed for at least 4 hours. Still, I'm alive – I'm surprised by this and deeply grateful – and when we pull into a very crowded and noisy bus park, a man with a wide but rather shy grin bounds up to greet me. Small wonder he has no trouble with recognition: there is no other white face among hundreds. I step out, and as the whole population stops and stares, he has to help me stay upright as I'm so shaky and stiff. After the introductions, he clicks his tongue. "You are very tired, Mwalimu (a title of great respect, meaning 'teacher') – we will go first to get something to drink and eat. No, please – it is *necessary*."

I murmur brokenly that a drink would be fine, but please, nothing to eat! My giant orange rucksack, bags and the battered box stand on the kerbside. Mr Wafula leads me away. I pull against his arm. All my worldly goods for two years! My essential equipment in the box! "What about the luggage?"

He frowns, genuinely puzzled. "What of it, Mwalimu?"

"Will it be *safe*?"

"But of course!" Mr Wafula stares at me as if I really am unhinged. "We do not have thieves here, Mwalimu: if they dare and if they are caught, the crowd would stone them to death."

I stare in return. He is absolutely serious. He leads me towards a shanty café with a few seats in the shade of a tree, and I gulp down several lemonades in quick succession as I can't risk water. He then persuades me to have some tea. It will be as good as a meal, he says. When it comes, I find up-country tea is made of full fat milk from a cow's warm udders, fresh Kenyan tea leaves and heaps of locally produced sugar. For good measure, it's sprinkled with cinnamon. As I drink, I can feel my body reviving like a watered plant, and energy slowly seeping back. Despite all this, I still don't want to go to the toilet. However, I go to the little rusty sink and mirror at the back of the lean-to, and make myself look presentable. We have to take another short matatu ride – nothing compared to the dicing with death journey just undertaken – and we arrive at our destination as the day starts to draw to a close. Mr Wafula says we must hurry. On the Equator the sun rises at seven and sets at seven: there is very little twilight, and soon it will be pitch dark. Apart from one bag, the luggage is left at the empty market place – he says it will be brought. This time, I don't worry.

As we break into a trot through a fringe of rustling trees, and lope across grass towards three houses, I see we are heading for the largest and smartest, an attractive bungalow, which, though a little roughly built, has a tin roof, a tiny verandah, pink walls, and decorative wrought iron bars on its windows and covering French doors.

"That is your house, Mwalimu. The best in the area, built for the headmaster's youngest wife."

I can see children's faces peering out through the windows. Even from here, I can see they are as big as saucers those eyes. People must be waiting to meet me. The children have probably never seen a white person before. My heart leaps.

"We must go to the back of the house, Mwalimu. The key to the front doors is lost."

Entering the house, we are almost knocked over by a wall of heat and blue smoke. There are no ceilings, the tin roof magnifies the heat of the sun, the concrete walls and floor trap it in and to top it all, there is a smoking fire in a grate. It is dimly lit in the kitchen, but the living room at the front of the house dazzles in the light of the setting sun. The interior is full of people, furniture, children, chickens and cats. I am blinded, bewildered, introduced to about five adults and innumerable children. There is a stronger sense of unreality. I feel like the Queen of Sheba smiling, shaking all the hands. I notice however two of the women are whispering, and looking awkward. One of the women steps forward. She is pretty, though with an oddly long face. She looks tired and careworn, but smiles warmly. "You are very welcome in my house, Mwalimu!"

At this point, she shuffles and looks imploringly at Mr Wafula. He whispers: "I am sorry Mwalimu – you see, they were told you were coming, but did not believe it. They said no-one would come so far to help us in this place. It was *impossible* a Mzungu lady would really come, so they did not move out into the next house as they were told by Our Headmaster."

I look at the very lived-in home, the children, the chaos and confusion. They won't even physically fit in the smaller house next door! I say as firmly as I can: "I'll take the next house. Truly! I'm on my own and I'd be happy to go there and not disturb everyone here."

Mr Wafula looks aghast, and the headmaster's fourth wife cries out: "No, no, Mwalimu! *This* is your house. My husband has said it! He will be angry with me as it is when he returns from his journey. But it is late now, and we will move out tomorrow if you permit."

Argument proves pointless, and, in the end, I am too depleted to continue. They see my state, and bring me cool water to wash. They bring a simple meal I can eat (salty omelette and bread) and cool water. We've been told never to drink the water, but I don't care if it gives me the plague – I empty the tin mug. Miraculously I finally go to the toilet – a thirty foot pit dug into the back garden – put on a cotton nightgown and lie down on the maid's bed in the kitchen. I have no idea where the maid will sleep and I can no longer worry about it. I'm trying not to think how dirty the kitchen is or to notice there are chickens on and under my bed, chicken shit all over the floor. There is no mosquito net. We've been told never, never to sleep without a net. Giant cockroaches crawl free. None of it matters. I sleep better than the dead and don't wake till dawn.

Next day, in remarkable quick time with so many willing hands, the house is stripped bare and I stand alone amidst the emptiness. A rickety iron bed has been brought from the school dormitory. I am to sleep on the bottom bunk. I have a stool, and a table. I have string, a sheet and a broom handle to hang from a beam to make a 'wardrobe'. At last, as if it's king Tut's tomb, I open my essential equipment box. It contains a set of tin saucepans, a kettle, a kerosene stove, crockery, cutlery, sheets, pillow cases, a blanket, tea towels, a hurricane lamp, two plastic bowls and a bucket with a cover. I note there is no mosquito net. So much for essentials! Someone has brought me a big jerry can of water and a bottle of kerosene. I fill the lamp and the stove, I pour the dirty river water into my bucket. Ah well – that's the housework done. This is my home now, and there's nothing else to do. It's strangely desolate and getting fiercely hot. Sweat runs in rivulets between my breasts and down my back. Panic gathers like an army for an attack on the fringes of my mind.

I go into the living room, large and bare except for the stool and table. The walls are painted hideous pink and lime green. There are no curtains. Suddenly, my eye is caught by a procession coming across the grass. I blink. The heat, the culture shock of it all – perhaps I'm really seeing things, a mirage. But the figures are still there, advancing steadily. As they come nearer, I see they are carrying a maroon '60s style plastic covered three-piece suite, a gas stove, a gas cylinder, a dining table and four wooden chairs. The gifts are carried in, set in their places. The bearers all grin, are introduced, pump my hand. I am overwhelmed, and the tears are threatening to spill. They see this, and are visibly satisfied as I stammer heartfelt thanks. They say it's very little. That I am an honoured guest and have come a long, long way: it is only fitting I have what they can give. I must be made comfortable and happy so I will stay!

I know this is an area where everyone is a subsistence farmer. Money is so tight people have to sell a cow or land to send a child to school. There is almost no spare cash – not always enough for soap, tea and sugar, the three material essentials here. Yet this morning I found fresh milk, some sugar and tea outside my door.

This is a life-changing moment for me, and I know I will suffer willingly *any* kind of discomfort for these extraordinary people. I thank my benefactors again, and offer them chai. Everyone beams and takes seats on the sofa, the chairs, the stool. Suddenly I realise how essential my equipment is: I will use the things that somehow survived a dozen crashing falls and an epic journey to make fragrant, sweet, creamy tea in the up-country way. I'm glad the house is noisy and full to bursting. I am wanted and valued. I looked for punishment: instead I seem to have come home. And suddenly, I'm richer than the Queen of Sheba in all her ropes of pearls and precious stones.

Armageddon

At seven o'clock precisely, on my first night alone, darkness falls with the drama of a thick, velvet stage curtain. With the hurricane lamp lit, the warm day-glo pink and green bungalow with its corrugated iron roof feels deceptively cosy. I'm at a stage now where it's starting to hover between oddly familiar, yet essentially *alien*. This is unsettling, but what is worse is that I have to put the lamp out. I've never experienced this kind of black-dark or solitude before: no-one from a town or city could imagine the vacuum effect of not having anyone within calling or even screaming distance. With no electricity supply to the area, the only light outside is a feeble orange glow from the windows of the two other houses on the school compound. But even if their windows dazzled white with spotlights, the challenge to the blackness would be Quixotic. There are no streets here either, of course, and no humming lamps. I read somewhere that the first streetlamps appeared in European cities like Paris in the late 1600's: well, all I can say is they still haven't made their way here.

Now I lie in bed, startled to find the darkness is the same whether I close or open my eyes. Above me, bats in the gables cheep and witter, pee and shit discreetly, silently. It seems to be what they do. They make me nervous, though I'm told they're harmless. There was no mosquito net in what I was told was my 'survival pack': it seems it isn't considered 'essential' equipment for living in these remote Western Highlands. Still, the rainy season *is* months away and I can't hear the malicious whine of the bloodsucker, so perhaps all will be well. Indeed, apart from the bat-song, the only sound is the busy sawing of insects outside. My window has bars on it, so I've been able to leave it open. There's no coolness, but a honeysuckle bush leaks its sticky sweetness, so that a scented breath of wind lifts the curtains gently. God's air-freshener covers the smell of the bat stuff and the sour, lingering odour of chicken shit . . . and plenty else besides.

Sleep won't come, and I try to force myself to be still, to be calm, to slow the acceleration of heartbeats, the quick-quick breaths. What can hurt me, after all? I've got to pull myself

116

together. The door is double bolted and padlocked and the windows have wrought-iron bars blocking human entry . . . but the window is *open* . . . there are *gaps* under doors . . . there is no ceiling! I have no net!! Insects and snakes can crawl through any hole, however small. Bats could fall or swoop. Maybe bite? Eventually, however, when soporific heat and exhaustion defeat anxiety and formless fear, I plunge into another kind of night.

Hours later, I wake. When I realise where I am, and what has woken me, I tense. It's not the echo of a dream, this mysterious sound, but a loud rustling, like the dry leaves outside seared by hot-season sun and rubbing against each other in the breeze. But this shouldn't be happening *inside*. A cold rill creeps over my skin despite the blood heat. I know I have to light the lamp and look. To put off the moment, I think of how irritated I've been by the Hollywood horror movies where people go into the attic, into the cellar, open the door, leave the safety of their room, bare their necks to Dracula's fangs . . . well, now, at last, I know why. When you're this scared, it's better to *do* something. *Anything.* The tension begins at painful and ratchets quickly up to unbearable. In the end, you have to break it. Face the fear, even embrace it – or be damned anyway.

Easily said, of course, and yet I amaze myself by managing to light a match. It flares. The wick catches. I adjust it, lower the glass, peer around. Shadows dance and crowd the room until I swear my heart actually nudges my larynx. Then the shadows steady. You have to imagine I'm on a low, school-issue iron bed. Beneath and around me, just inches away, I can't even see the pale concrete floor for a heaving copper-dark carpet of cockroaches indulging in what looks like a very successful insect orgy. They're even covering my flip-flops and shoes. I can't move. I can't make a sound. If I could, no-one would hear. If anyone did come, I couldn't get up to let them in. I'm stuck. Sick. Slick with sweat. If they come onto the bed – why aren't they *already* on and in the bed? – I know I'll pass out.

But the human brain, I find, is an amazing organ. There are times I steadfastly refuse to remember when I was a child when fear was so strong it couldn't be borne, and I learned to send it somewhere else. I have the ability to be here but not here. Beside me, the lamp will burn until the kerosene runs out, but I will see nothing, feel nothing until dawn. Nothing will come near me, as

117

I've become a not-thing. As light filters through the curtains and the insects head to whatever crack they call home, my mind will click back into place. I'll become sentient again.

When Francis the workman brings my jerry can of dirty water, I spill out my story. He's an oddly old-before-his-time-man, weathered by work and poverty. He looks like one of the Danish bog bodies come alive, his skin black and leathery, loose and bristled, scored into ravines of wrinkles. The impression is deepened as he wears a peculiar woollen cap, a torn shirt, ragged trousers, no shoes. His teeth are stumps and tobacco brown. He doesn't smile much, but when he does and you see them, it's a shock. His family are my neighbours in the mud huts beyond the school fence. I know he has two wives despite his poverty, as any man with just one is considered a feeble, pathetic kind of specimen. Francis has certainly proven his virility with a tumbling brood of children. I've waved to them across the barbed wire fence, and they all have huge eyes, white smiles, oddly dusty skin and swollen bellies. When I think of them, I feel ashamed, not only of my cowardice, but because this, for the moment, is my worst worry in the world.

Francis shakes his head, however, and seems sincere when he agrees this is *terrible!* Something must be done! We are both tactful, but we know it's because the headmaster's fourth wife was chosen for her voluptuous fertility and not housewifely skills. The house was filthy before she moved out. It's clean now after Francis and I swept and scrubbed it, but he explains the roaches will be hiding in every shadowed corner. He tells me I must go shopping today and get a net to sleep under – what was I thinking of to come without one! – and the biggest can possible of insect killer. I ask which type. He laughs for the first time since I have known him, and says there *is* only one type. I must go to the Asian hardware store. I can't miss it: there's only one of those, too.

I'm back from Bungoma town. My net is suspended from a hook in the bedroom ceiling. I can't stop admiring it: it's beautiful; bridal pure, virgin clean. Once it's tucked in, so will I be, and I will feel *secure*. I've bought two gigantic cans of insect killer. It's called DOOM. The cans are yellow, and there are red lightning flashes around the name. It says '*DOOM Kills All Wadudu* (insects)

DEAD'. I find this hard to believe, I must say: *wadudu* are very large here, and tough cookies. Francis returns as promised, and we set about our work with handkerchiefs tied over our mouths. When he goes home, I sit in a cane chair with a (warm) Coca Cola under the fig tree in the garden until the mushroom cloud of DOOM disperses. I have such a bad feeling it's pure DDT, banned in the so-called developed world, and I don't want it to kill *me* DEAD. When the sun is about to go down, I eat a scratch meal of beans on toast. You can buy tins of beans in the tiny town's 'supermarket' – you can't miss it, there's only one – and make toast by holding bread on a fork over a naked flame. I make and eat the meal hurriedly. Darkness falls before I have time to get too afraid.

Though snug under my net, I sleep very little, as the rustling continues all night. They can't get to me now, but, to tell the truth, it's not much consolation when I know they're sliming all over my home. Ah, well: so much for killing all *wadudu* DEAD. So much for DOOM.

It's a fresh Sunday morning and the sun's rays look as if they're being filtered through a pearl. Though it's heart-wrenchingly beautiful, my eyes focus on the heaps of baby roaches lying on their backs, making me pick my way gingerly to the door. Francis comes, dumps the water with a *plumph*, insists on sweeping them out. He urges patience: DOOM never fails. The next morning before school, we sweep away the medium sized mummy cockroaches. The next day, it's the turn of the daddy cockroaches. At the fourth, final, pearldawn, the biggest bastard roaches you ever saw or even had nightmares about are lying DEAD on the man-made floor. Why did I doubt DOOM? Not an antenna twitches. When they're gone, Francis insists on one enormous sweep and mop and one more spray. One or two Hollywood special effects monsters die overnight, and it's done. Armageddon is over, as all battles finally are. As in most battles, there's a winner. This time it's me, it really is, and I stand amazed as I survey my home, leaning on the broom stick like a warrior resting on the shaft of his spear.

Now I keep this house so damn clean you could lick your dinner off the floor. Margarine and cooking fat tins stand in bowls of

119

water, so insects drown if they try to get to the goo. Over the top of the cans is white gauze, weighted down. My dry goods, pulses and veg hang on strings in sisal bags from the beams, and the strings are impregnated with DOOM. Over my water (filtered, boiled and cooled) in the huge earthenware pot, there's more gauze, weighted down. Everything else is in tight containers. I'd lay a bet this is the cleanest house in Western Province . . . maybe in Kenya . . . possibly a contender in the world stakes. I can forget the Hammer-horror nights and the piles of dead because I'm busy. Taking precautions. Blocking it all out. I have an endless supply of DOOM and determination, and I will ban all things that creep like unwanted thoughts, filthy and disgusting, into my house, my bed, my dreams.

Riotous

I'm finding a new rhythm here almost-on-the-Equator where it's early to bed and early to rise in very rural Kenya where the nights are exactly twelve hours long. The sky is carpet-diamonded with stars and shooting stars stream, but each gleam or flash is, behind the shine, a barren rock millions of miles away shedding no light of its own. So, with the dark almost matte, the temperature varying only between warm and blood-heat, and insects joining the conspiracy to soothe you with a constant electric lullaby hum, even if you were the most desperate of insomniacs, you'd turn into Sleeping Beauty.

And if all that weren't enough, you're exhausted in a way people rarely are now in the developed world. There, most people *fancy* themselves tired: here you most certainly *are*. Dazed with the effort of survival, your bones ache and leaden limbs beg for rest. As what Kenyans call one of the 'upper classes' i.e. an educated wage earner, I'm spared the local women's endless labour – trekking to collect water and firewood, tramping to market laden with goods, squatting for hours over temperamental bitter-blue fires, making and serving beer, sweeping the dust and beating dirty clothes on river rocks, bearing and bringing up huge families, tilling the fields, grinding flour, feeding the domestic animals (and all this whilst pregnant, nursing, ill or *all of the above*) – but still by the time the sun disappears, I fall onto the bed like someone clubbed with a mallet.

I could make life easier for myself, to be honest, but in the face of people's struggles here, it would seem wrong. To the dismay of those who would if they could and think me mean not to give a poor person a job, I refuse to employ a servant. Thus I do my own washing (by hand), ironing (with a charcoal flat-iron last used by Noah's wife), the endless cleaning, the food preparation and cooking. Fortunately, all white people are considered hopelessly illogical and eccentric, so my Kenyan friends and neighbours simply shake their heads in tolerant wonder, trying to puzzle out why someone would do all this *if they didn't have to*. I almost give in to their urgings once in a while, but then one of the very old people I try to greet won't look me in the eye and calls me

Memsahib. Then I know I can't. My initial enchantment with this area and its people remains intact – as does a bloody-minded determination to do my work well – but I do flag, and at times am sorely tempted to give up altogether and go home. Sleep! I just can't seem to get *enough* of it. It's like a narcotic.

Anyway, it's a routine quiet evening by lamplight. Tonight I haven't even made it as far as bed, and my head has sunk onto the pile of books I'm supposed to be marking. As there's fifty to a class, it's a substantial if unusual pillow, but it feels like swans' down in cool Egyptian cotton to me. I've sunk fathoms deep in sleep, but, slowly, I surface, until I am aware the knocking in my skull is not part of some dreamtime nightmare. Then my heart hammers sympathetically to the rhythm of fist on shaking wood, and cold salt water seems to be running in my veins. I call out in Swahili, ask what's wrong. My voice is high-pitched. It doesn't sound like mine. Through the door, the school watchman shouts that there's trouble because the boys won't eat the evening meal! I should a) close my windows b) stay in the inner corridor away from the glass and c) *on no account* open the door. I am, frankly, astonished. Perhaps I am still asleep. As in the world of the subconscious, there's a semblance of normality but none of this makes sense. There's naked panic in his voice, for example, but where's the *panic* in boys not eating their dinner??

Of course I open the door, but when I've fumbled the padlock open and undone all the bolts, I'm even more confused. The ancient watchman who walks leaning on a stick and couldn't outrun a turtle has legged it. He's nowhere to be seen. I blink, hesitate only for a second, then grabbing the kerosene lamp I lock my door and stumble through the darkness towards the dancing firefly trails of cheap tin-and-wick lights. As I walk, the wall of insect sound morphs into the noise coming from the area around the kitchen where the boys sit on the grass to eat. No-one is in the other houses I pass. No-one in the empty classrooms or staff room or dorms. They look eerie as I pass: Ghost-town buildings filled with such poignant signs humans once used them. A breeze is springing up and a piece of paper scrapes along a concrete floor. Suddenly, the wind seems to have a frail, cool frill sewn onto it. I thought I'd welcome it but I shiver uncomfortably.

I'd better explain briefly that some students walk for five miles or more to school, but for boys who have too far to come, the school provides boarding facilities. It's not what you're thinking of when you see those words, I promise you! Compared to our fee-paying private establishments with labs and playing fields, theatres and swimming pools, this is fantastically primitive. For your money, you get four walls and a tin roof to sleep within and under, and you sleep on a cruel iron bed and thin foam mattress. You wash in and drink dirty water, using noisome pit-drop latrines for other essential functions. Your only furniture is a tin trunk (ants and rats can't chew through metal) holding your scanty possessions. And worse than all of that, remember you're a fast growing lad who's always hungry, and you have the most meagre and filthy of foods to eat. Slippery maize gruel for breakfast . . . rubbery maize and beans for lunch . . . maize flour stirred into boiling water to form a heavy lump of dough called Ugali with green kale (people feed it to cattle in the West) or gristle in watery gruel for dinner.

I suspect you've guessed the staple food is maize, and you're probably thinking now of Oliver Twist or Dotheboys Hall. That's more like it, but I doubt Oliver would have asked for more here. However, I do know that, grim as it is, the boys would fare little better at home. Maybe worse. They wouldn't have lunch, for sure: lunch is for wimps. In subsistence farming areas there's nothing to spare at the end of the hot, dry 'winter', and nothing to be done about it until the rains come, the planting is done and another harvest shoots up from rich, stinking earth.

Still, all things are relative, and even simple food cooked well and in quantity can be a treat. Here there's so *little* of it and it's cack. The cook is a slob – the Kenyan equivalent of a cigarette-ash-dropping-pot-bellied-greasy-spoon-chef back home – but it's a tough job and few want to do it. A woman can't be left alone in the dark with the boys, so it must be a male. Though backbreaking work and filthy, it's not *man's* work, so the cook is humiliated and his self-esteem low. He drinks to forget what he's become and steals food for his family to claw back some worth. This means the boys get even less. Today is a meat day. Even though I haven't been here long, I've picked up meat days are often trouble. I've never met a vegetarian in Kenya and probably never will. People long and salivate for meat here, and a small lump of grey fatty stuff in gruel isn't going to satisfy.

Everyone seems to be milling about as I near the kitchen, a malodorous and smoky hut on a little mound. The mood is ugly. It feels and looks like a hot circle in hell, everything distorted by flickers of light and yawning pits of shadow. One boy is gathering a little crowd by standing on a rickety chair and making a speech, raving like a demon evangelist. My mood turns fatalistic. Ah, well: *insh'Allah!* as my Muslim students say. I'm here now, too late to turn back. I move forward through a sea of sweating bodies that parts as I walk. When they see me, the boys fall silent and jaws drop. Moses must have felt like this! The trouble is this sort of stuff doesn't happen in real life. Ah: there's the simple explanation! I've sunk so deep into sleep now I'm having a bizarre but oddly realistic nightmare. I must make myself wake, wash off the sweat, fall into bed. I need to rewind the tape, start another, *better* dream.

But no: I don't wake, and the speaker also becomes dumb, steps down to the cracking earth. It's the apex of the hot season, and humid to boot: the rains are due any day, any hour, any minute. The breeze was a freak and is gone: I'm dripping with sweat again, and, like everyone else, I'm feverish, tense and throbbing like a boil about to burst. I get up on the chair clutching my lamp. Now I'm up here, I can't see anything. But everyone can see *me*. One hundred boys and young men pumped up and surging with testosterone can see me. I can feel the hysteria, smell the aggression. I don't think I'm a particularly small person, but I've shed a lot of weight having lost appetite and been ill on and off (more on than off) since arrival, and now I feel like a brittle stick figure. If I fall or am pushed, my bones will shatter on parched, rocky ground.

However, after a long pause, quite suddenly, strength flows and words come. They are reasonable and persuasive. My legs are steady, and so is my voice, though it still doesn't sound like mine. In fact, I don't feel like me *at all* . . . but *who* would want to take over my body and what on Earth are they going to do with it? No time to worry about that now: whoever it is tells the crowd we have to start at the beginning, and first they should explain their grievances. When the person patiently says she can't do anything until she *understands*, the story pours out. After a catalogue of daily depravations, frustrations and beatings, now *this*! A tiny piece of revolting gristle each! Less Ugali even than usual!

They've had enough! They're *starving*! The head steals a lot of the money their families pay while their parents and siblings suffer. This is why there are no books, no pens, no chalk, not even basic science equipment. Now the cook's stealing has gotten out of hand and he's run away as they threatened to kill him. They meant it. He believed it. If they had him here, they'd do it. Suddenly, I feel a chill again as I believe it too.

When the complaints peter out at last, the bodysnatcher who has invaded me assures them like some sweaty fairy godmother that they *will* eat tonight, as it's her week to keep the keys and see everything is opened or locked at the right times. Then, in the morning, she'll speak to the head and make him listen. As the only female teacher, she was asked to be boarding mistress (do the 'women's work'), but thought it was too much to take on. She tells the boys she's changed her mind, and will improve conditions whatever she's got to do. She seems to be getting quite carried away now, leaning forward until she almost falls . . . tonight, everyone will work together to make Ugali and greens! It's the quickest option! It can be made tastier with extra fat rations! She promises again they won't sleep hungry, and then delivers the coup de foudre: from now on, *she will eat with them every evening*. She'll control the stores, and the cook will behave differently if someone's there to supervise, to check, to taste!

Silence. Silence so deep I can even hear my own heart beating. That's definitely mine – it's pumping like an engine. I have no idea what came over me, and I'm very worried now this isn't a dream and I've just made outrageous promises, an overwhelming commitment. I wait for the howls of disbelief and derision, for the arms to yank me down off the chair . . . or maybe set fire to it. No-one warned me about this during the job interview or cultural awareness course, and I'm a pretty pathetic kind of Saint Joan. In fact, all I have in common with the French heroine is we're both been possessed and are obviously unhinged. As I start to lose courage and wilt, I hear a ripple of applause like that of a polite crowd at a cricket match. The ripple swells to a wave. They cheer. How strange that *they* believe me even if I have trouble believing myself.

As my legs start to give way, one of the boys helps me down almost reverently. He beams at me as he does, and his teeth shine fitfully in the light of the lamp. Well, I'm not to be burnt after all . .

instead, we open the stores, taking only enough for what we need. We lock them again. I assign boys duties like an army sergeant major. They obey. In a very short time, the food is cooked and eaten, the bowls washed, boys bathed and combed and in bed, lights out. After checking they are all asleep, I walk back to the house. I know I will take a long, long time to get to sleep tonight, even though it's extremely late.

In what seems just minutes later, a cock yells direct into my ear, but I smile to think I'm going to need every one of the 1,440 minutes of light and dark each day in which I will be English and Literature and History teacher, librarian and boarding mistress. This is going to be like having three jobs and 100 sons. I'll have the struggle of my life to get conditions here to approach acceptable. I'll get into a hell of a scrap with the bullish, corrupt and greedy headmaster, and an epic tussle with the thieving drunken self-hating cook. I have a feeling in my bones it will turn into a 'them or me' situation. I groan as I think of this and remember other promises made . . . especially the one about eating with the boys: if I do that, I'm sentencing myself to indigestion and dysentery for as long as I teach here. I suppose all heroic gestures are supremely daft and masochistic in the light of dawn, but I've given my word.

Those worries are temporarily eclipsed however when people creep back sheepishly into the compound. Soon I'm trembling as they explain that when Kenyan students riot, everyone with sense flees into the bush. That's why the houses were empty all night. That's why the head's fourth wife will be jumpy for weeks. That's why her skin is oddly grey-tinged as she whispers that during these riots, boys in their frenzy smash windows, burn and loot buildings, rape women, beat anyone who gets in the way. But while I quiver, of course, a loud whisper is going around that I'm not afraid of *anything*! Clearly, despite my struggles not to become a stereotype, people now think me the modern equivalent of the mad but strong Wazungu women who really ran the Missions and the Empire. They're already eyeing me differently. Only I know I went into the danger on impulse – not brave, just woefully ignorant. Not a holy breast-plated Joan of Arc, but a bumbling and naïve buffoon.

Ah well: I'm still not sure what the sod is happening, but I do know I feel truly awake for the first time in my life. After a hot and almost sleepless night, I feel like skipping. Adjusting to the alien environment and climate, teaching and starting to set up a library in these conditions with so few resources has been steep uphill work, but the rising slope was a steady one after the initial shock, becoming oddly and quickly *routine*. All the time, though, it's been as if I'm inside a spacesuit, able to breathe and see another reality but not to touch it. Suddenly I find myself without that protection on a rough crust that bubbles beneath your feet like an active volcano. But adrenalin is flowing like hot lava and the thing about lava is it can't go any way except forward, and nothing stands in its way. Today I'm alive and kicking like a mule, and I know, as all bewildered, terrified and happy new parents do, that even if I complain, I won't really regret abandoning the impossible comfort and luxury of being asleep.

Hot Spring

Having been in Kenya for three months, I know why what we call the winter months in the Northern Hemisphere are called simply 'The Hot Season' here. At first I thought that was absurd: on the Equator, it's hot all the time, so how can that word mean anything, let alone differentiate one season from another? But then the sun became violent and unrelenting in a way I've never known before, and a dry and baking winter set in more or less as I arrived. Every day for months, moisture has been sucked out of the earth, out of the leaves. As if petrified by a resentful Old Testament God, they've fallen to the ground to snap and crumble beneath the feet like brittle shards. Food supplies dwindle. Nothing can grow. Flowers and plants die, even tough grasses wither and are like thin strips of brown paper littering an Earth that cracks and yawns. The precious soil has grown too hard to till, but its upper layers are thinning to a red dust that coats everything, including your skin and hair.

As the Earth suffers, so do its people. We all feel as if our skin and brains bubble as we too become dessicated. The red dust mingles with our sweat. If the sweat dries, it binds with the dust to form a thin crust, a kind of dirty armour that chafes the skin. Our hair grows oddly brittle as the leaves and cakes together so it feels as if our armour is topped off with a helmet. And at a time when we need to bathe more than anything we've ever needed before, there's only a cupful of water to wash in as we have to dig into the riverbed for water. It's become more valuable than gold, and any water is boiled and drunk greedily when it cools. For the most part, we spare only a little to wash our faces and teeth, and that fools us into feeling a little better. The rest is left to stink, clothes and bedclothes to become greasy and gritty at the same time. There's no point in even fretting now: there's simply no choice. We're all thirsty, filthy, irritable, red-angry at the slightest provocation. All figures in the same Bosch nightmare, the endless scorch of a dun landscape.

Of course well-meaning people keep reassuring me it will pass, that the rains will come. That I'll get used to it. I'm starting to hate them and have long lost faith in all of those comforting murmurs. I can feel my nerves stretching like an elastic band and my patience eroding hour by hour like the soil. My body is not used to this kind of punishment. Not *built* for it. Pushing it from task to task is like trying to run a car on water. Water! Oh yes, I'm a fish out of water alright: I'm gasping for water, for coolness, for a breeze. I dream of the excitement of the first chill wind of autumn, the energising frost blue and pale gold of winter days. More and more often I think of the volunteers who have already retreated from the alien heat and lifestyle here: they'll be shivering but happy, waking to needling frost or falling rain. But somehow – I have no idea why – I go on. A tenacious nature I didn't know I had gets me up each morning and through the day until I can slip between dirty bed sheets and sweat through another long night . . but my jaw becomes so tightly clenched I fancy my teeth will shatter like the leaves.

I'm standing now in one of the four classrooms, teaching history. There's no ceiling. We're under a tin roof. I try to make it interesting, but the children's eyes have glazed over. One boy is falling asleep, mouth agape. His friends are mesmerised by the heat and unable even to nudge each other or raise a giggle. I have only the strength to set a test and am now writing a few questions on the blackboard. I'm sweating so much, I have trouble holding the chalk, and the salty perspiration is running down into my eyes. I swipe away the sting, but it keeps on running down from scalp to breasts to belly and back and hips and legs and right down to my feet. Dear God, it's like melting! Or, worse, like peeing yourself – and just as embarrassing in a different kind of way.

For the last few days, however, in the evenings, the breeze that springs up has been touched by coolness. That edge is so delicate and insubstantial, you wonder if you're imagining it, but at those times people sniff the air, pronouncing that the rains will come: *Soon.* They haven't yet, but today the sun seems to be losing power as I crawl about leaving a salty snail's trail. In the next class – a double English period – to get the children awake and interested, I start by standing at the front to read a paragraph from a story. Afterwards, I will ask quick-fire questions. The children enjoy this, and compete to call out the answers first, display the best understanding and memory. Suddenly, I feel that something has changed. I'm disoriented. Something is *different*. I look up, puzzled, but the children are fine. Attentive. One or two making sneaky little crib notes of things they think I may ask about. I still feel odd. Am I getting ill again? I go back to the story, and when I finish, I know what it is. I'm not sweating! It's simply stopped! I can hardly remember when I didn't sweat, and it's *turned off like a tap*. I'm stunned. Perhaps I really am ill now – so dehydrated there's nothing left to ooze out.

For a few moments, I stand still, staring down at my limbs, touching my hand to my dry face and neck. The children stare at me and then at each other. Teachers go bonkers here and have breakdowns just as they do in British schools. They're probably scared I'm going to go doolally. The tension mounts. With a huge effort, I force myself back to the present, finish the game and then write some of the words and phrases we've learnt on the board. The children have already forgotten my seconds of strangeness. I hold the chalk firmly between dry fingers, feeling the energy sucked out of me by the sun flow back into my body and my brain as if a glass is filling up with clean, life-giving liquid.

Later, while I'm still getting used to my new state of comfort and well-being, things get even better. It seems unreal, but, heartbeats accelerating, I'm watching the show of my life. As I sit on my little verandah, clouds of Biblical proportions approach rapidly, borne on high winds, swollen, purple-dark clouds that hurl spears of fiery lightning to the Earth and trail a grey cloak of rain to put out their flames. I've never seen such a performance as this, and my mouth drops open. When the coolness hits like a wall, the deluge brings visibility down to a few feet as if one is looking through murky glass and the noise is terrifying. I actually hold onto the arms of my cane chair, expecting to be lifted up and whirled away. The end of the world would be just like this. You'd be alone, beyond terror, and you'd have to watch the world rage and destroy itself around you. Shit! If this *is* it, there's nothing to be done but enjoy it.

Suddenly, however, the spell breaks and I'm galvanised into action. I run about in the rain, soaked to the skin, hair plastered by a cold power-shower that sluices away layers of dirt. I place every bowl and container and jerry can I possess under the waterfalls pouring from the roof. I take off my grimy dress and what people here call innerwear and stand under one when I'm finished, laughing like a lunatic, safe in the knowledge no-one can see or hear my madness. When the rain stops, the sun will come back out. In a kind of miracle, in just twenty-four hours, the grass and wildflowers will be growing, and we'll all be insanely cheerful, full of energy, friends again, clean. Our houses will be swept, wiped and mopped. Lines of washing will hang out like flags, its whiteness and paler colours contrasting with the acid green of grass and the indigo sky. Leaves and crops will grow again. People will eat. People will laugh and love and dance and celebrate. They and the land will glow and *burst* with Life. Oh *God*! For the first time in my twentieth-century pampered divorced-from-life, I thank a deity I have hardly spoken to for my first true experience of spring and the sense of pure joy, relief and utter rightness it brings.

Souvenir

Before leaving the UK, I had formed no proper image of Kenya. If I saw anything, it was a great transparent veil of heat shimmering above endless plains. Those parched grasslands were of course crossed by herds of beasts stalked by fiercer beasts stalked by a whispering David Attenborough – or others like him – while, in turn, curious animals and invisible cameras followed *them*. Yes: if I saw anything in my mind's eye, it was that image. If I tried harder, I could also see postcards of palm beaches on the coast, farms and mud huts baking in the interior, and the iconic spring-heeled spear carrying warriors wearing their stiff armour of haughty disdain, red mud and swathes of beads.

I found all those things, of course, but they were only scattered fragments of the story . . . the part TV, Hollywood and children's stories allows. The real Kenya is *huge*, a thousand times more crowded, complex and impressive. It's like four or five different countries – you even become quite disoriented as you travel and pass from one reality to another. Say you were to fly down from the North-East . . . first your plane would leave a shadow on diamond-white deserts so infested with 'Shifta' bandits that on the ground you'd travel with an armed guard. Eventually, you'd land on the wet golden coastal strip where trees ooze a bait of fresh palm wine while camouflaged mambas – their venom can kill a human in twenty seconds – twine around their trunks. There you'd stroll past oiled tourists frying on the beaches westerners dream of while the salty and impossibly buoyant blood-warm Indian Ocean rolls. Green coconuts would fall from the sky as you walked, exploding and spraying their thin, sweet milk onto startled, sizzling skin.

If you then took a toiling train far enough northwest again, more surprisingly, you'd find yourself in cool, lush highlands smelling as green and astringent as Scandinavian woodlands . . . but where tea grows on the hills. To get to those forests, you would pass – jaw dropping – through the indescribable chasm of the Rift Valley. In a misted, alien world rimmed with peaked and largely quiescent volcanoes, the land is gouged out in parts to form long, deep lakes. Then, in contrast to all of that, you'd be shocked by occasional noisy unexpected cities of concrete and glass, stinking of rotting mountains of refuse and streams of petrol. You'd feel a shiver of déjà vu as you see that people dress in suits, work in tower blocks, go home to a tiny new house on an estate, and dance only to the new rhythm of cash tills, electronic music and honking horns . . . and at last, if you got lucky, you'd go further, on to the parts tourists never reach and discover the Western Highlands.

Up here it's the Wild West . . . you're smiling, aren't you? I can tell, but it is, it is! Our local town has one wind-up telephone in a post office that regularly runs out of stamps, and one main street of stores opening onto verandahs on either side of a dusty dirt road. There is a place to eat and a saloon bar. No-one hitches horses to posts, but apart from that omission, I always expect a man in a Stetson to burst through its swinging doors and tell me to stick 'em up or get out of town. It's high up here alright: high and hot but mercifully dry – it's not like the coast, where your clothes become mildewed as nothing ever dries. The school compound where I live is miles out of town, however, and I if I nip to the shops between lessons marked out by old-fashioned bells, we're so close to Uganda I can see the river that marks the border. In the dry season, it's a thin dusty line like gunpowder. But when the rains come, it shines like a silver trail.

When I first stood and looked down, I simply couldn't believe it, because there *was* the plain I had imagined! There it is *now*, the silver heat shimmying to the constant throb of insect noise, the eerie shapes of Rider-Haggard rocks thrusting out of earth to break the waves of tan and green fields. Heading for that border is the main road to Uganda – an appalling moonscape more useless and dangerous than any rutted dirt track – and it runs past our school. The whisper is a coup is coming, and Obote will soon be gone just like Amin and all the others. I think people are right: in a hot, uneasy hush, police at checkpoints are looking nervous, fingering their battered Kalashnikovs, and we've all noticed the never ending flow of trucks is lessening. Everyone here shakes their heads when we talk about Uganda: they say it's fabulously fertile, but there's never peace for long enough for its peoples to benefit. Corruption and violence are so endemic Kenya is a veritable model of order and progress in comparison.

On this side of the border, it certainly is very peaceful. Perhaps it's because on this North-Western frontier where I work, the Luhya tribe predominates and almost everyone is a subsistence farmer. Women, men and children are focused on staving off hunger and surviving, locked in a harmonious if sometimes tense relationship with the seasons and the earth. Almost everyone lives in round mud huts with barely enough money for the essentials of soap, tea and sugar. There's no electricity, no running water. It's light at seven a.m., pitch dark at seven p.m. Sickness and Death are palpable forces and have absolute dominion here in a way people in the 'civilised' west have forgotten they can. Despite all of that, the local clan – the Babukusu – are tall, proud, handsome people, almost too friendly and generous. They have a great sense of humour and brew their own beer with maize they ought to use to make flour. They love life, and are always ready to dance, drink, eat, talk, laugh. I've read in a history book that they used to lose tribal battles because they always told the other side when they were going to attack to give them time to prepare. I believe it. Given their innate kindness and inclusiveness, they have taken a shine to me as I have to them. I work hard to improve the school that barely exists on the little cash people can collect for its upkeep and running, getting on well with the raw young teachers I have (unofficially) to train. And in Kenya, as I told you already, if you like someone and appreciate their hard work, you make them gifts.

And this is why I'm on my knees at the moment, contemplating what I've been given by one of my colleagues, unaware for the moment of the physical pain of kneeling on a concrete floor. Local people live in houses made out of the very earth, but I live in a 'proper' house, you see: underfoot it's hard and hot as packed sand in the sun, and the roof above is made of tin and magnifies the fierce heat at least ten times. I've always longed like someone whose lips are crusting for water in a desert to live in one of the thatched huts. Their interiors are shady and refreshing as an oasis, but I'm told people would be shocked. It wouldn't befit my status as a teacher: it especially wouldn't be right for what people call a 'Mzungu', a European, a 'shining one'. In here, the glass windows fenced by security bars let in no air even if wide open. My door must be shut, bolted and padlocked. I'm resigned to it by now

134

however, and impatiently wipe the stinging sweat out of my eyes as I squint in the dim blurring halo of a kerosene lamp at my present.

I keep on looking. I don't know what else to do. My benefactor has been on a rare and exciting trip to Lake Nakuru in the long vacation. He's brought me back a special and fitting souvenir of his journey, the most well known product of that area. As he presents me with it, his beaming smile is a torchlight piercing the gathering if short Equatorial dusk. Meanwhile, I struggle so hard not to look shocked my face feels stiff. Because it takes a few seconds to squeeze out words, the radiance of the smile dims and he looks disturbed. I rush to assure him I am pleased, thanking him profusely in the customary phrases. I offer refreshment as one always must, and he refuses politely as his family is waiting for his return. All is well again between us, and he says again he simply had to bring this to me: tomorrow would not do! He just *knew* how excited I would be, how much it would please!

This gift of friendship and regard is a baby flamingo. It looks impossibly delicate and it really is drooping like a tall pink lily left too long out of water. I know we shouldn't give human attributes to animals, but the jet-bead eyes are dulled with misery, and its whole demeanour weeps for mother and for home. It's paralysed with anguish and doesn't even shrink away as I reach out. As light as one of its silky feathers, my fingertip strokes its head and neck. I babble softly like a madwoman over and over how sorry I am. And like a madwoman I hope that I can convey the sincerity of my sympathy across a species divide and that it will help. Surely it *must* feel the sudden wave of tenderness and love that threatens to overwhelm? Surely it must be comforted? It isn't, naturally, and the flamingo closes its eyes as it splays to the floor like a drunk on ice. My breath is catching as I stupidly lift it up. I try to be gentle, slipping a cushion between the baby's body with its spun glass bones and the unforgiving man-made floor.

My brain ticks. It's utterly dark outside, and no-one sane leaves their house at night on this border, especially not now! I'm *alone*, and I know even if I venture, there will be no help. None of my neighbours will have seen a flamingo in their lives – Lake Nakuru is a whole day's journey away, and it may as well be Mars. Tomorrow I know they'll flock here like the birds crowding over that distant lake to see it. But tonight, always at night, I am alone. The minutes slide silently away, and I force myself to be calm and to think. This innocent creature *mustn't* be allowed to suffer. It can't have been brought here to die, and I will *not* let it die because of me! After a quick visit to the clay pot and makeshift larder in the kitchen, I'm feverishly trying to pour cool water into its beak, to tempt it with the smelly little dried fish I keep as a reward for my cat (a wild creature choosing to live with me for now) if he catches a rat. I feel absurdly glad he's out hunting now: what would the big grey tom make of this little creature to whom I offer his greatest treat? The water runs out again and again, and he's – she's? – supremely uninterested in the fish.

Eventually, I sit back on my heels, cooler now, even shivering a little as the thin cotton clothing is glued to my skin by sweat. It's time for a new tactic. This bird's world *was* composed of water and fish, but the fish and other organisms were *in* the water, part of it. It's a baby – you wouldn't give a baby a solid meal! My precious gas canister has run out, so, hand trembling, I light the wick of my little field stove to boil up a soup made of water and sprats. The bloody thing takes eons to heat the mess, and it seems like hours before it's cool. But at last I work gently but firmly to open the beak, tilt back the head and pour the liquid into the bird. My heart leaps with hope as the black eyes open and focus, but again the liquid trickles out. As our gazes lock, my own throat closes, my eyes fill with tears and I stop. It's an insane thing to do, but I know the right course of action is to bring in my mattress, curl up beside him, and go back to stroking, whispering that I'm sorry. Soon his eyes close slowly, the body relaxes and he looks as if he's going to sleep. I know he'll be cold and stiff by sunrise, but I'm *glad*. Someone – it must be me – is crying in an utterly abandoned way as if grieving for every death there's ever been, but then, apart from the wall of insect noise so easy to screen out, a heavy, dark silence falls.

All too soon, it's light. The school workman carrying jerry cans of water from the river on his rickety old bike shortly after dawn is puzzled and horrified in equal measure to find me trying to dig a grave for a strangely stiff, unreal looking bird. He's a practical and assertive man, simply clicks his tongue, takes the spade away and finishes the job for me. I know he thinks I really have gone mad as I lay the creature to rest wrapped in one of my favourite colourful scarves, but he's too kind and tolerant to say so, even with a look. When it's done, I hurry to wash off the caked on salt of the night, dress, eat something. It will be another long, very hot day. Wafula will be deeply upset, and I'll have to find the stomach and tact to comfort him and assure him the bird must have been weak and ill even before it began the stifling, nightmare journey on a bus taking it from all it knew to certain death in a world suddenly become terrifying and hostile. I can't tell the truth, let alone express anger, as the former would hurt and the latter offend him beyond measure.

I've even offended my poor cat. He's laid, with a flourish, a huge and very dead rat at my feet, but my congratulations and caresses are perfunctory today and I have no fish to give him until I go to market.

I'm like a stranger in my own skin this morning: a hollow-eyed, slightly nauseous Shaman after a drugged journey. I'm caught drifting between worlds, dislocated but brought too close to a pure distillation of grief. That little creature's mother will be as sick with longing for her disappeared young, but I must try not to feel her hurt too as there's so much to do. I must follow the artificial little routines that attempt to organise and conquer Time, and of course I have to avoid self-pity and be pragmatic. I decided once I fell in love with this place and its people that only circumstances beyond my control would make me bale out before the end of my contract, and I'm used to making my upper lip as stiff as an ironing board and plodding on. And on.

Every morning as we all stand to attention and the Kenyan flag creeps up the white pole, there is a moment of deep, respectful silence. This morning it's the same, but then we all jump like cartoon characters simultaneously into the air as an unmistakeable and unfeasibly loud noise erupts on the border. Yes: carried on air that is still and very warm even at nine a.m. comes the definite rattle of automatic gunfire, and the ordered circles on the school parade ground dissolve like ripples when a stone is lobbed into water. We watch as the children scatter comically, yelling, in every direction: we know from experience just to let them go, as they can run faster than we ever could. They will stop eventually and come back. My heart is skipping about in

137

my chest, and some of the teachers look as if they want to run too, but the headmaster rounds us up and takes us to the staff room for a pep talk. The worst that will happen is that refugees will start heading over the border, he says. The Kenyan Special Guard is prepared, and the frightened and dispossessed will be ushered into camps. They won't bother us. All will calm down soon enough, and they'll be sent back. All will be as it was. But it won't harm to be vigilant, of course. Now the children are gone, it won't harm to go home and lock our doors until tomorrow. At moments like this, desperate people like to take advantage of the panic.

My absurd little house with its tin roof is as hot and airless as ever, and it feels oddly empty. I imagine if I shout I'll hear an echo. It's an eerie feeling and I can't settle however hard I try. Already it's as if the flamingo was never here, but I know it unwittingly set something inside me free, and I will remember this gift forever. Last night, in one space between sunset and sunrise, I was dragged to the bottom of a pool of sorrow, and floated to the surface as the innocent are supposed to do. One day soon, if I survive this next trial, I'll have to go home. That's just the way it has to be: if you have a home, however distant and unreal, you can never truly leave it. For the most part, if we humans do, we don't sicken and die because we're programmed to adapt and fight. What breaks the heart is that for some that fight is lost even before it truly begins, but if you survive you cling on because there's no real choice: drift too far from home and you're bereft . . . let go all together and there's nowhere to go but into a dangerous dark.

Coastal Idyll – Coastal Idiots

To some, just being in Kenya would seem like a holiday. Indeed, people flock here for comfortable *safaris* and to ignore the rest of the country by lazing under palms by anodyne pools next to the warm and beautiful Indian Ocean. In the evening they dress up to show off tans, eat real wildebeest steaks and watch mock plastic African tribal dances. As VSO's however – and as you can tell – we definitely don't see ourselves as tourists, and probably find them and their behaviour as alien as Kenyans do. We are especially surprised how their flaunting of gold jewellery and even worse, bare knees and shoulders, offends us: Kenyans are often deeply religious and find this unacceptable. Even on our holidays, we still wear 'decent' clothing. Our sphere is 'up country', where we work very hard in term time, not just at our jobs, but in combating all the other challenges that come our way. We have all been stunned by the deprivation in our remote rural areas, as Kenya is one of the more prosperous African countries. Away from the tourist zones, however, the deep pockets of the one-party government ministers and the westernised cities, we see too many of the children having to drink river water and become sick, their bellies swelling due to lack of nutrition, their skin and eyes dusty and dull. Despite this, they smile, play and go happily to primary school as it is free. Disease is rampant, and their parents are subsistence farmers living on the edge of hunger and disaster at all times. But their spirit too is very strong, and they not only survive, but relish life, love their land and children, somehow scrape shillings together to send a son or daughter to secondary school. That's where we come in, we realise, and our help in fundraising and helping children get qualifications/paid work can benefit the whole community. There is however – as we came trailing clouds of luxury and over-indulgence since birth – also a deprivation factor for us. All is relative, and we are human, after all: *Mzungu* may mean 'Shining One', but it refers to our white skin and fair hair gleaming in the sun, and does not mean we are little golden idols.

Although I increasingly enjoy spending weeks in the long holidays visiting students and their families, I also pant at these times for a kind of regression, release. There are, as we have been warned on orientation courses, high expectations of us in our projects in terms of behaviour. We relish the hard work – it's what we signed up for – but what can often ratchet up the tension is we are expected to behave like informal ambassadors: to local people, like it or not, we do represent all *Wazungu* and we are guests in another culture. Teachers in any case are high status individuals, and we are expected to dress smartly but decently, and not to offend customs, drink too much or, if unmarried, get involved in any liaisons. This is especially important as white women are thought to be either prim virginal missionaries or very promiscuous, and we all want to counter this double myth: a strong reason to be careful not to go to local bars, as they are also brothels. It becomes second nature to follow the rules after a while, and though there is friendship, laughter and socialising a plenty, being ever decorous, well dressed and polite at our projects for 3 months at a time is tough going.

Volunteers also rarely have running water. I don't, and though you can keep surprisingly clean washing in tepid water in a plastic bowl, you long, long, long for a bath or shower especially given the heat, dust (or mud, depending on season), and the throbbing insect bites that need cleansing and soothing. Food too is restricted to what is available locally, and, though pleasingly organic, is often stodgy, dull and vegetarian. There are times when a fellow VSO will visit, and after a dinner of Kenyan beans and rice, you will sit in the soft light of a lamp and whisper what you most would wish to eat: Cream éclairs; steak and kidney pie and chips; the juiciest, spiciest chicken curry; hot toast dripping with butter and honey; fresh bread; eggs and bacon and sausage and tomato and beans and mushrooms and fried bread and lashings of HP sauce; marmite; beef and Yorkshire pud or luscious lamb dinner with mint; chocolate mousse; lemon meringue pie. In the end you are literally slavering and the game gets wilder as you shout for things you've never even eaten: Caviar! Poached salmon in watercress sauce! Tournedos Rossini! Syllabub! Lobsters in garlic! Suckling pork! Puffer Fish!

You could cook some of these things, of course, but the time, effort and expense involved is extreme. An unlucky chicken has to be caught (try it), its throat cut in one merciful sweep as you stand on its wings, plucked after immersion in boiling water and, last but not least, gutted. This bit has an added dimension of horror as there are usually eggs waiting to be laid inside. After all that, you don't have an oven to roast it. Actually I do in my first project, but gas runs out fast and is expensive and most volunteers cook on charcoal or small paraffin stoves. I am proud of the oven I make composed of a huge pot a third full of sand with a tight lid held down by a brick: if you stick it on a charcoal stove, it will get hot enough and work – but there are no controls and boy you have to be clever not to produce blackened inedible cack. Wasting food is taboo, so it's a risky option. All fuel can run out totally in an area, too, and then you have only a wood fire. You find ways to cook in some way and enjoy – up to a point – local staples, but Maxim's it isn't. It's not even a greasy spoon. You can buy luxury items in some city shops, but we only get to a city every few months or so.

What I'm getting at is that holidays are not just a break from slog and routine, they are for us a sensual and fun riot. Being with other volunteers, you can talk and talk until your eyes pop out and swear and even complain bitterly if you want. You can rail against corruption. Stay up late. Drink beer or palm wine (utterly lethal) and even an occasional g and t. You can dance to sweetly bouncy Kenyan pop or moondance to Michael Jackson in a disco. Oh yes, and you can sleep in, shower & scrub so your skin nearly peels off and EAT IN RESTAURANTS. A few – not me, through genetically inbuilt caution and conditioning – even end up in the Nairobi police cells for a night, to the amusement of the policemen who enjoy demanding a decent bribe for early release.

Sandra and I are growing to be close friends quickly, and we meet in Nairobi for our 1st proper holiday. We've both been through the mill in different ways, and can only afford a cheapo hotel – but it has a warm shower! We can't decide who goes first, so we go in together, whooping like idiots. Then, squeaky clean, perfumed and coiffed, in our Sunday best, we go to a good quality Chinese restaurant: we are as happy as two people can be. We go to the coast regularly too, though on our first arrival by train we walk out into dripping blood heat, turn on our heels and go straight to the ticket office wanting to hop on a train back to cooler Nairobi. A notice says there isn't a train back 'til next day, however, so we make the best of it. In the end, we grow accustomed and we *do* laze under palm trees in a soft sea breeze by the Indian Ocean. Our friend John lives and works on the coast, and we often stay with him in Malindi. He is an archetypal Yorkshireman and very dry-humoured. Under the palm trees, he wears a hankie on his head. He never disrobes from white shirt and black trousers (all men here are allowed to dress only in a kikoy if they wish, a type of sarong), and paddles in the ocean spume with trousers rolled while we float on it blissfully. When we explore Gedi, a deserted Arabic city, solemn, eerie and strange, he breaks the mood by making us laugh, voicing ridiculous theories as to why the population ran away leaving a kind of stone-strewn Marie Celeste. People in the 'modern' village tell us of Lamu, a paradise Island further up the coast, and once we know, nothing will do but that we go there.

Sandra and I both have amoebic dysentery, but we have reached its symptomless stage. It's caused by parasites which are very good at what they do: she's down to six and a half stone, and, always heftier, I'm down to eight and a half because the greedy bugs consume a third of the calories you eat. Sadly, it's too hot to eat, and, if you go hungry, they double you up with cramps until you feed them: I never thought I would become the plant in the Little Shop of Horrors. We plan to get antibiotics on the way back to Western Kenya, but, for now, we go with it. A bus will take us north, and we buy our tickets, pushing as if our lives depend on it against a crowd to get on. For some reason, this is the custom, even if there are plenty of seats. We grab seats towards the front, and as we settle, are puzzled to note we are seated just a short way behind soldiers with Kalashnikovs. Still, we expect the unexpected here. Finally, when the ramshackle bus is packed above and below with people, goats, luggage, chickens, baskets of fruit and vegetables and the ubiquitous tin trunks, off we go at a cracking pace, onto a dirt road like the surface of the moon. It's so hot, our seats are quickly soaked with sweat as if we've weed ourselves. A soldier dozes. My lids also droop. Sandra digs me in the ribs to alert me his gun has slipped and is now pointed at my chest. One extra big bump and I am history. I lean towards her so the bullets will get the unfortunate people behind me and we giggle. This travelling delight goes on for hours. We cross a huge swirl of muddy river on a raft pulled by ropes. We stop for tea, bread and marge and fresh peanuts and get to visit a malodorous long drop. There is nothing to see out the windows as the land gets drier and scrubbier. Some stunted grasses parch apathetically in the sun.

Suddenly when we know we are about an hour from the island, my tum is sending me worrying signals. We breakfasted on chai, mandazi (African maize doughnut) and a huge mango. On top of that we thoughtlessly placed our weird lunch. The bugs are temperamental: they like to consume, but are quite fussy as to what. I try to pretend I can't hear the warnings and that this simply can't be happening. I wish I were back in the stench of the long-drop. Sandra's gone rather quiet, so I sneak a look at her and her face has the tell-tale grey tinge. She confesses she cannot hold on. I confess to the same. We are getting distressed. John asks what's up and when we tell him he calls us names for not speaking up sooner and lurches his way to the driver. They exchange words and the bus screams to a comedy stop. Everyone and everything is flung forward a foot or so. Amidst the mayhem, we streak off, and we have no choices. Our insides are dissolving into something akin to the muddy river and we just have to close eyes and hold hands as we squat and suffer. Getting back on the bus is a humiliation and we sit, drained, with heads bowed. John tells us to cheer up: as you would expect with Kenyans who are such kind people, as we did what had to be done, everyone turned their heads the other way and found things of fascinating interest on the right-hand side of the so-called road. We wish we could thank them, but the bus is bucking like a Zebra stung by a bee and it is noisy, so we can only smile and nod round at everyone. The soldier is now thankfully awake and his gun pointing at the ceiling. We have learned from people sitting nearby that armed bandits attack any vehicle for booty in these parts, intent on rape and pillage, so the soldiers are our protection. We feel a warm glow and love their guns.

Well, we have arrived and my goodness people were right! This is a *wonderful* place, an island that is surrounded by white beaches, palm trees and the warm, salty Indian Ocean. We float and laze. John, in his own heaven, paddles happily with a hankie on his head. We eat grilled fish on the beach we have caught ourselves on a dhow trip. We visit the one charming falling-to-bits museum, drink in the one surprisingly pleasant bar. This is a strictly Muslim island, and this is strictly for tourists, if they behave. The streets are mediaeval Arabic, with intricately carved doorways hiding courtyards with cooling fountains, and fretted balconies make beautiful patterns against creamy walls. We inhabit another world and time for a while, and, with its little shops and restaurants, it is a pleasing and relaxing one. Our tums are behaving. We are not looking forward to leaving. Our hotel may be cheapo, but it is clean, spacious and has flushing loos AND showers: bliss. We say we will come again, but Sandra is quite unwell for a time in the months after and we don't get round to it. Paradise sleeps.

Two years later and Sandra and John are elsewhere in the world. I miss them badly but I'm visiting the coast with two other friends, Ian known as Snaily Boy as he is always in a hurry and Tilly. They too have heard of Lamu, and I tell them by lamplight, like a shadowy Scheherezade, of its magic. This time, we also hear that if we dig a little into savings we can take a light aircraft to the island, flying over the silver, blue and green glittering coast, over the rough road and its chasms, over the rushing filthy river and the vicious bandits. Hooray! Tickets are booked, and from the terminal our pilot Joseph walks us out to the plane. He reaches an arm out, proudly as if to say 'Ta da . . .' My first thought is '. . . but where IS it?' and the second is 'No, that can't be it! It's like a mini with wings'. But of course it is our Chariot of the Gods, and we approach it gingerly. I wish now I had a stronger belief in a God or gods. If I convert and repent sincerely now, will it count? Some mediaeval European heretics thought so and caused uproar by living to the full, confessing all and then committing suicide. The 'plane' is a 5-seater and there is a Japanese volunteer already inside, smiling and bowing fit to bust, telling us his name is Hiroyuki. We climb in, the lads in the back seat, pilot up front, Tilly and I in the middle, next to the doors. We notice the pilot can't see as the windscreen is too high up. Maybe this is normal, but we gulp. There are no cushions to perch him on. It is too late now in any case, as we are speeding to a smooth take off and soaring into a blue and gold haze.

As we are sideswiped by the slightest breezes and wisps of cloud, it feels more like a boat ride in space. Hiroyuki has taken travel sickness pills and passed out on Ian's shoulder. I laugh as Ian squirms. I stop laughing abruptly however as I feel my diaphanous cotton skirt being sucked out of the door on my side which doesn't quite close. Tilly is holding onto me tight in case I get sucked out too. We are laughing again now and loving the sights below, the lush green ribbon of trees inland, a strand of white, almost silver, merging into the colour burst of sea and reefs. Oh, this is the life, and despite only being able to see out of side windows, the pilot is doing great. Even our landing on the beach is perfect. As we alight, after waking a groggy Hiroyuki, we are trembling, but it is with the thrill of the ride, and a kind of daft, bubbling happiness. We have made it to Paradise Island!

We are huddled miserably in our beds after walking to our hotel through several inches of water, composed of sea, drenching rain and sewage. It is the rainy season here (we didn't check) and high tide (we didn't dream of checking). On our first night, I am tired and tetchy, and one of my friends is tickling my leg. My sense of humour has gone on its own holiday, and I announce if he or she does it again, blood will flow. Both my friends put their arms and legs in the air to demonstrate their innocence, but the tickling continues. I check under the sheet. It is a cockroach as big as a mouse. I leap like a gazelle and there is a flurry of Anglo-Saxon cursing and frenetic activity as we shake out bedclothes and spray our beds and all corners with *Doom*, more in hope than conviction. We do fall eventually into an uneasy sleep. Next day brings another shock. In our first damp exploration, we discover everywhere is closed: all shops, all restaurants, all cafes. There is no way to break our fast. It dawns that it is Ramadan (we forgot this of course) and no-one is allowed to eat or drink between sunrise and sunset: *12 hours*. I still have dysentery, I never really get rid of it now, and this will mean cramps that will break me in two. Clever plans must be made.

And so each day we wander disconsolately around the island under lowering clouds or in the rain, hiding in mangrove swamps to eat and drink things we bought, looking innocent, in shops the evening before. There is no lazing, no floating, only daily trips to the museum with rain dripping through the roof until we know every damned item and can recite the history of the coast sideways. Evenings are better, as we can eat in restaurants and have a drink in the bar in an effort to forget how many days we have to endure. There seem now to be more cockroaches and rats than inhabitants, driven from their cosy sewers and niches by the floods. This then is how a quaint mediaeval town with no proper drainage looks and smells when the sun is not shining: not quaint at all. In fact, the stench turns our already unstable tums. At last, we get to leave, and it is a more sober party that journeys back on our little plane and the train north. The angels in Paradise clearly had the week off – or have a twisted sense of humour.

We are philosophical after many blows endured over the months and years, and we have learnt lessons, accepted the disappointment. Ian is one of my nearest VSO neighbours and we arrange for him to visit the weekend after we get back. He does not come. This is very unlike him, and I assume he is unwell or his bike is broken down. However, the village grapevine extends to many other villages and word reaches me quickly he is so ill he has been taken to hospital in Kisumu by Lake Victoria. I tell my head teacher I am sorry, but there is an emergency and I will be back in a few days. When I reach the hospital, I am taken to see him looking wan and wasted, attached to multiple drips and tubes. I must not touch him or anything in the room. He tells me in a distant voice unlike his that Tilly is in the next room. They both have typhoid. He tells me it is, of course, courtesy of Paradise Island. We were all inoculated, but someone failed to tell the microbes. Except in my case of course . . . as they recover, Tilly and Ian become uncharacteristically bitter that I remain hale and healthy, eating the tasty meals provided for them that they don't want and enjoying fresh squeezed passion fruit juice in the days and a few ice cold Tusker beers in the evenings after hospital visits. Under the cheerful taking-grapes-to-the-sick surface I am actually quite spooked, as I remember horrible and even hallucinatory times spent in this hospital with E-Coli (disgusting) and malaria (you wouldn't wish this weird plague on your most hated enemy).

Having been assured they will both make a good recovery, I am bowling back to my school in a ridiculously full *matatu*. To distract from the agony of both legs being crushed and my head pushed way too close to the nipple of a nursing mother, I reflect once again on Paradise, on how it can tempt, deceive and let you down, catch you napping in sinister coils, inject poison from invisible fangs. If you think about it, however, that is what it does: It is in essence its job. We are glad to be alive to tell the tale and may even laugh at it with a little distance between us, the stink and the rats. If there *is* a third time, before I buy a ticket, I will be checking weather charts, tide patterns, levels of bandit infestation and local religious festivals: nothing will be taken for granted and

I will travel with a trail of donkeys laden with macs, umbrellas, *Doom*, guns, parachutes, lots of books, antibiotics and wellies, even in the boiling sun, even to Paradise Island.

Shadow in the Sun

Now I have been here some time my body is adjusting and I'm mastering the heat and tiredness that so enervated me at first. Just when I feel a little smug, however, there follows the next challenge of how to rise above the indignity of the bent-in-two cramps and watery brown African rivers of dysentery. Even that you can grow used to, as well as the unfamiliar language, the customs, the food. Though chai too can give you dysentery and brucellosis, it gives you strength in the short-term and I'm becoming ever more appreciative of this energy-injection concoction of equal parts of warm cow's milk, coarse local sugar and river water slick with weed. Somehow, I've found ways round teaching classes of fifty without any books. Oh, yes: I'm on top of it all. Well . . . at least I am during the twelve-hour sunny days. In public, I am fiercely determined to Get On With Things: what the hell else is there to do? But at night . . . alone in the dark, cocooned in the mosquito net, hemmed in by a cage of bars on the windows and a padlocked and bolted door . . . at night, in my bed, after initially thinking I could take it, I am a pathetic creature. I ought to be glad my house is like Fort Knox, but I'm not sure. You see, people tell me its defences will keep out the bandits common in this border area, but Francis made me buy a machete at the market. It's at the side of my bed. He knows this area through and through, and all he has advised has been necessary.

Though to tell the truth, I'm even more worried about what may be small enough to slip in like a silent, pale shadow through the gaps: I'm told snakes are rarely seen, but the ancient school watchman has fashioned me a snake-stick with a great knobbly head. It's at the other side of my bed. Everyone assures me the insects – except the blasted mosquitoes of course – are harmless, but they advise having a huge yellow can of *DOOM* to hand just in case. It's underneath my bed.

I may be exhausted beyond words, but most nights, as soon as I lower the wick of the kerosene lamp and am blinded by the deepest dark I have ever known, I am eye-wide-awake. Tense as a whip. Uselessly scanning the impenetrable blackness, ears straining at every noise. Dry wood cracks like a gun. My heart

148

hammers. Something knocks a tin cup off the kitchen table. My heart almost stops. Because the windows must be left open, my nerves are wound up tighter by a backing-track to my torments. It is always at full volume, performed by manic sleepless insects creating a Phil Spector wall of sound. I jump in my skin again as a flying beetle bumbles into the room and crashes into furniture. I can't see it, but I know it's horribly opaque, has bullhorns and is the size of a small Volkswagen. Oh, God: a noise in the kitchen again: a rat? A *snake*? I am nauseous at the thought of either. As well as the open windows, I am aware there are no ceilings and spaces between walls and roof. Thus, right above my head, I can see and hear the bats nesting in the eaves. Yes, even the bats that I at first tolerated and even found cute . . . now I know close up, they are furry and monster-faced with Dracula wings. They probably have Dracula fangs. They chirrup and tweet and crap constantly . . . and now it's the wet season, and, around and above it all, comes the whine of mosquitoes stukka-ing the net. If I fall asleep and allow flesh to rest against the gauze, they and the bats will feed and I will sicken or die. Small wonder, I suppose, amidst the cacophony, that the world of rest and dreams has become the foreign land. I am a victim of torture: where is Amnesty now?

It's late afternoon, Saturday. The rains have been, shorter in duration now, and the sun is losing power after drying and warming the earth. In a very short time it will be dark and the night's warped entertainments will begin again. Slumped in my wicker chair in the shade of the fig tree, I finish a drink cooled in the clay pot full of water nearby. Too torpid to cook, I've eaten a plate of corned beef sandwiches instead. I pretend to read, but am nodding. Apart from the fact I can smell the sweet blue wood smoke it's one of those moments when it's hard to believe there are other people living on the compound, in the fields and the village nearby. Suddenly, my brain registers a message, but another part of it denies. You see I don't want to admit I just saw a shadow that moved. Glimpsed what my brain does confirm was a green snake slipping into my house through the doorway. If I do believe this, I'll have to face the fact that now I know it's in there, I won't be able to go to bed at all. It may not be a deadly green Mamba, it may not even be poisonous – but I *don't know*, and that's the rub. Someone once told me you can easily tell a snake is venomous by checking if it has teeth or fangs. What sort of idiot was he? Who in their right mind is going to ask a serpent to open wide and say 'AHHHHH'?

At last, the messages are passed on and my brain gives orders crisply. I move in several strides to the entrance hall where I keep the snake-stick during the day. I'm glad now I've privately been practising swinging it to hit a spot nine times out of ten. Gripping on tight, I stalk the snake. It's not too hard: my house is neat. There are concrete floors, no cupboards and few places to hide. And there he is, coiled up in a warm, dry corner of the living room in a shaft of dancing light. The minutes till the frightening dark drops like a bomb will tick away, so it will be good to get it right first time. I manoeuvre closer, closer, crab-like and quiet, but he seems very sleepy and content. As far as I can tell, his snaky eyes are shut, and I make myself wait till I know I'm in the right position to bring the stick down with both arms. I'm like a golfer patiently perfecting his stance, and when I'm satisfied, the stick creates a wind and a *whoosh* as it arcs gracefully through the air. I can hardly believe it myself, but it crushes the neck of the snake, and, before he can react, it cracks down again and again. Sweat sprays from me to spatter the walls, the floor. Mercifully, snakes don't seem to have blood – but it's wet and messy all the same, and he's almost in strips. I am sobbing and catching for breath now. Shaking. My legs go and I plump into a seat. I have to swipe sweat from my eyes as they're stinging and I can't see. Then I stare at the remains. Remembering a hundred Hollywood surprise endings, I still feel insecure. I know there is one more thing to do: it's him or me, and it won't be me.

I'm in bed, and what's left of the snake is at the bottom of the thirty-foot long-drop latrine (or shit-pit as my fellow VSO's call it). I carried him out draped in strips over the stick, let him fall and listened for the *plop*. I know he won't be crawling out of there. Even the Alien couldn't get out of there. I don't stop to wonder why I assume he was a he or why – though I'm not proud of what I did – there is no remorse. I'm just glad my net is tucked firmly in. Outside, insects saw and hum. Inside, the bats cheep sweetly and mosquitoes blitz my bed. But for the first time in a while, I fall asleep almost immediately. I will wake rested at cockcrow, and, for the most part, that will be the pattern from now on. The exceptions will be when I go away to visit friends in the cities, stay in a hotel on holiday or go home on leave: then I will have trouble sleeping because I miss my bats and the rhythmic lullabies of the insect choir. At those times, I also miss the manic cock crow. There is a faint unease now I know what I'm capable of, but I'm too shocked to think much about it. Awake, I have determined to lose no more sleep, even though in my dreams I still seem to be trying to outrun fear's pale slithering shadow. But now at least I CAN sleep, I'm conserving what courage I have. I've learnt that adjusting to fear's dictates progresses in stages, and you can slip back as well as leapfrog forward. I will keep trying to get stronger, preparing for a time I can move beyond the impulse to kill and forget to be able to stop, prise open the jaws and coolly gauge the threat.

Echo

In Kenya, some things are very different. You don't get post delivered, for a start. Upcountry, there are no streets, no letterboxes, no postmen. There *is* a post office where you can do your business at a booth next to a 'phone on the wall you have to wind up and into which you then shout 'Hello! *Hello*! HELLO!' at frequent, increasingly desperate intervals. The ritual ends when at last, and quite unexpectedly, a ghost-operator appears to explain why you probably can't make your call. This post office is a neat, tiny place . . . and often has no stamps. The first time this happened, I was dumbstruck. After a while, I found I got used to the fact that the stamps do run out and you simply have to wait for another delivery. The stamps come from Nairobi via Kisumu on Lake Victoria, so it takes as long as it takes. In the end, of course, you get clever, and, each time you go, you buy a wodge. That's why they keep running out, I suppose, with mail-neurotics like me building stamp-mountains. Anyway, outside this little post-hut is a battery of shallow metal lockers where you pick up letters and small parcels. Renting one is quite expensive, so I get my mail via the school's box. This means if I come into town I take back not only my mail but everyone else's, and it's hellish disappointing if, after rifling through the pile, you're left with nothing. But today is a good day! Today there's a magazine and four letters for me. Three are from home – and one has a German stamp.

Suddenly, from looking forward immensely to my stroll down the wild-west type main street, shopping and chatting and sharing milky tea and lukewarm sodas with shopkeepers as I go (shopping is a different experience here too), and then – treat of treats! – taking lunch at the *Bungoma Tourist Hotel*, I feel sick and restless. Micha! Though I find it hard to believe, he still writes after conning my address out of my poor soft-hearted mother. I am no longer soft-hearted for obvious reasons, but there's no point in getting angry with her. She would turn into a red-haired fury telling him in no uncertain terms where to go if ever I told her the full story of why I left him, but I can't. Some things you really don't tell your mother, unless you have one of those

152

cringeworthy 'we are just like sisters or best friends, really' relationships. When Micha rang her, he cried into the 'phone. Of course, she couldn't bear it – a *man* sobbing! In her world, women should be too strong to cry and the male of the species would only shed a tear if his entire family was wiped out and he was told he had leprosy. So Micha got his own way as he almost invariably does. Now I turn my eyes up to thank God there are no 'phones here other than the useless wind-up one, so he can't pester or sob down a crackling line to me!

At least with his occasional letters I can scan and bin them before trying once more – though it seems a hopeless cause – to convince him that I'm very much somewhere else, starting to be someone else. To point out again how truly relieved I am to be away from him and will never come back. I keep it simple, and add mentally that I am stunned I stayed with such a selfish, immature and – now the rose-tints have cleared – rather silly man for so long. His behaviour destroyed my feeling for him as fast and as finally as lightning hot-slices a branch from a tree, and, most of the time these days, he doesn't stray even onto the edges of my thoughts.

When a letter comes, though, despite my scan/bin/one-last-rejection attempt routine, I am deeply unsettled. Something is worrying at my mind now as I walk across the smelly wasteland at the back of the hotel (if I'm going to feel bad it may as well be in the shade and with an iced drink at my elbow). Yes . . . it's something about the envelope. Unable to wait, I pull it out of my bag. German handwriting is oddly standard, so each person's echoes the next. But this is neater than usual, the ink sloe-black when Micha's is always blue. It's from Maehringen, however, from the huge, half-timbered house we shared with friends in a traditional Swabian village. No, it must be from him – who else?

Composing myself in the shade of a fig tree, thumbing my nose at the fairly early hour, I sip at an iced G & T until I feel calm. Here, I've learned endless patience and Saharan stretches of solitude have taught me to take time to steady myself, to focus. When I'm ready, I open the letter. It's one of those occasions on which you take nothing in at first, as it's too unexpected to be real. I force myself to read the words again slowly. It doesn't take long. It's very short. What's so startling is it's from *Annette*, the groupie he queued up for like a soldier in a cat house and who gifted him (thank God not me) several revolting sexually transmitted diseases. I reflect that if he had passed them on to me, I wouldn't be in this dilemma, as they would both be in neat, German graveyards and I'd be serving a life-sentence in a neat, German prison.

I've heard from old friends of general amusement at the spectacle of Annette deciding he was the only man for her, pursuing him relentlessly, and then moving in when his resistance was low. From the letter, it appears he's now got her pregnant. I do suspect however she may have engineered that, as he genuinely never wanted children. Why would a child want a child? It would be pretty easy with him dazed with drink and drugs to be careless about contraception. But any road up, she's pregnant now and her groupie days are clearly behind her. He hasn't had the courage to tell me – no surprise there – and I wonder why on earth Annette's informing me now. We were and are hardly likely to be what a dictionary defines as friends of the bosom, sharing confidences and jokes. My God – is she *gloating*? I remain surprisingly naïve about these things and thus sideswiped by people's capacity and appetite for active malice.

I concentrate on the relatively neat lines though and suddenly, inside and out, I feel cold. Even my veins run with ice water as I feel an echo of pain for my, our, dead babies. Then, as my heart and brain tick like bombs, I hit the nub of it and the mists clear. My eyes widen and my breath catches. Then I start to laugh, and the laugh has a wild, brittle sound. The Kenyan waiters here know me well, as I teach some of their sons and or assorted relatives. They always ask after the boys and chat to me when the manager isn't looking. As the blade of my laugh grates like knife on stone, they are growing concerned, and one approaches to ask gently if I am OK. There's a very long tradition of white people going doolally in alien, boiling lands and even the quiet ones can crack. Aware again of everyone around staring, however, I burst the bubble, bring myself under control, cough, sip my drink. Cool my skin down as discreetly as I can with a wet-wipe. Time passes.

It's so hard to believe, but this woman is asking me to leave 'her man' alone. He doesn't know she's writing, she says, but she's telling me that she's pregnant so I will back off and stop trying to 'steal' him back. Something stirs deep inside, a kind of fluttering like a baby shifting in your guts. I don't know if it's a dark

154

amusement, anger or pity. Has *she* lost her marbles? Ah . . . no . . . I realise suddenly she's where *I* used to be in more ways than one. I escaped: she's trapped and very insecure, hostage to an unborn dependent and slave to Micha's selfish, lethal and shabby charms. There is an audible click in my head: she's seen my letters to him arrive, and I'm still in the continental habit of writing my address on the back of the envelope. Clearly, though, she hasn't read them. If she had, she'd know I write only to tell him I'll never come back. If she had, she'd have picked up the sincerity in my pleas to leave me the fuck alone and get on with his life.

For the moment, it's anger that swells to a flood full enough to drown any other emotion, but this is white anger, pure and strangely controllable. So, for once, I decide it's safe to let it loose, to *use* it – and then lose it.

When I can trust my voice, Wafula the concerned waiter is puzzled, but happy to respond to my whispered request for some of the smart hotel stationery. The reply is quickly written. It's even more succinct than her missive. Will leave her in no doubt I am not a threat, but also in no doubt I am now skimming thousands of feet above Earth in clean blue heavens while she sinks in the mud. I end by telling her I pity her deeply, but not to write again. I urge her to have the courage to tell Micha she wrote and to show him this reply. If he sees the message in plain language to a third person that I truly hope never to hear from him again, it might actually do the trick! I stick one of my blot-out -the-sun wodge of stamps on the envelope then Wafula glides away with it on a tray like Jeeves the Butler. I know he'll put it with the hotel's outgoing mail, so I don't even have to walk back to the hut that sometimes so gamely pretends to be a post office.

I have no appetite now for my yearned for civilised lunch, but glug down another G&T and relish the relief. It feels as if it could finally be *over* . . . maybe this time it will be for good. Well, whatever the impact of my letter, I've grown adept at forgetting and getting on. I will now go back to my shopping, and I will have plenty of physical and mental work to do back at the house when that's done. There are visitors to prepare for, too, as some friends are coming to spend a few days with me when the holidays proper begin. Mentally, I consign Annette to Hell (though a little half-heartedly as I suspect the poor cow sweats in a steamy anteroom already) but Micha . . . Micha I trap in its innermost circle of flame where he will be anally raped by sadistic daemons with spiked and warty penises. I always did have a vivid and comforting imagination. As I pay my bill and leave, I smile to myself, and give Wafula a wink and leave him goggling at the kind of tip he might earn in a week.

****

I am back in the house in Germany. Although I know this is a dream, I can't wake up, and, at the same time, I can't understand why everything is so real. Indeed, everything is exactly as it should be. Dreams are not like that. Everything should be slightly alien and askew, everything and everyone not quite as they are, or even downright Dali-symbolic and surreal. As I move into the kitchen from the corridor outside Micha's and my room, I note the main kitchen light is on. It's tidy and quiet as it can be when the house is empty. It smells of fresh-ground coffee. The bright cloth is on the table under the hanging basket light. The Heidi stove is on and it's warm. The kitchen feels empty. The house feels empty. The only sound is the purring of the fridge and of my beloved cat Sapse, who sleeps in the corner unseen. I walk past the table, but then do a double-take. Step back. Stare. A doll is lying on the bright gingham cloth. She's dressed in traditional Swabian costume, a white lace-frilled cap hiding her face. It's very inviting, the doll. It's a substitute child. Like any female of any age, I must pick it up, so I do.

Then, at last, the dream-madness roars in. I can see the face now the frill has fallen back, and it's vomit-inducing ugly. Gnarled, lined, the eyes evil and living sloes set into raw, soft dough. They beam pure malice at me. I flinch. Worse, the limbs are also soft as dough, and I know they are stuffed with warm, wet, squashy shit. I can feel the heat of it and how it slides greasily about between my fingers under the cloth. But I am paralysed. I can't move an inch. Cannot throw her off, cannot look away, cannot cry for help into empty air. The vomit rises in my throat. It's the only living thing around here. Apart from the doll.

I don't know how long it lasts, the paralysis. Dreams can last five minutes in the outer world, hours in the inner. Then, so imperceptible I missed it, something unlocks. I find to my amazement that I can move my foot. Inch by inch, sweating from the effort, still having to endure the kill-hate-stare of the thing in my hands, I move towards the sink. In the end, sweating even more with effort, I reach it, and more eons have to pass as I prise the fingers of one hand painfully one by one from the warm cloth. With those fingers, I can ease on the tap. I find more strength from somewhere inside to thrust the thing under the flow of icy, clean water, and she – it – begins to writhe. Now the irony is I know I must hold on even though I can let go. Gritting my teeth, I grip so hard I'm amazed my fingers don't burst the bag of shit so it spatters the walls. At last, in front of my streaming eyes, she begins to dissolve. She melts away. There is smoke, a hissing, the smell of grease burning. In the end, there's only a little shrivelled slip of black material curling at the bottom of the basin.

Time ticks loudly by. I can't believe she's gone. I can't believe I'm free. Where will I go now after this struggle? What will I do? The water washes all the filth away and the smoke dissolves into air. It's safe to turn the tap off, so I do. The kitchen is quiet, empty, warm, neat. The fridge and the invisible cat purr. I lean on the sink and finally breathe out for what feels like the first time in hours.

I wake.

My little house is empty, clean, neat, quiet. A very different cat sleeps unseen, a warm furbag on my feet. Slowly I become aware of the constant clatter of insects from outside. It soothes. The echoes reverberate for a few seconds, then recede. To the cat's consternation, I get up and light the lamp. In its soft, buttery light, we both blink and I see all is exactly as it should be. My taut muscles relax. I will drink a little cool, clean water now and then use some of my precious supply to wipe away the sweat. Then, cooler and cleansed, I can go back to sleep with the echoes of an older and alien world fading as I sink into a sudden and comforting forgetfulness.

Lifting Up Thine Eyes

Pius, one of my pupils, has nagged me all year to visit his family. He is a delightful boy, very tall and well built, which contrasts strangely with a childishly innocent face. He is deeply Christian, so his forename is more than appropriate. All I know about his family is they are exceptionally poor, and don't live locally. Pius is one of the cleverest pupils in the school, but old Toad-Face is threatening him with being sent away due to arrears of fees. I have decided to help out with the fees, and, as the long Christmas Holidays approach, Pius puts his very large foot down: I must now meet his parents, as they wish to get to know me and offer their hospitality in thanks. The reason the visit has been delayed is they live on Mount Elgon, many miles to the north, and I will need to stay 2-3 nights to make the visit worthwhile. As the mountain is over 14,000 ft, I assume he means they live in its foothills, and off we go. It is very hot just now, approaching the driest part of the seasons, so I wear as always a t-shirt, cotton skirt, straw hat and flip flops. I have a locally woven shoulder bag of necessities.

After the usual sardine-torture *matatu* ride, we roll out onto a dusty roadside. When we have painfully unlocked our squashed limbs, we are eager to get on as it is beautifully cool in the trees, and we relish the fresher, greener air. I am very fit, as is Pius and another pupil, Emily, who comes with us as a chaperone, and the gentle slopes are no problem. Foolishly, I ask how far to go? Absolutely typical of Kenya is the reply, as Pius smiles and says 'Not far now, *Mwalimu*. Not far.': this is always a terrible lie, and means a good few kilometres (perhaps 8-10), but, hopefully, if we keep at this pace, and it stays cool, it won't be too demanding. After all, I am a veteran now and have walked 10 kilometres or more through the bush on some visits, over different and challenging types of terrain.

Quite suddenly the wooded slopes give onto a more open area of the hillside and I blink, thinking I see a sort of mirage in the middle distance. I ask Pius. He says it is real: the ruin of a big house, from the time a *Mzungu* owned all the land as far as our eyes can see. Amidst all the mud huts, made from and melding into the landscape, they built houses of stone, glass and tiles that would have looked more at home in Surrey. As I am interested in history, we walk over. While the sun soaks into a few stones and ruined walls, I explore and find a 'room' where a fireplace has survived. Suddenly it's not hard to imagine the *Wazungu* dressed absurdly for dinner, dining on four courses of defiantly British food, sipping wine from crystal glasses that know it's a joke and wink mischievously in candle and firelight. Now, however, there is nothing but birds circling and crying and tough grass whispering as it grows and stretches. Out here too is a steady, cooler breeze and it is suddenly an eerie place, a bony graveyard of so many things that are dead. Pius senses my mood, touches me arm, and we move on, all three of us are glad to leave it behind.

Many hours later we are still trudging. I am beginning to fear darkness will not be so very long before it falls in its usual instant equatorial fashion. We have climbed . . . and climbed. It's as well I'm used to walking in flip flops as they are not usually de rigueur for this kind of ascent. If anyone could see, I would look like some eccentric *memsahib* of old. I'm not out of puff, but all my muscles are screaming silently. Where in the name of the Lord do his family live? We passed a little iron roofed kiosk selling basic provisions a while back and I expected it to herald a settlement, but no. Finally, just as I am getting genuinely uneasy, we emerge onto a partial plateau, and there are people ahead, waving, calling. There are huts with smoke creeping out of their thatch. Oh, this is wonderful! As we slow down, however, I realise I am numb with cold. I don't want to think of how high up we are, but the air is like thin trickles of iced water. Talking of water, as we cross the last boundary, a bubbling stream with stepping stones, my legs fail to work and I fall into it. There is hilarity from me, shock and much concern from everyone else. People pick me up and whisk me helpless to a hut in which a smoky but welcome fire spits and crackles. We are served immediately with creamy, piping hot chai and Kenyan red beans mixed with curry powder. This simple and weird meal, however, tastes like manna – and we are WARM.

Later I venture to ask the question of why people live so high up, and at last Pius tells me. He said he was worried I would not come if he told the truth, but his family lost all their land, had to sell what they had to survive and pay his fees. He is it seems to be their saviour by getting qualified and into a good job. Thus they are now squatters in a kind of illegal encampment, with others who are in a similar boat. As the mountain straddles two countries, covers a huge area and no-one else wants to live up here, they have until now been left alone. There are a native people up here who are supremely shy and seldom seen, but, if you in turn leave them in peace, they do not seem to object to an alien presence. They hunt and gather while the squatters try to grow a little food, keep a few skinny animals. The squatters' life is fantastically hard, and they often do not even have the luxury of being warm as fuel, like all other supplies, is finite. They scrape a living, grind their own maize or millet, survive against the odds and sometimes have a few shillings to buy tea and sugar from the kiosk that sells such luxuries. I think of the tea we guzzled earlier and feel a bit sick. Pius knows me well and smiles. He tells me quietly I must forget these facts: they have prepared for weeks for my coming, and I must not refuse *anything*. Their welcome is all the more appreciated, and I steel myself to accept all they offer unquestioningly and with gusto.

We retire as we are, as we literally cannot keep our eyes open. Although the fire burns all night, we stay clothed and there are several thin blankets on the bed, I am relieved Emily and I are sharing, as it is still hard to stay warm. For all the days of my stay, I never once undress. Though they bring me warm water in the mornings, like a naughty little boy I splash it about a bit – but only wash face, hands and feet. Someone has lent me a woolly jumper, shoes and socks, and I figure if we have come this far and these folk are so hardy and brave, I should climb to the top. After our first insane, endless climb, it does not take long and I am entranced by the views of green and rust gold heat-shimmering plains of Kenya and Uganda and the mountains of the Rift Valley to the East. Better still, when we hit the summit, I gasp aloud. I had not cottoned to the fact that this, like so many of the nearby Rift Valley mountains, is a volcano; an extinct volcano, thank Heaven, with, in its deep crater, a lake. Amazing . . . here, on top of Kenya, a freezing cold, pure lake reflecting the blue of the sky and a trail of white, scudding cloud and around its waters grow a

160

profusion of weird plants, tropical but immune to the cold, survivors in a lost world. People her call it *Wagagi*.

It is literally breathtaking, haunting. I am a little jumpy when I think I see a movement of shadow at the corner of my eye. Pius and Emily have seen too, and he whispers like David Attenborough that it's one of the secretive native tribe. He assures me they will just be curious as they are very peaceful, and will do no harm. Some *Mzungu* climb up here but not as many as flock to Kilimanjaro, and probably not many white women. Most are on other parts of the mountain, too, exploring elephant caves, waterfalls and strange, tortured pinnacles.

Part of me wants to stay in this fabulous place, but my teeth start to chatter loudly and it's time to go back to those poor huts with their blue woodfires and eat whatever has been prepared for us. From somewhere, people will produce a thin, tough chicken, and they will proudly offer me as an honoured guest the breast meat and the gizzard. As a guest must, I will eat as much as I can and ask for a little more. I know already this will be one of the strangest visits that I will make here, and I will never be able to forget this mountain. It's been here for 24 million years, a fellow teacher told me, the oldest in the range. It was thrown up by earthquakes, shaped by fountains of lava, fire and grinding rock, cooled by rushing titanic waters and skiing glaciers, pummelled by endless winds. It's eternal and indestructible, with tiny, desperate ant-people, watched over by shadows, clinging to its slopes for dear life. No-one knows how long they can stay or if they can continue to survive, but they have stiffer upper lips than the impossibly rich *Wazungu* of Empire who lived in that huge silly house on sunnier foothills, and I am certain, for all their misfortune, they will be nurtured roughly by Elgon and survive a great deal longer than their oppressors.

161

None so Blind

Train journeys here in Kenya are a treat to look forward to. I love them for themselves as well as associating them with the first hilarious up-country trip and with holidays down to the Lake or the impossibly sophisticated cities of Nairobi and Mombasa. I relish the long, deep and sensual sleeps in a cocoon of cotton and wool, lulled by a strong, clattering rhythm. Have certainly never enjoyed so much waking up to a full English as I do in the faded Art Deco dining cars, awake but gazing still at dream landscapes in the volcanic Rift Valley or golden game parks. Forking up bacon blind as the train glides past teeming herds or the waving stalks of giraffes' necks above parasol trees. Whenever term ends, with me wound up tight and yet weak after another three months of hard work and illness, I head for the train station. And, as soon as the old locomotive pulling far too many carriages labours away from the platform, I feel myself relax and shift into holiday mood. Eight weeks free to visit friends! To travel! To wallow when we are in towns or cities in showers, electric light, well-cooked meals, gallons of gin and tonic – *with ice*. Oh, heaven on a plate with parsley garnish – and the train taking me slowly but surely to it.

This time, however, I'm on a return journey and a little deflated to be going back to work after a wonderful holiday. I'm settling rather glumly into my assigned seat, but, as usual, my spirits lift as the whistle blows and the train departs. There's always a sense of excitement as we do this, a feeling of heading off into a warm open night and the unknown. Nothing exciting will probably happen . . . but then it might! We're gathering speed now as we all try not to look too hard at the sun setting over the shanties that stain the dry skirts of the city with their sticky orange mud. When we finally build up speed, equatorial darkness descends so quickly it's like entering a tunnel – and the train shudders to a halt. We sigh, knowing we have no choice but to resign ourselves to a horrendous delay as some sort of repair takes place. I've been here long enough not to be surprised how remarkably patient people stay as we wait. The lady sitting opposite me is a Muslim called Fatima. She has just performed her evening prayers behind her veil with quiet dignity and you can almost touch her simple piety. She nods and smiles to show little pointed teeth, shrugging as she whispers 'Insh'Allah! As God wills!'

On this journey, when we finally move again, nothing is as it usually is, and we're passing through the Karen Blixen green and dappled Highlands to the north of the city in stark morning light. Normally, you never see these hills unless you travel in a bus or in a car. By the time the night's journey on the train is over, you are almost at the Lake and in an equally green but more tropical plains landscape. Now, as we leave Karen itself the sun's light is so powerful the beams are like spotlights picking out every tiny detail of sky and leaf and cliff. Suddenly – how can it happen with no warning? – we're all on the most terrifying journey of our lives.

It's hard to believe that this old fashioned train that must already weigh many tonnes and is packed with a thousand passengers is teetering across a wooden bridge that decays and crumbles even as we stare at it. Below, a brown river foams around giant rocks. We feel dizzy if we look, so we all close our eyes and hold our breath until we are safely over it, but then the python of carriages slithers around impossible corners and leans out over the edges of sheer cliffs. This is worse. We can actually see the terrified faces and whites of eyes of the people crammed into the third class carriages, and hear a child screaming fit to bust somewhere. The Muslim lady moves like lightning, and is being very sick out of the window with no dignity at all. Normally, this would upset me deeply, but I'm too scared and it's all too unreal to count. God! How much happier we were when we couldn't see this danger: on all the other journeys, when it was dark, we slept utterly content. I wish I didn't know it was only because we had no idea what lay outside the black train windows . . . if the train would stop, no matter how difficult it would make the journey, we'd get off.

But this knowledge and fond wishing is pointless. We all know there's no station for many, many miles. There's no getting off for any of us. From ancient men and women gnarled like old trees to a baby born slick with blood and water last night in the dining car, from chickens scuttering in the rack above my head to the nabobs in first class: this could be the last second or minute or hour or day of our lives . . . and in a flash I realise that *I'm happy*, happy as I never thought I could be again. I'm busy and fulfilled as any human being has a right to wish for. *I am alive* and I truly want to stay that way. I want to get off at the other end and go back to work, back to everyday humdrum life. It's what we have, and it's probably more than we deserve. But we've been robbed of freewill, and we're at the same time one and alone and silent as we trace each sway with our nerve ends, suffer each jolt with beats of the heart. The journey becomes interminable, and we keep climbing. Slip in and out of dark tunnels cut into sheer rock. Cross more swaying and creaking wooden bridges. Barely stick to steep cliffs. It's beautiful beyond reason and description, but we see only the danger. No-one speaks or drinks or eats, though our mouths are full of dust. We concentrate as hard as we can, willing the train to safety and fervently hoping the driver isn't as sick or scared as the rest of us.

It's hard to believe that we've long emerged from the wooded highlands and are rushing down onto hot, silvering plains with the Lake in the distance vast as a blue ocean. We're like a thirsty herd thundering towards a watering hole. We can smell the bitter wood smoke and the toasting *ugali*, the wonderful burnt maize flour and water of a thousand evening meals as we slow down and near a stop. Hear the children whooping as they run among the trees on a little ridge, see them waving and tripping over in their ecstasy. We return the smiles of the graceful women in multi -coloured wraps carrying on their heads food to sell. The mood changes to one of sheer, bubbling happiness as we pull into the dingy little station that no-one would normally remark. We rush to buy cold beers from the bar. We break into the food packages we've all bought from the vendors and stuff ourselves with spiced *samosas*, fruit and fresh-picked and roasted peanuts. We eat like pigs. We drink like drains. We laugh hysterically and tell all our worst travel tales. We declare that we will always from now brave the crowded buses and the risks on the roads. When we calm down, of course, we'll remember that would be equally if not more dangerous and we'll have no choice but to forget, to close our eyes against the unaccustomed sun and get back on the train.

Prophesies and Witches

The Supernatural – what on or off the Earth does that mean, really? Do you believe in it? I didn't at all until I heard a ghost many years ago on holiday in Scotland with Micha. People are always sceptical: how can you 'hear' a ghost anyway? Frankly, no -one can persuade me I didn't, but you can make up your own mind by listening to the story.

In his usual madcap way, in 1978, Micha had decided we should holiday in Scotland just after New Year. He says in his Dietrich voice he has heard how beautiful it is, how mysterious. So, as soon as my doubts are suitably vanquished, ready to do battle with snow, ice and wind, off we rattle in his beat-up VW rust-bucket with no heating: the VW that people honk and laugh at as they speed past when we are chugging along on motorways. With him as driver – reckless, putting our lives at risk even in this thing that couldn't go faster than the speed limit if it tried – me as a nervous passenger. He is a man on a mission however, and we travel ever northwards, over-nighting first in the Lake District with its waters like glass, mirroring spoiled white hills streaked with toboggan trails and echoing with shouts and laughter. On up the motorway we go, unbelievably SHUT WHILE WE ARE ON IT due to extreme weather conditions, and on which we shiver under blankets sipping single malt while we wait for the traffic to flow again. Up, up even further north past Glasgow's smutty, dangerous sprawl and along the side of blue, misted Loch Lomond, through an eerily musical Glencoe (the winds sound like bagpipes) and – finally – with chains on our wheels, we toil past red horned cattle and mediaeval castles reflected in Arthurian waters – to the Kyle of Lochalsh and the ferry to Skye.

Soon after we touch land again, I do confess to utter weariness and that my stamina is reducing by the second. Micha admits I look very pale, and we have travelled hard and long. Fortunately within minutes he spots a hotel sign and turns onto a driveway that curves behind a hill to a stunning 19th century mock gothic house. It looks as if it was a lodge to a much larger house. Best of all, it stands on a bank of its own small loch, which reflects back the cold winter sky and the few black, bare trees that cling to its edges and to the hills. It is eerie, moody and magnificent here – but the hotel looks closed. Ever optimistic, Micha parks the car, leaps out and rings the bell with gusto. To our amazement, the door opens after a few minutes and I see him in earnest conversation with a pleasant looking man. He returns beaming. It seems they are closed, but as it was just the two of us . . . and we are on our honeymoon (barefaced strategic lies are a speciality of Micha's) . . . and cooking dinner for four is as easy as for two . . . we're in.

Inside it's even more marvellous: a grand stair and hallway, complete with baronial fireplace and cracking log fire. There are stags' heads on rich damasked walls, enormous bedrooms with four posters and a tasteful lounge with a view of the loch from deep, inviting sofas around another log fire. Admittedly it's very chilly away from the flames' golden power, but there are electric fires in what will be our bedroom, and it will soon warm up. In the meantime, the owners will cook dinner, I can have a hot bath and wash my hair, and Micha can sit in the lounge by the fire on one of the worn, shabby-chic sofas with a single malt in one hand and a book in the other. This is definitely the life after our catch-as -catch can nights at pretty ordinary B and B's and one night with a kind native who put us up in Fort William in his cramped spare bedroom as there were no hotels open at all.

In our room, I am on my own, drying my hair, very cosy, indeed glowing, in front of the fire. There is a delicious silence as we are far from the road or any other habitation. I hum softly to myself and realise I am very hungry, looking forward avidly to dinner and a glass of wine. I don't think it's possible to be more relaxed and this is all I hoped a Scottish holiday would be like. Then I hear – or more accurately gradually become aware of – the sound of heavy footsteps on the stairs. Nothing odd about that, but they go up . . . and down. Up . . . and down. Over and over and over again. I stop rubbing my hair and listen properly. Tune in. How weird is that? Who would *do* that? You go up to a room, stay there or do what you need, go down again, end of. And then for the first and only time in my life so far, I experience what I have read of in books, seen in films: I am terribly cold, paralysed and terrified. I couldn't move if someone threatened to shoot me. I can't think. There is only hair-pricking and skin creeping fear. I don't know for how long. As suddenly, it's over and I burst out of the room, hurtle down the grand stair and into the lounge. I give Micha a huge fright as I appear from nowhere and throw myself at him. It takes a while to tell the story as my teeth still chatter. He definitely believes in the Supernatural. He looks thoughtful, and leads me through to the kitchen.

Our hosts are there, cooking, laughing. He asks if there is anyone else in the house. The laughter stops. They hear my story. Look at each other, again as people do in films. They assure us they have been in here the whole time and there is no one else in the building. They take us back into the lounge and pour me a whisky.

'We didn't say, as only a very few people hear him, the old laird. We think when we're busy, even people who do hear the footsteps might think it's other guests.' I am really frightened now. He goes on 'But others get the full Monty. We never have. He was laird of the big house to which this was a hunting lodge. He came here often in the 1870's. No-one knows why, but he seems gradually to have moved in here and become a kind of hermit. He hanged himself at the very top of the stairs one evening. He hardly spoke even to the servants at the end, so they didn't find him till the next afternoon: Someone raised an alarm as he had not taken in his breakfast tray by lunchtime, poor man. They cut him down and he's buried down by the loch, there, where the stones are. They wouldn't let him lie in the kirkyard. This house wasn't much used after, but we bought and restored it 10 years ago.'

Micha is curious as ever and to the point 'Why up and down, up and down like that?' Both shrug. 'We don't know. Only he would know that. He left no note. We think maybe he was just so agitated, taking time to decide . . . life or death. It seems he was retreating from life anyway.'

The rest of the evening is oddly uneventful and I warm up quickly. Dinner is excellent, the wine good. Micha comes up the stairs with me. The house feels peaceful. As I am not alone and exhausted, I even sleep a dreamless sleep. But we leave very, very early and I am so relieved when we turn the corner that my shoulders relax down. The lodge on the loch and pagan grave of its sad laird disappear from sight. We drive on, and, over the years, though I can't forget, I think of it less often.

Now, this morning, here in Kenya, in my too-hot little house with no four posters or stags' heads, I am deeply shaken and why I'm suddenly thinking of it again, I don't know. I find as I come to a little that I am bolt upright in bed, sweating profusely, with trails of a strange dream still swirling around me. I remember slowly all is well, this is the real world, and it is the eve of the new term today. All the boys who board will trickle back, with us all behind closed gates by sundown this evening. This includes two brothers of whom I have become very fond. One, Gerald, had polio as a child and is twisted in body wearing callipers and using crutches. He is very sharp in mind, however, full of character, determined and mischievous. His brother Joseph is more conventional, but a bright and handsome boy. They are very close, always supporting each other. In my dream I see them wending their way to the school through mountainous territory in a packed matatu, which of course careers along very poor roads with deep ditches on either side. It takes a corner too fast, crashes into one of those ditches, and, in the chaos that follows, I see Joseph on the road, decapitated. There is no blood, but his head is definitely several feet from his body. I am terrified. I can't see Gerald at all, and someone is screaming. I wake to find that someone is me, making strangled noises.

This dream lingers, and I walk across several times to the school to greet arrivals, talk to the cook about the evening meal, and to see if the brothers have arrived. No sign, no word. They are *always* back on time: their parents are a little better off than most, and always have money for the fares, so the boys arrive punctually, neatly turned out and with Joseph carrying their boxes on his head into the compound. When it is dark and the gates are locked, I am really worried. Can one really have prophetic dreams? In this under-the-white-sunshine dark and dangerous place, where witch doctors are secretly more popular than the white coated doctors in the town hospital, strange things feel more possible than in our spiritually barren concrete cities.

Next day, word comes. Both brothers were in a bad matatu accident. I feel sick. And Joseph was hurt, Gerald just bruised. They will arrive later today. The nausea retreats – both are alive

168

and walking! I ask calmly what happened to Joseph and they say they are not sure. When the brothers do arrive, Joseph is wearing a neck brace. I am a little perturbed, but predominantly relieved. No-one knows of my dream. I have no idea what if anything being able to tell a (twisted) future may mean. It was half right and helped no-one at all . . . I think again of my hesitant and tortured Scottish ghost, and quickly assume this is another 'one-off' mystery, meaningless and probably best forgotten.

It's happening again, months later, but this time, I am very much awake. Every holiday these days, I spend a fair proportion of the time visiting the families of my pupils, repaying their generous hospitality by staying the night or several nights, and appreciating all they offer, which they seem to love. They can then bring me hot water to wash in the morning, followed by breakfast, and we can spend a lot of time in talking, me telling them about the UK, them explaining Kenyan life and customs, taking me to other compounds or villages to listen to traditional tales and songs, watch dances, circumcisions in season, eat a lot of chicken and ugali and even drink hot, home-made maize beer through a straw. This liquid is lethal but does not give you a hangover – I've learnt to love it and the hilarity that can ensue. One day I went outside a drinking hut for a breath of air, my head a little woozy, and saw a man I half-knew staggering happily off up a pathway. Several people were doubled up with laughter. They would straighten, point at him, and dissolve again. I was puzzled and asked why: They told me the man lived in the opposite direction, and was heading for the Ugandan border and bandit country, where there were also caves eaten into the landscape holding bones of the dead. I laughed too, loud and long, and only wondered after sobering up if he had been chased by offended ghosts, eaten by giant ants or shot by bandits in his drunken meanderings.

However, there is no home-made beer here, only chai and coca cola. Patrick's family is very respectable, his father a Christian and local community leader. There is food galore, as usual, though, and it will be ready soon. One moment I am chatting happily to people, and the next, I have an urge, no, a compulsion, to return home. Danger! DANGER FOR SOMEONE. The only person left on the compound in the holidays except me is Rose, a close friend of mine, another teacher. She is pregnant and her partner John is away. It must be her. I have never felt this urgency before, but I know it can't be ignored. I explain fervently that I must go, and people are shocked, then truly devastated: There are even tears. I never fully understand why, but these visits mean such a lot to the people here and it is taboo to offend by rejecting hospitality. However, those trying to dissuade give up when they see how determined I am, and Patrick's parents give me an escort so I can get home safe. It is several kilometres, but less if you cut through the bush, and it will be dark in less than an hour. I have never been fitter, and I opt for the bush. My pupils jog in front of and behind me, and we set off at a good pace. I am glad we have not yet eaten as we speed through the bushes. We weave and leap, effortlessly skimming over stones, rough ground, little ravines, holes, a slow and sad waiting-for-the-rains-river. With my weak night sight, I pray we are not doing this still when it is dark, but we make it with minutes to spare. The boys set off back gamely with torches lit. I light my lamps hurriedly, then rush round to Rose's.

Rose clearly thinks I am nuts. She seems fine, and is very puzzled I left whilst on a visit. She says solemnly 'They will be very offended, my friend!' I nod sadly, deflated, and after a cool drink with her, go home to eat a scratch dinner instead of chicken, gravy and ugali. Ah well – at least I won't have to eat a gizzard!

It is not yet light but there is a knocking at my back door. Oddly feeble but insistent. It's interrupting one of the oddest dreams I ever had. Rose in my dream is giving birth in a swimming pool. The baby looks too big and has almost Chinese features. He is plump, very black (children here are often lightish skinned when born) and there is hair on his back. She has bought nothing in preparation, and while they float about I have to rush to market and buy all I can find that will help; baby lotion, shampoo, soap, cloths, talc, little baby clothes, a blanket. Just as I am about to take these to her and the odd baby, that damned knocking is waking me up and it's still dark. Fully awake if groggy now, I light a lamp, pad to the door. It's Rose and she actually falls into my little hallway. I get her somehow to my wicker chair, and she tells me

170

she has been in labour she thinks most of the night, didn't want to disturb me as no matatus start running anyway till about 6 am. It is almost that now. The mission hospital is only 45 minutes away if you drive straight there. I dress quickly, grab my purse and we head for the matatu stop, Rose leaning very heavily on me, riding the pains with enormous bravery. I see the lights of a matatu as soon as we emerge onto the road and in case they miss us, flash my torch at my face. At the same time I also hold up into the light a couple of 20 shilling notes. People here see a mzungu and cash bells ring anyway: *This* is every matatu driver's dream. After it screeches to a comedy halt, I explain, all the other passengers are turfed out, protesting loudly. I don't care. We lift Rose in and I promise another 20 shillings at destination if they hurry. Rose holds onto me for grim death and we fly through the countryside. I can't believe how fast we get to the hospital with its low, white bungalows. It's not as good as a private hospital, but it costs little and is a thousand times cleaner and better than the utterly filthy hospital in the town.

Rose's waters broke some time ago and the birth of her first child is very close now. Staff helps her to a delivery room but the lusty cry of a healthy baby wafts on the air only after what seems a very long time. I sit for what seems hours on a bench in the corridor, winded and shaky, gradually calming, readying for what will come.

Afterwards I am told the delivery was complex as the baby was BIG and it was touch and go; they had to break one shoulder bone to get him through. He and Rose though are well enough now. She will sleep for a good few hours after the painkillers they have given her. Thank God, they say, she got here quickly! Another hour, they would both have been dead. One of the nurses stays to talk to me. As Rose's friend, she says, can I help? There is nothing for the baby and they do not keep things here. Also they are short staffed and would appreciate if I sit with her and the baby today. I nod eagerly. I like challenges! It will get me away from here as an older, very tired looking woman is now giving birth and her screams are awful.

I whizz round the local market and get a whole basket of things for the baby. They sell Johnson's baby products here for those who can afford them, and there are 'baby gros', cloths and

171

towels. There is even a pretty shawl. Lots more shillings are shed, but I don't care. I earn the same as the local teachers, but I have no family depending on me so I have plenty compared to them. Then it's back to the hospital, and a heavy-eyed Rose. She kisses my hand and tells me to look at her son. I peek into the crib and my eyes pop. He is very black and plump, his eyes are slanted and welded shut so he looks Chinese. I check, hardly able to credit this, and, oh yes, there is hair on his back. Rose says he is beautiful . . . beautiful . . . and drifts away again. I don't think he is beautiful to anyone but her just now, but he might be one day! I marvel though that apart from the tight binding on his shoulder/ chest, he seems fine. I frown as I notice he is definitely not very clean. I doubt he's been washed. I am outraged, look for a nurse, but they are so ferociously busy I know this is too much to ask. How hard can it be to bathe a newborn?

There is a plastic bowl in the corner and the water comes from a tank outside so is actually quite warm. I've heard you don't use soap at first or fully immerse, just gently wipe with a clean cloth and warm water. So that's what I do, lining the bowl with a towel, relaxing into it with him as he doesn't struggle and seems to feel better for it. I can then dry him and dress him in a clean baby grow. It's a bit tight, but then he is a big boy. . . Loving the feel of his weight and warmth, I survey the sleeping Rose and her boy with satisfaction; when she wakes, I will help her have a blanket bath and find some cool drinks and food for us. Baby will have her breast.

Later, I have time to reflect. Rose says she can't name her baby 'Helen' for obvious reasons, but she and her partner had even before this agreed my second name is perfect. So he is Nathaniel Wafula, and I feel absurdly proud. I also feel very unsettled still because of that dream. The family I left has been told the story by now and they have forgiven me: everyone puts it down to instinct that I left. Only I know it's something more, but then I don't know what and would rather keep it to myself in any case. I am grown so close to the people and integrated into the environment here, and it is such a strange, magical place, the unexpected can happen. I don't know if there will be more Mystic Meg Supernatural moments – I fervently hope not – but if there are, they seem to be getting useful, and I will take them very seriously indeed. The jury is still out on the Supernatural, but it feels as if there is something almost within my reach, nudging me gently now and again, but preferring for now to lurk in dreams and shadows.

I have had no more 'moments' up to this time, but I am puzzling now what to do for my adopted daughter, the lovely Emily. Emily is a gentle girl, very clever and capable of going to university, but her family is poor, and can barely send her to school. One day she tells me she may have to stop coming as her family has had a poor harvest. This I can't accept, so discreetly arrange to pay her fees myself. She and her family promises not to tell, but this is the huge village that is Kenya and everyone knows within minutes. To make it seem more acceptable, I do what pleases everyone and I move Emily in with me. I will miss my privacy, but no-one else has any so I will grow to accept it. Actually, I think I may adjust quickly: I have a kind of daughter now, people will stop nagging me about employing a maid (in their view Emily will take on that role and I will pay her fees instead of wages) and it feels wrong here not to have responsibilities or dependants.

Emily is over the moon, as she will live so comfortably with me and no longer have to walk miles to and from school each day, but can visit family at weekends and in holidays. She can look after me too, as a mzungu should be looked after. There however she is swiftly disillusioned: people may think she is my maid, but I explain I can't be waited on. We'll share tasks, but I do make her smile when I say I guess I won't object if she takes over the two I hate most – doing the washing by hand and mopping the concrete floors. She is happier then and says it will be a pleasure. I know it's true: she is young, healthy, has a sunny nature and does a great deal more when at home, including carrying huge jerry cans of water on her head for long distances. The younger sisters will do that now. If she did so well at her studies when tired out and having to do so many chores, she should now absolutely fizz academically. She will even be able to do homework as I have a pressure lamp as well as a cheap hurricane one.

Why I am puzzling now is that Emily is no longer sunny. She is really worried, losing weight, with dark semi-circles shadowing her eyes. She is happy living with me I know, but something is eating at her. In the end, I make her tell me. I tell her if she has gotten pregnant after all our talks, I may have to beat her. That makes her smile wanly and out it all pours: some people are jealous of her for having her fees paid and for living with me. They have paid the witch doctor to put a curse on her. Everyone is saying so. She has found strange items in the garden and, one morning, when she went out early, pinned to the door. She kept them secret so as not to frighten me. She shows me now. They are nasty little things, grasses with bits of cloth, bone, feather, fur and what looks like dried flesh and blood attached. Suddenly a rare, ferocious white anger rises in me. I remember books I have read when interested in religions and rituals/the occult. I look into Emily's eyes and tell her I have never said anything, but I have power too.

I tell Emily we must wait until the moon is full to perform certain rituals so she will be completely protected from these spells, as will I. Emily I know believes in me totally. On the designated night, we are in the garden, and all is silence except for the insect concerto. The moon is huge, so we work behind the fig tree as we don't want to be seen in its blue light. She watches, rapt, eyes round, as I lay out my charms on the blood red cloth (cut from the skirt of a favourite dress. Ah well!). I have collected pieces of twisted wood and dug out of a box a beautiful cowrie and feathers garnered from my coastal holidays. I have plucked hairs of hers and mine, lit a perfumed candle, pricked tears of blood from our thumbs. I arrange everything, making strange passes over the objects, drop our blood into the candle flame, and burn the hairs. I write a message in what looks like sigils on thick paper, fold it several times and burn it too. I say things under my breath, then make her close her eyes. When she opens them, all is wrapped in the cloth and bound tight with strips of red. We bury it deep.

The moon shines approvingly on the earth once we have tamped it back into place and covered the area with dried grasses. We both shiver though it is warm. I am desperately tired, but smile at her and tell her firmly it is done, can't be undone, ever, and that our life essence and futures are protected and hidden. No curse will have any effect whatsoever, and anyone who tries will get the curse right back in their faces. I can tell Emily believes it 100%. She looks different already. Anyone who looks at her now will know she cannot be frightened, cannot be a victim. She will feel in control. I have told her to say NOTHING so that she will,

174

of course, tell everyone. It's a calculated risk – I hope people won't lose respect for me, as you can't function without it here – but worth it. Emily is soon her sunny self again and the frustrated, jealous, cursing and cursed people who have always inhabited the Earth are, at least for now, vanquished. As one with power, I also tell her she WILL get to university and be a teacher, maybe even a headmistress, with time and I will come to the graduation ceremony. She needs only to believe, and learn to screen out the malice of those less able or less hardworking who so hate to see others succeed and prosper.

I may not know what to believe of the Supernatural, but it has, yet again, been very useful. I only hope if it is out there that it understands and approves of why I used it so shamelessly . . .

Woodpecker

There is a group of us in Wafula's hut, drinking too-hot sugared tea out of tin mugs. The mud walls and floor and thatch roof mean it's mercifully cool, but the space is also cosy in the amber light of a lamp ingeniously made from an old tin. Wafula is very proud of his home, as walls and floor have been smoothed by many willing hands for months, treated carefully with layers of cow dung so they have become hard and free of cracks. I can't quite pin down the resulting smell, which hovers somewhere between dust, sweetness and decay. Wafula has painted murals on them of abstract designs, trains and cars. His sisters have laid the table with freshly picked peanuts, boiled eggs and bread with margarine. They are there to 'take the edge off our hunger' as people say here. There are no ready-made snacks except bread of course . . . everything is organic, everything comes fresh from the fields or animals.

Dinner will be served later, and it will be chicken with *ugali*, as there is nothing else people here feel worthy to be given to a guest. Sadly, as the honoured guest, I will be given the gizzard. I have grown to loathe this custom as much as the tribes here hate each other. It's a terrible insult to refuse it, however, so I have learned to use my incisors to slice it into slivers to swallow: otherwise it's like trying to chew a rubber ball. Once it's gone, I can do my best to plough through an enormous meal. It's expected. It's also expected that one eat with one's hands and strew bones and food about liberally. I love this as it feels like being Henry VIII for an hour or two. As a very special treat, there will be some bottles of coca-cola for me. People here are not well-off, but a guest is king (or queen) and there will even be some cigarettes on offer as they know I smoke.

In the meantime we chat. As is often the case, we talk of the different customs in Africa and the developed world. People have heard a lot about Western customs, very little of which is accurate. When I visit pupils and their families, people love to check out the truth with me. Wafula now asks quietly: "*Mwalimu*, in your country, I have heard that a man is allowed one wife only. Is this really true?"

"Yes Wafula, though if he doesn't get on with his wife – or she doesn't get on well with him – they can divorce and both can marry again. But if he marries two women at once – or a woman marries two men or more at once – the man or woman can be arrested and even put in jail for bigamy."

Wafula looks puzzled. Even shocked.

"That does not sound right, *Mwalimu*. I think it is much better to have more than one wife! I will have many. A man must have as many wives and children as he can afford for his honour, and to support each other and do the work of a farm. And some can be educated and all members can help to look after the family and the land."

I explain I understand all that, but I ask if it is not also true that many polygamous marriages are very unhappy, with wives jealous of each other and even sometimes poisoning or trying to bewitch an unpopular younger wife. There has been a famous case recently in the area, and Wafula has to agree. He points out though that many are also very 'harmonious', and work as in the olden days to everyone's benefit, as long as the husband treats all equally, wives help each other and the children grow up surrounded by a big, loving family. In the rural areas, he tells me, there is seldom a divorce: any woman who wanted to leave her husband would be made to stay by her family, as it would bring dishonour to them, and, he admits, they would not want to pay back the dowry the man had given for his wife. He tells me there is only one woman in the whole area known to have been helped leave her husband by her family: this family is poor, but she was being so badly mistreated they thought she would die, and beggared themselves to pay back the cows her husband had paid for her. Now she is felt to be a failure as a woman and a burden to all. I feel a rill run along my nerves as I am told her only hope is that a very old man will be willing to 'take her on'. His desire to possess her young flesh and the fact she will come at a rock bottom price will perhaps outweigh her reputation as a 'bolter'.

After we have sat in silence for a moment, drinking our tea, one of the other boys, who is what is called here Wafula's stepbrother from his first mother i.e. his half-brother from his father's first and oldest wife, asks me a more direct question. I teach this boy also, so I know he will not give up asking questions until he has an answer that satisfies. The teachers call him the woodpecker. I

177

know he is also frighteningly good at debating. My heart sinks and I take a gulp of sugar-thick tea.

"*Mwalimu*, having now seen and understood both systems, which then do you think is best – polygamy or monogamy?"

Tap.

I struggle. I explain it's hard to answer. List some pros and cons. Waffle. He shakes his head.

"No, Mwalimu, I already know all of that – I would like to know which *you* think is best. You personally."

Tap, tap. I try to wriggle about, but he will not have it. Wafula and the other boys are rapt. They are all waiting. I sigh.

"Well, I suppose if I had to choose, it would be monogamy."

My interrogator is very fair. He nods kindly.

"Yes madam. I know a lot of people here now are starting to think the same. The old ways are out of date, they say. They like the way of the West."

I feel he has given in too easily, and I am right. He leans forward.

"So, madam, if every man is allowed one wife, is he then faithful to her until he dies?"

Tap, tap, tap.

"No." I tell the truth. "Sometimes a man is, but I'm afraid not always. Some men have . . . a girlfriend or even girlfriends."

Into the silence his voice glides.

"And the woman he marries – is she always faithful to him?"

TAP!

"No. Again, some are but many are not."

"How then do people know whom the children belong to?"

I shrug my defeat.

"And he can marry as many women as he likes, this man, and be as unfaithful as he likes and abandon his children as long as he is married to one woman only at a time?"

The tapping is giving me a headache. I take another gulp of tea. It can't delay the answer long.

"Yes."

The sharp beak seems to be tapping into my skull.

"So, madam, all these women, especially the girlfriends, why does he not treat them well, honour them all with marriage and status and homes of their own? Why does he not look after all his women and children like a man should? They cannot have a very good place in your society if he does not!"

"No. No, sometimes they don't. But it's complicated as many women insist on their right to choose how they live. And as you said yourself about polygamy, no system is wholly bad or good! There are very faithful and successful monogamous marriages too."

I know it's a weak point and we're back to square one. But it's the best I can do.

"Indeed madam. It is true. You are right."

Silence has fallen again. Behind it my mind is very busy, fresh air rushing in. All the things I believed up to now without question – all the things I took as a given – start to appear less solid. I think of the free-for-all that passes for organisation of relationships in the developed world, all the brothers and sisters with one mum and a different dad each, all the illegitimate children, all the spouses cheating on each other, the big expensive weddings followed by big expensive bitter divorces and meeting the children once a fortnight in the park or some café, all the absent parents and children grieving, brothers and sisters hardly knowing each other, the living together, the common-law marriages, the heterosexual, gay and bisexual pleasure seeking and infidelities, the lack of any real rules at all. With the veil rent to reveal the chaos that is the reality, I try rather weakly to smile. I'm relieved to see Wafula's sister, Alice, who brings more tea and a special treat for all of us from his father, a packet of biscuits from a shop at the market. They are called *Manji* Biscuits, and they are a joke among volunteers who say they are Manji by name and mangy by nature. But I know how difficult it is to spare even a small amount of cash – especially when you have four wives and nineteen children – and I am very touched. Wafula's step-brother by his first mother is still looking direct at me. I put the biscuit down.

"No – I'm not the one who is right. I was assuming what is familiar is the only and right way. I didn't think it through or look at the real truth of what has been happening around me. I needed to face it. I should not have – no-one should have – a closed mind or . . . an assumption of superiority."

He smiles so widely I think the top of his head may fall off.

"Yes *Mwalimu*. Please take another biscuit, and then my mother would like to meet you. She is a very good cook, and she is cooking the supper for you tonight. Wafula's mother cannot cook.

My father must have married her for her looks, people say. It's why Wafula is so handsome and thin, and I have a plain face but a good belly."

Everyone laughs and Wafula throws a pillow at his half-brother. Then we talk of other things. Well, the others talk. I nod or smile occasionally, but am distracted as the fresh air continues to waken my sleeping-beauty mind. It has to get used to the world as if new, and to the odd sensation of being cleansed by a cool wind as the clean-up of cobwebs begins.

Nuns on the Run

Though I've mentioned the dinky and often stamp-less post office in Bungoma, I realise all of a sudden this story is reading as if there is very little contact with my family back in Swansea while I am in Kenya, but that emphatically isn't so: I'm allowed two periods of leave and visit them twice, once after two years for a few weeks the second time after three and a half years for a few months. We write regularly too, and I know they read and re-read my letters about work, friends and travels in Kenya: I can see in my mind's eye my mum stashing them carefully in a box they keep for important documents. Their letters sometimes have me rolling with laughter: The best relates to the first time I was on leave. A Swansea man saw an article in the Evening Post about my work in Kenya (sadly the article mostly focused on bugs and diseases, but he saw past that), and through sponsored table tennis matches raised quite a lot of money for our school library. He was also heavily involved in promoting various cultural events, and we discovered a shared love of Dylan Thomas. When I had decanted with the doubloons, he invited my mum and dad to attend a Dylan Thomas recital: my poor deaf dad had the perfect excuse not to go, so Aunt Sylvia was drafted in to accompany my mum, not without reluctance and trepidation. They hoped to sneak off early, but were made quite a fuss of so this seemed churlish. They described the state of semi hysteria they were in during, and how they almost expired laughing afterwards when safely outside in the car. The letter looks long and interesting, so I settle further back into my maroon plastic sofa. She describes the gathering, with everyone dusty and eccentric, looking for all the world like the residents of Llarregub come to life. The poems were declaimed in the epic style of the Man himself, every consonant rolled and vowel stretched, by a man who did not look unlike him. Then, just when they thought they could finally get away, tip-toeing to the door, they were caught mid tip by strains of *Mae Hen Wlad Fyn Hadau* and had to stand rooted to the spot – where they were easily caught, tyrned round and introduced to all the strange, trapped-in-amber people, forced to discuss the poems and drink gallons of weak tea. I can see it in my mind's eye, and laugh aloud several times when reading it. Neither of them has *ever* read any Dylan Thomas – and they thought I was weird for doing so with such relish – but they had heard and seen some of his stories and Milkwood on radio, TV and in film form, so they just managed to keep their end up. . .

One genius thing mum does for me is to send contraband wrapped in magazines. I soon discover that no-one can send me anything here as import duty is crazily high – more than original goods are worth. I can't afford large, unexpected expenses as we are on local wages, and it is all I can do to save some cash so I can travel in the holidays. What I really need, as washing powder here has arsenic or something similar in it and rots your clothes, is undies from M&S. So mum wraps two cotton bras and on another occasion 2 pairs of knicks in magazines so tightly no-one can tell they are there. Wonderful! I thus have a steady supply of cool and good quality undies for which I am deeply grateful – and I know she loves beating the system like this. I do manage to get some parcels free of duty, such as the medical supplies I get a friend who is a nurse to send so I can run a first aid centre for the lads and local folk in my house. I have a seriously well stocked box, including sterile dressings and antibiotic powder, and I can deal with all minor things. This may seem a bit of a strange and *memsahib* thing to do, but there *is* no local clinic. The state hospital in Bungoma is filthy and has no supplies as the doctors sell them all for personal gain: people truly only go there to die. I just can't bear to see people struggle so much for the want of basic first aid – a cut can turn septic here very fast and kill – but must say sometimes I almost regret this impulse. I have to deal with very unlovely things at times like a boy covered in boils, one who is scared as one testicle is bigger than the other and one with ulcers on his legs. Everyone tells me that there is no help for the latter, and even doctors can do nothing. This arouses my scepticism: I find out what I can and discover they are due more to malnutrition than anything else so I arrange for him to have lunch at school daily (he's not a boarder) and when he comes for treatment every few days with said antibiotic powder and clean dressings, I give him milk and high protein snacks. The ulcers do clear up after a few months, and I am as delighted as he that there is a cure after all! I insist he keeps taking lunch and the ulcers know better than to try again and stay away.

Every now and then we arrange a phone call – you have to book in advance! – and I can speak to (shout at) everyone in the close family unit, including my gran or nana as I have always called her. If anything, being so far away from Swansea does make the heart grow fonder and though I always feel uncomfortable at 'home', at this distance it seems we can have an easier relationship – ironic, but true. However, this occasional contact is not enough and mum is very keen to visit. Though she has never been abroad and has never flown, it seems a great idea. As with anywhere you have grown truly to love, I long to show any interested family or friends Kenya and Kimaeti. What dampens all the fun of anticipation though is that given my dad is not allowed to fly due to having Menieres Disease, nana insists on Aunt Phyllis coming too. Our relationship with her is a complex issue. I am ashamed of my own reaction to the news but I really can't help it: my heart sinks to my flip-flops. She drives mum nuts too, but my mother would never disobey nana.

Truth is Phyllis – though no one in the family will ever admit it – clearly has a learning difficulty maybe combined with being on the autistic spectrum. This happens periodically in the family and there was a weird great aunt Elsie I remember doing odd things and whom people talked about in whispers. Phyllis *is* a truly out there person (focused predominantly on money and gambling) and can cause a war just by walking into a room. I instinctively don't like to have contact with her, but then another part of myself berates nasty-me harshly that I ought to show basic affection to an aunt. However, I promise if you were to meet her, your good intentions would also fly away, and all you would want after several seconds is to knock her head off with a mallet and/or get away. Fred used to say her mouth works faster than her brain, and was sometimes so exasperated by her tactlessness and selfishness that steam came out of his ears. It is certainly true we can be happy and getting on brilliantly, Phyllis will enter the room and – Bingo! – there is a family argument. Bookies should take bets on it. The worst and darkest part of it though is you just can't be sure if she is as dim as she seems: She always gets what she wants so she is astute on some level.

When Uncle Fred was dying, Phyllis was living very near to my gran's – on her own, with no responsibilities – but didn't help out at all. Indeed, when in desperation they asked her to help with washing as my poor uncle became incontinent in the months before he died, she grumbled and brought it back crumpled and still wet, making more work for them not less, and, of course, causing umpteen family quarrels. Her most infamous trick, half-hilarious half-infuriating, is to turn up at Christmas, eat through food like a beaver through a wood, drink all the drink and scoff all the chocs, figs and nuts. She criticises everything, doesn't bother to help in any way at all and only brings along as a contribution something she has won in a raffle at the pub. Her 'presents' are extraordinarily bad, bought we swear in charity shops from the 50p shelf. They are entertaining, but we all buy her nice gifts and it seems shall we say a little one-sided? As a coup de grace, when everyone can bear no more, she causes an especially horrific argument to disrupt the day, going home in a huff clutching half the cooked turkey and whatever other treats have survived her rampage. As nana insists we be nice to her, she gets away with it all – as she has since the day she was born. Aarghhhh! And now this force of anti-nature is coming *here*, to my sanctuary. The embarrassment factor when she is unleashed in public if I'm truthful is very high too – at least 9/10. Well, I must try (oh Lord, how many times have I said this?) and a more welcoming and charming people than the Bukusu you cannot meet, so I know we will all make a good shift of it.

Mum and Phyllis fly out on a Jumbo and the fun starts at Heathrow: Sylvia tells me by letter that my mum sees the 747 on the runway, and refuses to get on as she says it won't get off the ground. Once persuaded on by caring staff, she sits at the back smoking her head off chatting with a few BBC wildlife programme cameramen for 6 hours, having a whale of a time. I meet them in Nairobi as I am still on holiday, and whisk them south for a few days to stay at a beautiful safari lodge beneath Kilimanjaro. Oddly, on the way back, we go through the smaller Nairobi Park and see much more exciting wildlife there, including the gruesome yet fabulous sight at sunset of lionesses bringing down a giraffe. We cannot believe the speed and order of the hierarchical devouring of it: huge shaggy father lions begin, followed by lionesses then cubs, with hyenas and vultures picking the bones. The giant beast is a clean skeleton in about 15-20 minutes. Then we travel up to Lake Naivasha and the Tea Hotel. Mum and Phyllis are both enraptured, especially with the pink clouds of flamingos on the silver lake and the colonial luxury as we drink fresh local tea on the green lawns of the hotel. In stages, we work our way to my school, as my mum, fair play to her, is more interested in the school and my friends there than any tourist trail. They even believe me now re the *matatus*: I pay extra for them to go in the front seat, but they experience the screams and excitement as the *matatu*, crammed full, leaves its stand and then screeches to a halt so everyone shoots forward and a few more people are pushed in. I am in the back, but well used to it by now.

At the school, mum is so lively and appreciative, people love her immediately and she and Phyllis make enormous efforts to come out into 'the bush' and visit many of the families I know. When mum dances happily to local pop music, everyone whoops and claps: this is the best entertainment for many a year! We have a great visit one day but goodbyes take forever, and we are trudging along the road to Uganda later than hoped. I mention it will be dark quite soon and we must try to go faster as we still have a couple of miles to go: not the best idea to be on this road after sundown, given there is no pavement and bandits come out to play in the dark. There are no buses to hail today as it is a National Holiday, so mum just steps in front of a car. I wonder idly why she would commit suicide when she seems quite happy just now, but the car swerves to miss her, screeching to a halt. A handsome young Kenyan man looks at us, eyes popping, with some consternation. She tells him we are nuns visiting the faithful of the area and we need to get to Kimaeti before dark, and, lo and behold, we have a lift all the way home. My favourite bit is when the man says 'Goodbye, sisters' as we descend, and my mum replies without missing a beat, 'Thank you and God bless you, my son'.

To backtrack a little it is their first night in my little hothouse and they are coping quite well. Emily and I have prepared for weeks to ensure the house is squeaky clean and they will be comfortable. We give them a plain but tasty meal and later warm some water for them to wash in my so-called bathroom. This is a small, bare room off the kitchen with a sloping floor and pipe in the wall through which water runs out. The facilities are a stool with a plastic bowl on it. They clearly feel cooler afterwards, however, and climb thankfully into what are normally our beds in the bedroom. I've warned them re the bats, and both have mosquito nets of course. We tuck them in. They are exhausted by now, and so are we: the lamps are put out, with torches and a potty right between the beds so they will not panic too much if they have to get up in the night. Smugly, we think we have covered all eventualities and can retire to our own makeshift beds in the living room. Quiet settles against the background hum and an occasional horrendous fart from Phyllis (something is having a dire effect on her digestion) and we are all lulled to sleep by 10 pm. It must be about 3 a.m. when my mother starts shouting. Hearts in mouths, we rush to the bedroom and find pandemonium, with both of them charging about shouting. We calm them down, and my mother manages to stammer out a lion tried to get on her bed. A L-L-LION - onto her FEET! A LION . . . I start to laugh and she tells me angrily it's no laughing matter. We must find it! Where is it? They are terrified. In reply, I pull up the sheet draped over what is usually my bed and there is my huge grey Tom ('Puss') cowering, green eyes flashing through the dark. We all sit down and laugh until we are weak, and I explain it's the one damn thing I forgot: Puss is a wildcat who has adopted me, and he goes out hunting every night, coming in at 3 a.m. to slip under the net and sleep on my feet. He must have been excited to find me back, but found it harder than usual to join me as I always leave the bottom bit of the net loose for him, but, of course, cats never give up. Fortunately, they are both cat lovers, are introduced to him, and peace returns after I take him into the living room where he can curl up with me on the couch.

It is time for mum and Phyllis to leave, but by now term has started. They have seen every inch of the school, met everyone locally and charmed everyone they've met, but it's time to move on. I can't take them back to Nairobi, but I can take them to Bungoma Station and they are booked into a hotel in that city from whence a taxi will take them to the airport. Fate can be unkind, however, and, a little earlier than usual, the second rains come with a vengeance. In Bungoma we actually have to wade through about 3 feet of swirling brown water to get to the station while Biblical torrents also roar from the sky. They are very brave once again and we make it intact and even laughing. I wave them off with a hankie as the long, long train pulls majestically off out of the small station: I know they will be fine on there as guards and passengers will be delighted to help them dry out and wash/change. What's more they will have hot tea and dinner in the faded restaurant car, then be wrapped in wool and crisp cotton to sleep. It is sad to say goodbye, but there is an awful lot of work to do and I am determined to get back to school and start on it, floods or no floods. This will be my last term here, and there is limited time to complete some projects – and be ready to welcome my replacement.

Later on Uncle Glyn and Sylvia come too, with their good friends Joan and Walter. More widely travelled than my mum, they adapt even more quickly. They can't believe though just how friendly Kenyan people are, how helpful – so naturally people here respond well to them, to their humour, warmth and genuineness. I take them on roughly the same route as mum and Phyllis, and they are in Heaven. Well, they are until the second big stage of the trip: we have returned to Nairobi and must now travel to Kisumu. I am stunned that the trains are full for a few days (this just never happens), but think fast and remember you can hire a long-distance taxi. Sadly, after several hours weary wait, our driver turns out to be a raving madman. It's a pity the journey is in daylight and though we try to pretend it isn't by closing our eyes, imagination is even worse than reality. The driver who is stick thin and seems to have only one tooth is zooming along at about 80 mph, on a twisting, turning and climbing road. That road is doubly dangerous, packed with traffic, in seriously bad condition – and 20 mph would be pushing your luck. He overtakes nauseatingly close to precipices and on blind corners. I think the others are starting to feel seasick, and though more used to danger, I am afraid too for me and for them! I can really smell the fear oozing out of everyone though all four are paralysed and deathly silent. In the end, I know I have to act, but wisely, in case I make him angry. This is him in an OK mood – what would his driving be like if he were infuriated? I inflate my bosom and tell him imperiously 'Ngoja, Dereva!' (STOP, driver!). He does and turns, skinny arm on the back of the passenger seat. I tell him if he

187

doesn't drive us more slowly to Naivasha, I won't pay him and he can call the police if he likes . . . But if he does what I ask, and lets us out there, I will pay him for the whole journey though we have done only half. He may be a lunatic but he sure understands economics, so he does what I say and we are soon sitting traumatised drinking hot *chai* in a cafe in the town. People of course are lovely, and not only arrange someone to take us to the local hotel for one night (cool and clean) but on to the Tea hotel next day. This driver is quite a contrast, in no hurry at all, and takes us to see the flamingos on the lake as an extra. We walk out towards them as far as the mud will allow, and it's like being on an exotic alien world. All my guests, as did mum and Phyllis, adore the Tea Hotel, and then we travel, calm and recovered, with the same laid-back driver, to Kisumu. There we stay in a hotel with balconies leaning into Lake Victoria. The sunset of black, rose and gold is the loveliest any of us has seen – probably as we feared we wouldn't live to see it: bliss!

Next day we decide no more entrusting our lives to anyone but Glyn, and we hire a car. It's not huge, but we and the luggage are squeezed in. They want to stop at the Equator and straddle it, a photo opportunity, but even more they want to see my house and school, so we factor in a few days there on the way up to Kitale. On arrival, I cook them corned beef hash, and they cannot believe how good it tastes with organic potatoes/onions and local butter and milk: every bit is scoffed with fresh bread. They will speak of it for years to come! Walter is also delirious with joy as he sets up a washing and shaving post in the garden, whisked back miraculously to his youth and happy army days. While they're here, and before we take a look at Northern Kenya, I ask if they can do me a favour: my good friend Ian has made me a lovely wooden bed, but I need a proper double mattress for it. We do have the car, and it's not far to the town. Everyone loves the idea, and off we go: *Five Go to Buy a Mattress* . . . In a small car. Doh! None of us wondered where the mattress would go given the boot is petite too. Ah well, we're British are we not and people expect us to be verging on the insane, so we buy one anyway and no-one blinks when Sylvia, Joan and I wrestle it into the back seat on top of us, and we career back as fast as we can to my house. We are hot and squashed but laughing when we get back, and le voila – I have the best bed and mattress since I came to Kenya more than four years ago. There are few people for them to meet here as it is still the school holiday, and the compound deserted. Soon it's time to head for the mountains and gorgeous, almost Scottish, scenery around Kitale.

We still have the car we hired in Kisumu, and so far the roads have been hairy but not too scary. But now I have to explain to Glyn we will really be in even wilder country, and there will be no road markings or signs or lights at all. Main roads are quite busy and it's a free for all, with eye contact used to gain right of way. The only rule is we will periodically have to bribe armed police to get across checkpoints. He nods solemnly, and the others' eyes grow round, but off we bounce up the dirt track to join the main road. He is daunted by nothing, not even the hand-made sign that says 'Deviation' and takes us 20 miles off route for no apparent reason. Glyn is recently retired from BP and having driven tankers, he is clearly the right man for this job: indeed, he is magnificent. I bet for years *matatu* drivers will be saying 'Oh *Bwana*, that *Mzungu*! He fixed you with his eye and you knew *he* was the co-o-olest driver on the road! No messing with *him*.'

But this, too, is all too soon over, and they are as sad as I am. We have had a superb time, but each of them except Walter (who insisted on eating boring European food, mostly chips, at all times) have been unwell, and I think they will be relieved to get home to coolness and comfort. This is for them a holiday, though a special one, and I know they will be delighted to get back into the gentle rhythms of everyday life punctuated by the pleasures of bowls and bingo. They are waved off with many thanks as I have also enjoyed myself hugely, appreciating the loot they brought, and gained such pleasure from seeing their enjoyment. The trouble is Kenya has become my reality now, and has made me happier and more fulfilled. Like it or not, I will now have to start the process of deciding whether or not I can leave it. There's no wish for routine or familiarity or love of Bingo to draw me back: So what's next?

Interlude

Moving Within Kenya

I know when the contracted time at my first school runs out that I have not completed my work there, and I sign up for one more year. Now that year has ended and I know I have gone as far as I can. I'm glad to have played a part in helping the school attract government funding. Here, the government will only fund a school if it reaches minimum standards. Ours has: it has a well stocked library with a part time librarian and trained assistants; there are more, if still not sufficient, text books; we have raised funds for a better lab; there is a system now – with all the ditches dug by our pupils! – of clean, running water from standpipes; one day it is now sure electricity will come as it is creeping out from the town like a sparking crab.

Most excitingly of all, the hated Toad Face is gone. He had bribed local worthies to let him stay for long enough: with the government funding the school, the head has to be qualified and Toad Face isn't! He simply set the school up to make him money, played the part of the big man, and had now been found out. He never even qualified as a teacher . . . I am truly sorry life will be harder for the 4 wives and many children he can no longer keep in the manner to which they have become accustomed, but feel no pity for him. The local children and their parents now have a school which will continue to improve, for which fees are affordable and where corruption isn't impossible, but at least unlikely now to be so blatant or on such a grand scale. Whatever one's views on the fact secondary education for poorer families is not free and is in English, qualified young people do get better jobs and their whole family and community benefits as bonds are so strong you simply have to help your family financially or risk being outcast.

Despite an aching sadness at leaving its people and my pupils, I know that I simply have to move on from this particular school. I could not in any case work as a VSO at a government school: Volunteers have to work at 'Harambee' (Let's all pull together) schools that even qualified Kenyan teachers often avoid as they are so poor and remote, lacking the most basic facilities. I could of course still work there if, as my friends wanted, I stay by marrying and settling . . . they speak with serious faces of how to get the cows for my dowry to my father. I have to look equally serious, even while imagining his – and even better – my mother's faces as the horned, protesting beasts are driven into the neat gardens of their semi-detached in urban Wales. Friends have even brought a very handsome and quiet young man – a teacher like me, but more than a decade my junior – to tempt me. He says he would be honoured! They say I will have a young husband, a home, children, status. Be a full member of this close community.

These are my friends and sincere, so I tell them very solemnly that I am deeply grateful, and tempted. Part of me is perhaps – better the Devil you know – but I know it isn't the realistic way ahead and that I will regret it deeply this time if I take a path of least resistance. So would he of course, especially as unknown to them I can have no children. I have seen what happens even to high status barren wives, pitilessly cast aside or humanely pitied, used as always-available babysitters by their fellow wives. And so, when they finally accept my decision, there is a fabulous goat roast and beer-fuelled leaving party, with speeches of gratitude and sad farewells on both sides. But in the end, not long after sun-up, I leave the way I came, with my orange rucksack and box, heading for Nairobi. I am ten times tougher and wiser, however, and, truth be told, excited as well as sad.

It still makes me uneasy that I have deceived my friends: I hope there *is* a big gulf between omission and commission of sins. Knowing they expect it and will better understand it, I let them think I am returning home to Wales. But though not wanting to stay and settle in Kenya permanently, I know I'm definitely not ready to leave the deadly beauty of this country. Not yet. So, until another full two year contract becomes available in Western Kenya, I've accepted the challenge of keeping a project alive until the volunteer allocated can take over. It's on the other side of the country, a teacher resource and training service in the sparsely populated and semi-arid country North-East of Nairobi. I did this knowing the area is prone to devastating drought. That people there live on pulses, maize flour paste and the occasional high-day-and-holiday vegetable or piece of tough goat meat. That

191

every cup of water is ineffably precious, often obtained by digging deep into parched riverbeds and carried home on the creaking backs of donkeys. As there's next to no public transport, and none at all to the remotest settlements, I will have to learn to ride a great yellow monster of a farm bike needed to get to far flung schools. I hate driving a car, but hey, there's hardly any traffic on the roads there and how hard can driving a nice, steady farm bike be?

Edge

For the first time, I'm in top gear and gingerly letting out the throttle – millimetre by millimetre – of the motorcycle I've been given to get to very far-flung schools. For just a few months, I am teaching part-time at a surprisingly well equipped school with the rest of my week occupied by taking books and materials to remoter schools in the area, and working with teachers there – and at occasional meetings in my school – on how best to use them. What I didn't know of course is that this is the very last place on earth one should even attempt to ride a bike, and that if you are bonkers enough to try, you spend over 90% of your time on the hard ground as it:

1 Keeps running into patches of sand as soft as any on a palm-shaded beach and stops dead so you fall off.

2 Keeps running around corners into sad, plodding donkeys, heads hanging, so you have to stop dead and fall off. If you don't, you may kill the hapless creatures and/or the dusty girl or boy leading them.

3 Keeps running into patches of road so eroded or rough that you stop dead and fall off. I shudder to remember that once I got lost and ended up freeze-framing just in time at a sheer cliff's edge. If I hadn't stopped dead, I'd be dead.

An incident that maybe sums it up is when a desperate teacher at the school begs for a lift to get to see a sick friend. We are doing fine until the first of the above happens. Defying the laws of logic and gravity, he flies into one ditch and I into its fellow on the *opposite* side of the dirt track. With customary Kenyan phlegm, he dusts himself down and we both remount silently and carry on hoping for the best. He doesn't ask for a lift again. Neither does anyone else. This is the same thing that happened when I learned to drive a car. No-one would travel with me, and eventually, neither would I.

Such incidents are semi-comic, but sometimes what I'm doing is truly exhausting and so surreal I'm disoriented. I get to a school, for example, after hours of muscle-screaming and brain-busting effort, and am very dirty indeed. Sweat is mixed with sand making me feel as if I'm wearing a rusty suit of armour. On arrival, I'm whisked like a dirty secret to somewhere dark and private where I can wash and change into a clean, more demure outfit of cotton skirt and blouse. This has to be done as no-one will look at or speak to me otherwise: indeed, I appear not to exist at all until I fit their idea of how a female should be, especially a 'high-status' one. Then, after concluding my business, people nervously divert their eyes again when I have donned the filthy uniform of Khaki trousers, T-shirt and jacket, jammed the helmet on my straw-stiff hair and whizzed away. Each visit takes a whole day, and I get home dreaming of a hot shower and an iced G&T, neither of which exist outside of big city or tourist hotels and my fevered imagination.

Anyway, all of a sudden, here I am, starting to enjoy a bike ride for the first time since I learnt the basics of driving my machine on the (empty!) Nairobi racetrack. I lean back, breathe out, drop lower in the saddle. My shoulders loosen. I start to drone a daft popular tune to myself. *Malaika . . . naku laika Mala-a-ika . . .* all the usual guff about loving your sweetheart. I pull the throttle a little more and the engine seems to hum along with me. Because I'm going at a steady clip now on a wide and hard dirt road, it's quite cool. Oh my, this is the life! I had no idea, and, obviously this is why people risk death and injury on these things! At last I'm getting somewhere fast and for the first time in my life, I imagine I must look quite cool. Not quite Marianne Faithfull in leathers and shades, of course, but pretty damned good.

Then, as the once-a-day packed bus heading for the northern desert overtakes, people cling to the roof with one hand so they can wave and armed guards hang out of the windows to salute with their Kalashnikovs and cheer. Despite the racket and the instant dust-bath, I wave and smile back. A *Mzungu* is entertainment value in any shape or form, of course, but a *Mzungu* woman on a motorbike in trousers . . . now that's show time! I see one child being held up at the back window for a look by its mother and its eyes and mouth forming into three huge O's of surprise. Then child and gun-toting soldiers (there are inhospitable bandits in the even more inhospitable deserts) and waving black arms disappear into a mushroom explosion of cloud. Soon I'm blissfully alone again. Insects buzz themselves to sleep. The air shimmers. The sun's rays are palpable, loud, liquid. I whistle as I take the turn off leading to the most remote school I've visited so far. Bloody hell! I can *do* this! I must be getting used to it and becoming more skilled than I thought. Perhaps people are right and practice does make perfect!

As I turn again onto an even narrower track, I see that the recent much appreciated but rather short rains – of which there is now no other evidence at all – have after all left a deadly legacy. There are no road signs here. No markings. No bum-crack maintenance crews. No plastic cones. No roadside rescue. And the once-road has simply slid into the two ditches on either side of me. There is nothing left but for a single elevated switchback with a bone-breaking tumble on both sides. If I go over with this metal monster on top of me, then I will be a shattered shell, a skinny Humpty-Dumpty oozing stickiness into the sand. But the wonderful thing is that in this split second I have no time to process information, no time to think further or plan. There are no alternatives to sift through. I've had to slow down and go into a lower gear on this winding road and, without conscious thought or hesitation, I change up smoothly and let the throttle out full. A roar comes from somewhere nearby, and my stomach tilts as if I'm on a roller coaster. It *is* a little like that as the bike speeds across the narrow isthmus, skimming every incline and dip. I forget about breathing until I hit the other side and suddenly – it's hard to take in! – I'm on safe ground again.

That must be an illusion of course, but, by now, even though I can breathe again, I have to work hard to believe it. Realising what I've risked and seeing the vision of Humpty-me, vivid and horrible in my mind's eye, I shake like someone in a fit. I should stop gradually, sensibly, put down the stand, get off and sit down. Take a drink from my water flask. Breathe deeply and evenly for a while. But of course I can't unlock the fingers on the throttle and run bang into a patch of sand. I stop dead. I fall off. I lie in a stupor, amazed to be alive but too shocked to enjoy it. Suddenly, it seems very silent and very hot. There is a long, long way still to go. Now I have the leisure to think and plan again and the duty to take decisions, I know I can't go back and that choice is as illusory as safety. There *is* only one way. I get up and try to steady my breathing, my limbs. Nothing broken. One or two bruises tomorrow, perhaps. Purple and yellow. Yellow. I give my jaundiced beast the evil eye and wrestle him into an upright position. I sigh. After all: it's not his fault. He's a victim of his environment. I dust us both down. Mount. Set off to find this school. By the time I get there, I will have a smile fixed on my face. I will tidy myself, make myself acceptable against the odds as I have always done and will always do. Somehow, after concluding my business – though I have no idea how as this way back is definitely blocked – I have a firm conviction I *will* get home somehow in one piece this time . . . though not for the first time I wonder whether that will always be so.

Spotlights Not Suns

After the short but satisfying stint in my 'troubleshooting project' East of Nairobi, I've been given another two year teaching post. While I'm pleased it's in the Western Highlands again, it's disorienting to find things are so different to before. This school is at a lower altitude, slap-bang in the steamy middle of sugar-plantations. The sugar processing factory is a distance away from the school, however, and not all the local people benefit from its dominance. Still, it's the most prosperous area I've worked in up to now, and this means there are more people who can send their children to a local school. This in turn means there is no need for children to board. I find this makes life very dull after my intense experiences at the other schools. When all the children disappear at the end of the day, it's eerily quiet: a graveyard would be like a night-club in comparison. I do find my lips curving into a smile at times to think that after years of being on what amounted to 24/7 duty, and dreading being disturbed at night, I never expected my first real nine-to-five job to be here in Kenya!

There's still plenty to do, but I struggle to get used to such quiet evenings and weekends. A sad knock-on effect is I don't develop the same sort of relationships with the students, and don't get to visit the local people as much as I did when at my first school. There, I got to know students' and the school staff's families and lives very intimately, taking a part in those lives and in the life of the community – and I felt a real sense of *belonging*. Once again, one of the headmaster's wives lives next door to me with her children, but, unlike my former friend, she's rather standoffish. This is very unusual in Kenya, but I suspect she cottons to the fact I dislike this headmaster as much as I did old Toad-Face at my first posting. This one is an outwardly urbane and more handsome man, but at bottom he's a Mr Piggy with his nose sunk in the swill. Several times none of us teachers has been paid because he's taken all the school fees for himself. VSO has to pay me so I don't starve, and he has to pay them back. I think they have a devil of a time getting the money – this little piggy isn't even prepared to pay for my services as a teacher, librarian and fund-raiser extraordinaire. He wants to have his *ugali* and eat it.

It's irritating for me but hell for the other teachers – they need their jobs and money, and no-one is going to sub them. So they wait in growing desperation until he deigns to pay them: this is usually when he feels they really are about to leave and questions will be asked that he cannot answer. As with Toad-Face, the school board are in his pocket because he shares his choicest scraps, but even they all know they can only cheat the community and its children up to a certain point.

This is a big compound, but there's only one other tiny house beyond the one next door. It's a much meaner looking dwelling, in which the hard-working school secretary Hafsa lives in a medium size 'bedsit' with her little girl and boy while two of the unqualified male teachers share the other, larger room. It's crowded but it's very cheap, and they all prefer it to living in the tiny, ramshackle rooms for rent – called quite accurately 'cubes' – behind the shops in our market. The market is not a place to bring up children or for a young teacher looking for respect to live: it's hot and eye-wateringly smelly, with scents of rotting veg and piles of decaying offal balancing with hints of human and animal sewage. There are bars there too which double as brothels. I'd got used to the wild-west look and atmosphere of rural places, but, just a few months ago, we were all very shocked when there was a bandit raid on the shops in the dead of night and one of the bandits was shot in a gun battle. The police it is said had a tip off and that's how they managed actually to turn up during the raid. The children were all agog, of course, and went eagerly to view the dead body on the way to school the following morning. It made them all late, and left the head and all us teachers standing like wallflowers at assembly. Nothing much fazes me now, and I went home for another cup of tea, returning later when I could tell from the raised noise level that the children – still over-excited from their grisly treat! – were back.

I can't pretend to like this school as much as the first, or even to enjoy the time here as much as my short period at the second. I find the people more distant, and the experience less involving. Items have been stolen from my washing line, and though it's common practice here to have a tiny padlock on your water tank tap, when I went away, someone smashed it off and took a lot of the water. I'm ashamed of how angry I was, how betrayed I felt. It's a lesson learned however: Though this area is lived in by the

198

same Luhya tribe, it is a different clan, a more materialistic mindset, and not as traditional as the area around my first school, where thieves were so reviled they could still be stoned to death! The headmaster wanted the prestige and money I could bring, but largely I'm liked by some, only tolerated by most, and it's best to calm down and get on with it. A part of me realises this situation may be helpful, as at the end of my contract, there will be no agonising about whether to stay.

However, I'm used to all the rhythms and different challenges of life here now and always enjoy teaching. So I roll up imaginary sleeves and am soon deep in the process of raising money to improve the library. Also, after noticing and hearing the staff talk about how many of the good students' performances suffer due to social or family problems, I've been allowed to start a pupil counselling service. It took time to persuade the children personal issues would be kept confidential, but more of them are coming by now to talk out their difficulties. They seem relieved to get them off their chests, or even go away with ideas or some advice/ assistance on how to improve things. It turns out to be a suitable substitute for the work of boarding mistress, and it's good to feel I can genuinely help some students through a truly amazing variety of anxieties.

One thing that might surprise is that the children and young people's difficulties are not much different however exotic the surroundings: most of the problems would sound familiar in the West. They range from: teenage romances, teenage pregnancies and sometimes more sinister types of mistreatment, bullying and/or sexual harassment through the usual personal hygiene and health problems to frantic anxieties around the onset of puberty. Sometimes the difficulties are very Kenya-specific, however, like the grief and frustration of the boy whose brother (who used to pay his fees) is in jail for subversion against the government. He daren't talk about this to anyone else, as subversives disappear, and not only do family and friends have no redress, but also have to try hard not to attract any more negative attention to themselves or their friends.

A lighter activity has been doing all I can to make my two bedroom house very comfortable. Indeed, a good thing about living in a less poor area is how much better off materially I am than before. The house has the unspeakable luxury of ceilings, and, as if this weren't enough, I have two other amazing facilities in the form of a water tank as mentioned and *electricity*. The latter is only available as we are on a direct line between the town of Kakamega and the sugar factory, but it means my 'des res' sports electric light, a fridge and a little two-plate electric cooker. The cooker gives me a tiny shock every time I touch it, but I haven't died yet and it otherwise works very well. Strange how hard I am finding it to get used to modern conveniences again: to tell the truth, for old times sake I still use a hurricane lamp when I want to relax and just listen to music or do nothing much at all, and I find it almost a comfort that I still have a 30 foot long-drop toilet at the back of the garden.

There are other advantages that make my life quite pleasant, including a chilli tree by the back door, papaya trees and pineapple plants in the garden and as at my first house, a honeysuckle bush outside my bedroom window. There are also plenty of fellow VSO's to visit at weekends and in the holidays or have them visit me, and many Kenyan friends back in the area around Bungoma. So, all in all, despite having to adjust to some changes, I am not too unsettled. Another consolation that comes with time is a developing friendship with Hafsa. She is a widow who has not remarried, bringing up her delightful little girl and boy on a pittance. But she is proud, and the children are bright, choc full of humour and character and already doing well at primary. They adopt me as a kind of aunt, and spend time playing in my house and in my garden. They bring me strange gifts they have made themselves, including mud sculptures made from the churned earth at the riverside. Sadly, this mud that has been formed into weird, misshapen figures is mixed with the dung and urine of animals which drink on its banks, and, as a result, it stinks so badly there's a sort of miasma in my room and an influx of flies to admire my works of art. I say nothing, however, and the statues stand proudly on a shelf. As they dry, they smell less, the flies look elsewhere for fun, and the children are very proud. In return I tell and read them stories, teach them new games and play them music so they can dance like disco divas. They are so innocent they make me feel happy. I dance sometimes too, and they are enraptured.

I can't believe the first year has already gone, but I have been away for my last long holidays. Today is the Saturday afternoon before term begins, and I am trudging up the driveway to the school gate and to my house. It's the hot season and very humid. After a sweaty, endless, tooth-rattler of a *matatu* ride over hard dusty roads and dry, dusty river beds, I am looking forward to some peace, a cool wash, fresh clothes and something cold to drink. As I draw near my temporary home, however, I can hear shouting and what sounds like weeping, and my brow crinkles. I speed up. As I arrive at the gate, the strangest tableau is set out on the grass before me: indeed, it looks like a scene out of Victorian England, with the bums in action. Hafsa and the two children are crying fit to bust as their meagre and rather pitiful belongings and sticks of furniture are removed from the house and piled up outside. She has ceased to remonstrate now, as the school workmen have finished and are putting a new padlock on her door. I understand enough Swahili to pick up that they are urging her it is *not their fault* – they have their orders and they need their jobs – and they will of course help her carry her effects to the market. Even bums are polite here, and they insist there's an empty cube behind the butcher's shop. She'll get used to it and the smell and it's very cheap!

It happens so seldom I am shocked as a tremendous anger rises like a hot white tsunami from my feet to my brain: they haven't seen me yet, but heads turn as I bear down on them and I notice as I do a face peeking out of the other window of the small house. One of my fellow teachers at least is in, but obviously keeping out of it. Foolishly no doubt, I don't. I demand to know exactly what's going on. The two children cling to and pull at my skirt, while Hafsa droops with exhaustion and despair onto a tin trunk and tries to explain it all. The two workmen break in. They are quite adamant. It's the headmaster's orders! It must be done! Someone else needs the room. He will be arriving today and *must* live at the school. I am deeply puzzled: none of us was told at the end of last term of any changes. People who know me when this mood does hit would not be surprised to see how my (much depleted due to continuing weight loss thanks to malarial interludes and dysentery) but still visible bosom starts to swell. I am equally adamant this stranger will *not* have Hafsa's home, and I am here, right now! I will take full responsibility and deal with any repercussions, and *I* am telling them it's a mistake. They will take off that padlock and put everything back. I am not moving until they do and will break the padlock with a machete (I still have one by my bed) and put everything back inside myself if they don't. *Then* see what repercussions will ensue!

I need to pause for breath and in any case I can't think of any more threats. I'll have to rely now on my so-called 'high status', and on staring out the workmen with steel in my eyes so they see I really mean it. Finally, they lower theirs and re-open the door. When despite their mutterings and hesitations all the effects are back inside, with the timing of a comedy sketch, we hear a terrific noise approaching until a truck bumps and grinds in through the gate. As the engine sputters into silence, a young *Mzungu* leaps down from the passenger side. To me, he looks about twelve, very pale, but fresh faced and eager. He, it turns out, is Andy. He is American. He's come to teach 'math' here for a year, as he is part of a gap-year Christian college project in his home state of Idaho. They are offering super-bright but FREE unqualified young people as teachers for a year to remote Kenyan schools. He is so excited, so pleased to meet us and looking forward to working here!

As we make introductions, however, the workmen are talking to the truck driver, who has asked them to help unload the young man's luggage. He's getting irritated as they stumble through some explanation that there's been a change in plan. They wrangle, and my brain ticks on. Of course! It's all become clear to me now. Our un-esteemed head had a chance of this young man's services and the extra kudos and money/equipment *Mzungu* teachers bring *for free*, and he took it without telling anyone else – and of course decided to throw Hafsa out as she's a woman, can't fight back, costs the school some money and has no power at all. I take a very deep breath and explain the situation rapidly to Andy. He frowns, and I inflate my shrinking bosom ready for another battle. However, I have to deflate it immediately – the frown is because of the headmaster's behaviour. Andy doesn't approve of it! He didn't come here to make some Kenyan lady homeless! No sir! That's not right. He can go somewhere else or back to the town until something is sorted out. Despite his youth and the fact he looks very fit, I remember my own tiredness and dazed state on arrival at my first school and the chaos I faced. And so I take control again, ordering the men to bring his luggage to my house. My second bedroom is already made up for when anyone comes to stay. The house is big enough for two. He can live with me. Andy seems a little taken aback, and the men and Hafsa are utterly horrified. Unmarried people don't share here. I tell them openly I am old enough to be Andy's mother, and we will do very well together. *Mzungus* as they well know are different. The rules can be adjusted. That's the decision. That's what's going to happen.

It happens.

Music is playing softly, the hurricane lamp lit. Andy is drinking an ice cold coke after he and I have eaten the dinner I cooked. I meant half of it for tomorrow as well, but he ate it all. He is delighted with the dinner, the house, the room, and everything around him. He's even tickled by the washing and toilet arrangements – gee, it's just like camping! We agree to share everything: there will be a kitty for food. I will do the cooking (men are not allowed to, that really would be too controversial!) and shopping, and he will – with the doors closed and curtains drawn – do the washing up and help with cleaning. He is 19, and cannot cook to save his life, so we are in any case both happy with this arrangement. We agree also to give each other privacy as well as company, and to stick to our guns about the arrangement. I try to help with useful advice and support but balance this out by letting Andy find his feet as much as possible on his own. So far it's working extremely well. The local people are getting over their consternation and Mr Piggy didn't give two hoots about my high-handed actions once he knew his problem was solved at no cost to himself. Hafsa and the children still have their home, and our friendship has deepened further.

Most good tales must have a twist, however, and this one is certainly no different. Local sensibilities I suppose can never be underestimated – they always have to be pacified somehow. The people have strong, traditional beliefs and must find a way to maintain an illusion we are 'a couple'. Ergo, they decide to believe we are married, and that Andy has come to join me from whatever distant cool blue planet *Mzungus* hail from. If they want to do that, we really don't mind. However, we find it doesn't end there, as status is a complex issue. In something of a reversal of all they know, they still need to recognise I am the higher-status, older and more forceful of us two, and they decide to call Andy

'Mr Nathaniel'. We are both highly delighted, and, knowing how short a time remains for both of us here and how infinitely elastic and strange so-called reality can be, we are more than content to live out the lie.

Epilogue

Fool's Gold

Though outwardly I remain calm and organised, as decision time creeps nearer, I often feel like a spooked gnu scrabbling on a Maasai Mara riverbank, with pressure from others piling up behind and a slippery slope and murderous torrent in front. What helps, ironically, is that these last two years in Kenya have been less satisfactory than the first four, and that makes the choice easier. I certainly didn't want to go 'home' while I wasn't sure if I had one and where exactly it was, and I still have no idea why – no matter where I have chosen to live – Swansea never draws me back. I know whenever I do return visits will have to be time-limited: However warm the welcome, immediately I cross the line into the Land of My Fathers and head west, my nerves come painfully to the surface of my skin while my brain feels as if someone has thrown a thick blanket over it. Filled with an overwhelming urge to flee, I do. Why I have simply accepted this without deep questioning, I can't truly say, but I have.

Over the last twelve experience-packed years however awareness of how wrong I was to think I was completely alienated from my family and culture is finally dawning: why did I not see before the plus points of the narrowness of focus, the toughness? Where in the name of God would I be if they had not passed on – with their love-by-osmosis – the determination and strength to endure, no matter what, and the kind of chin-tilting pride it confers? Together with the absorption of their unlikely but irrepressible love of life and fun (no matter the poor hand they may have been dealt), that grit has saved me. I am grateful for that inheritance now, for the fact steel was bred in my genes and bones and given me with my baby milk. It has buoyed me up, invisible but strong. Perhaps the only real difference is a *generational* one: I've been offered chances, choices and mobility that they, in different times, were not. South-Welsh women have always ruled the roost whatever their men may think or believe, but too many of them up to now have still not been able to break old, unspoken rules about the extent of their spheres of influence or personal choices in careers and relationships. I can, and to a point I have, but it is about time I faced the fact there were not-so-good effects too, the legacy of emotions denied, even mocked, and their open expression taboo.

I am thinking for the first time in many years of *Mamgu* ('Big Mam') my maternal grandmother. In a rented house, with Big Dad's wages from the chemical works put in her hand every Friday, she brought up six children, doing all the washing, mangling, and baking by hand. She managed budgets so there was money left over. She kept the house sparkling and beat her rugs half to death. She kept her children clean, healthy, well-dressed, happy and loved. She somehow found time to clean the house of a little old man next door who still had a big, black range. She lent money to neighbours interest free when they otherwise may have been crushed beneath life's wheels. She was a force of nature and I found it hard to believe Death could conquer her. When I saw her in her coffin, I am quite sure that was the first time I saw her at rest. My other gran was made of very similar stuff, and pulled off the same conjuring act, though she had only four children and was widowed even earlier by the poisonous effects of industrial working. Those women's genes are in me: I have to be worthy of them. In a modern world, I imagine they would be successful company directors juggling home, children and awesomely responsible jobs.

This gives me a little extra courage now to talk of something so personal it upsets me as I write, but it must out: in Kenya, I have had several relationships with men, but avoided mentioning them AT ALL in these pages: how bizarre is that? I focused in on the stories, and kept pushing the uncomfortable facts away. I meant to be honest as one can be, but failed dismally. And so I must address this now: I think my reluctance and shame stem from feeling I should have learned a lesson but emphatically did not. What I still do, every damned time, in an effort to appear and feel 'normal' amongst a sea of normal people, is to drift into a relationship with someone who finds me attractive. That makes me feel good initially, somehow confirms I am not as unworthy as I think – but I don't feel anything much else thereafter. These are counterfeit relationships, and I am being very unfair to some good men: like my other sallies into this minefield, these so-called relationships in Kenya end by puzzling, disappointing or angering (all three at times) the partners involved. Sensitive ones can guess I'm not really there and are better prepared, others are completely fooled. I would *never* do this to friends or relatives: I have a code of kindness and loyalty. So why is this so different? Without excusing the behaviour, I am beginning to recognise it is not at all purposeful: I seem to be pre-programmed.

To give an example, I meet a lovely young man called Kipungu, a student at the university, younger than me by a few years. He is handsome, intelligent, funny, a little shy, a gentle man. He lives on the coast, so we meet in my earlier sea-side holidays. I never ask him to visit me, but keep him like a toy in a cupboard. When he comes unannounced mid-term to my school up-country, I panic, making the No Liaison Rule an excuse. I make him unwelcome in subtle and not so subtle ways. He leaves, crestfallen: I am nerve-cringingly ashamed yet relieved at the same time. Essentially, I repeat that idiocy four times at greater or lesser levels of seriousness. On my last attempt comes natural justice: the man (a fellow VSO) is made of tougher stuff and cheerfully does the same to me. I am not hurt, except a little in pride, and that, too, is *worrying*. There is a gaping emptiness in me, so when I attempt to connect emotionally and sexually with men across the chasm, it is as if all my feelings stay elsewhere. I hide them as a miser conceals his coin, and, on one level, I am comfortable with this. I am a mechanical woman giving the appearance of normal service, but very badly in need of repair. I worry now that like a machine, if I keep running on empty, I will one day blow.

With gritted teeth I am making a promise to myself now, perhaps more important than any other as a whole vital part of life, perhaps the only truly vital part, is closed to me: There will be no more sexual relationships until I can work out what is holding me back and making me into a deeply unsatisfied and unwittingly cruel person in this sphere. It is in effect an oath of celibacy, as I know pretending is no longer good for me or men who get enmeshed with me. I don't know yet how one works out what the damage is, let alone how to repair it, only that I must try. This engenders the clutch of fear in my guts allied with the feeling of a heavy stone being lifted off my back.

While in the mood for honesty, I have also admitted to myself that despite my initial feelings, I know I'm not really part of this or any other African community. The two quieter years in this school have helped me to detach a little, realise the sense of belonging and homecoming in this huge and ever alien country was powerful but illusory. I've worked hard and learnt so much, but this is not the home I'd looked for after all. I understand more than most about life and the culture here and can counterfeit being part of it, but I'm *not*: this is not in my genes or deep enough in my bones and cells. The time for pretence is nearly over: In personal terms, it feels I've been allowed to get too comfortable and am still following an old pattern without properly questioning its suitability or attractiveness. Now I have admitted it, I know I must leave this dangerous safe-haven for the unknown.

Some partings are painful, but even there I have found comfort as well as pain. Emily has graduated now from Kenyatta University. She will be a teacher herself, one day a headmistress. She is to marry another former pupil, and he calls me mummy-in-law, which I find delightful. Emily invited me to her graduation, and it was a stellar day. However, to her great upset, several of the students, swayed by government and media propaganda, tell me I'm not welcome, that I am a White Imperialist. I tell them I am sorry they feel this though as a lover of history I can fully understand why. I came here full of guilt for my ancestors' deeds, but have loved my six year stay (at the invitation of their government), and learnt so much from meeting and working with so many special people. I am leaving anyway, but will miss Kenya very badly. They do cast down their eyes, suddenly very interested in other things, and Emily gives them a death-stare before whisking me away. She will go back to them when I am gone and tell them any racism, direct or inverted, is utterly unacceptable, the hateful and lazy weapon of the weak. She is starting a new life, personal and professional, and I hope I will be able to keep in touch and visit her and hold any children she may have. They will call me granny-in-law.

Thus, gradually, in so many ways in the last year, I've been steeling myself for a return. I haven't applied for an extension of contract this time, and the few loose ends that remain are short enough to be securely tied. I can plan my departure, say sad but on the whole, controlled goodbyes. I can follow the pull to what I feel will lead to a permanent career, perhaps even making a settled home for myself somewhere. Somewhere that isn't rented or comes with the job, a place that I create. This will be less like running away, and more like purposefully heading for what could be the right destination.

Several things have successfully seeded an idea in my brain, and it's growing stronger day by day. My time as a boarding mistress, dealing with everyone's problems . . . the campaigning for improved conditions and fairness for the pupils and their families . . . fighting old Toad-Face until he got the sack when the school had improved enough to be taken over by the government. Then later there was coming here and having the idea for the counselling service, with the immense satisfaction that led to . . . enthusiastic letters from a friend doing a post-graduate university course in Birmingham. Something one of my VSO friends said a couple of months ago:

"Bloody hell, Nelly – you're more like a social worker than a teacher these days. Thank God it's too hot for a woolly jumper and sandals with socks."

So even if it leads to more of the same jocularity, I'm going to look for a way to attain the same kind of total absorption and rewards I've experienced here but working in the UK. Something tells me this might be the right way, but of course I'm afraid as well as a little excited. But I remind myself that's how I felt before I came *here* – indeed, I was terrified. This feeling of being on the cusp of something exciting, maybe even a bit risky, is potent and addictive. I can't explain what's happening much better than that, but I do now have the power to move onto the next stage of something, but purposefully, and it feels good. It also feels positive that I have already sent out enquiries about applying for a place at university to study social sciences.

I know I will never forget all the people, the experiences and lessons learnt here and know this is the end of a phase. Of course there is a nervous-Nelly part of me whispering, asking if it *is* after all the right time to leave . . . and the temptation to keep drifting, avoiding, may always be there. I don't have definitive answers to important questions, and can only repeat to myself and others like a *mantra* that this feels like the right thing to do at the right time. Kenya has changed just as I have: when I came here like the walking wounded I could hardly help myself . . . somehow Kenya and its people worked a magic that helped me get stronger by working with and for them. I've had to be solitary so often, adaptive, practical and resilient always, and there has been a process of healing in body, mind and spirit. Very belatedly – I am almost thirty-five years old! – I feel I am finally maturing. In the meantime, however, Kenya itself is growing up fast and that can be such a painful bloody process: already, the country is destabilising as people chafe against the oppressive authority and awesome corruption of the one-party state and start to revert to older tribal jealousies and hatred. I worry about Emily and other friends, as you can almost smell a growing scent of violence in the air. Like me, the country has outwardly appeared calm and even capable, while under the surface there is the drag of fragmentation and a wound held together only by threads, leaching blood.

Well, here it is: house emptied, goods sold or re-distributed, bag packed, ready to move on. I feel I am right to go, but unsure yet what I might be capable of if I keep on working hard, developing inner strength and trying to be honest, especially if I am re-trained and can start a new career and different kind of adventure under a gentler sun. I don't kid myself that it will be anything but hard work and have learned to mistrust: so much has been illusory, and I seem to create most of the illusions myself, throwing them up like smokescreens. There's nothing to say I won't do it again . . still, I *am* more awake now than I have ever been, and slowly, very slowly, I am becoming more adept at recognising fool's gold for what it is. What still niggles however is that deeply uneasy and sometimes queasy feeling – still too far buried to reach – that some hidden but relentless force is in turn paradoxically driving me AND holding me back. I may be getting braver and less passive as time passes, but I will still be, unless I can find the right time and strength to fathom and master it, always the passenger

210

and not the pilot. I no longer believe in the possibility of Eden, but I am beginning to wonder if I could, with a following wind, perhaps navigate my way towards one of its more peaceful suburbs.

Helen Nathaniel-Fulton was born in 1955 and is from Swansea originally but now lives in the town of Paisley in Scotland. She studied History and the History of Art at Aberystwyth University and, later on, Social Studies at Oxford. She lived for many years in Kenya where she was working as a teacher with VSO. She's a retired social worker who paints and writes full-time and is based in the WASPS studios in Glasgow. She has had one pamphlet of short stories called *Da Vinci's Cuckoos* published by Something Like Chalk Press in 2017, and was co-author of *The DTs* (Controlled Explosion Press, 2014) along with her husband, the poet Graham Fulton. Individual stories have also been published in literary magazines *Laldy!, Southlight,* and in the anthologies *Bridges or Walls?* (Dove Tales, 2019) and *Of Myths and Mothers* (Fly on the Wall Press, 2022).